Mastering CA-SuperCalc for Windows

Janet Swift

I/O Press

First Published 1994
©I/O Press
Cover Design: Jane M Patience
ISBN 1 871962 24-2

British Library Cataloguing in Publication Data
A catalogue record for this book is available from the British Library

All Rights Reserved. No part of this publication may be reproduced, stored in a retrieval system, or transmitted in any form or by any means, electronic, mechanical, photocopying, recording or otherwise, without prior written permission.

Products mentioned within this text may be protected by trade marks, in which case full acknowledgement is hereby given.

Although every effort has been made to ensure the correctness of the information contained herein neither the publisher nor the author accept liability for any omissions or errors that may remain.

Typeset by I/O Press

Printed and bound in Great Britain by Cromwell Press Limited, Broughton Gifford, Wiltshire

Contents

Preface

Chapter 1   Getting Started With Sheets   1

The Windows tutorial; The first five minutes; Inside the Sheet; Selecting cells; Practical - Expenses; Edit mode; AutoSum; Cells, formulae and the equals sign; Practical - Expenses II; Moving around the sheet; Saving a sheet; Opening a sheet; If you make a mistake

Chapter 2   Pointing, Moving and Copying   19

Selecting a range; Object -> Action; Range references; Using the clipboard to copy and move; Cut and Paste = Move; Copying once and many times; Using Edit,Fill; Shortcuts for moving and copying; Drag and drop; What your right mouse button is for; The toolbar; Extending ranges; Using Formula,Goto; Practical - Costing a mailshot

Chapter 3   Calculations   37

Operators; Pointing; Absolute and relative; Moving spreadsheet entries; Row and column relative; Functions; Pasting functions; Range expressions; Multiple selections; Names; Relative names; Names from labels; Converting to names; Undoing names; Formula names; Row and column ranges; Circular references; Controlling calculation; Autosum; Practical - The mailshot sheet

Chapter 4   Formatting   65

Format basics; Applying formatting; Number formatting; Numeric place holders; Text in formats; Advanced numeric formats; Practical - See when you are overdrawn; Scientific format; Other formats; Alignment; Fonts; Borders; Using borders; Patterns; Pop-up; Controlling the display; Clearing formats; Controlling colour; Column width and row height; Styles; Practical - Formatting the mailshot

Chapter 5   Charts   95

Basic principles; Editing charts; Data series; A five minute chart; Categorical and non-categorical data; Chart types; Categorical data and XY charts; Selecting a chart type; Customising charts; Axis control; Legends; Controlling colour; Front and back; Chart editing; Chart templates; Duplicate categories; Mixed chart types; More than one X series; Error bars; A Hi-Lo chart; Curve fitting; Practical - A pie chart of sales data; Transposing a range

Chapter 6   Making Sheets Work   129

Windows and workspaces; Spreadsheet surgery - Inserting and deleting; Organising sheets; Title locks; Sheet merging; Sheet links; Practical - Links in action; Links to other documents - DDE; Managing links; Templates and protection; Practical - protection in action; Debugging sheets; Notes; Formula and Map mode; Info window; Audit trail; Select Special; Verification

Chapter 7   Printing and Reports   159

Windows printing; Printer setup; Fonts; Simple printing; Preview; The print range; Page setup; Titles; Headers and footers; Making it all fit; Scaling; Layout; Practical - the mailshot report

Chapter 8   Using Functions   177

The arithmetic functions; Range functions; Using the IF function; Conditions; AND, OR and NOT; Multiple IFs; Checking validity; Checksums; Logical functions; Text functions; Converting to a format; Other characters; Numbers to text; Lookup functions; Practical - Sales commission spreadsheet; Practical - Post Room Calculator; User defined functions; What's missing

Chapter 9   Dates, Times, % and Precision   211

Date serial numbers; Entering dates; Times; Mixed dates and times; Formatting dates and times; Working with dates and times; Entering today's date and time; Date arithmetic; Time arithmetic; Practical - Days360; Practical - Named day of the month; Practical - A calendar; Practical - Graphing Biorhythms; Percentages; Fixed decimal entry; Accurate arithmetic?; Rounding, rounding up and truncating; Rounding existing values; A user defined RoundDn function; Practical - Calculating VAT

Chapter 10   Database   249

What is a database?; A database as a table; Form view; Entering data; Finding and editing data; Criteria; Database commands; The database names; The criteria range; Find and Delete; Extracting data; Practical - Salary database; Database functions; Practical - Summing salary; Sorting; Practical - Sorting the database; Importing and exporting dBASE files; Practical - A holiday flight database; Data series

Chapter 11   Models and 3D   275

Meet the model; A 3D model; Ranges; Absolute and relative; Relative offsets; Importing SC5 3D sheets; 3D spreadsheet to model; Global formulae; How far?; Pivoting; Models or sheets?; Importing 2D CAL files

Chapter 12   Macros with CA-ble   295

Writing macros; CA-ble fundamentals; Print and Input; Making choices with IF; Loops; Counting loops; The link with SCW; CA-ble functions and SCW functions; Dialog boxes; Recording a macro; Importing SC5 macros; Translation - an example; Debugging; Assigning to keys and menus; User defined functions; Example 1- Auto 3D; Example 2 - Age in years; Example 3 - Codebreaker

Index

Other books of interest

Disk and Update Service

Preface

SuperCalc for MS-DOS has long been my favourite spreadsheet and the lack of a Windows version has been problem for myself and many other users. Now with the arrival of CA-SuperCalc for Windows (SCW) there is a sensible upgrade path and it has plenty to offer the new user.

SCW is an economical spreadsheet in the sense that it doesn't occupy much in the way of disk space and it will run on a fairly minimum Windows system. However, anyone approaching SCW with the idea that it is "just" a Windows version of the old DOS product is in for a difficult time! There are many similarities, enough to make SCW the only sensible choice for an existing SuperCalc user but to take advantage of the Windows environment there have to be differences.

While writing this book I have been mindful of my two audiences - the newcomer to SCW and the SC5 user. I have deliberately tried not to burden the newcomer with repeated references to how SC5 did this or that. Where such a comment has been necessary it has been separated out into a box which can be read or skipped as required. On the other hand, I have not avoided using the examples from my two earlier books - *SuperCalc Professional* and *The Expert Guide to SC5*. I am sure that readers who are familiar with the original versions of the examples will find the comparison useful and interesting.

All the examples in this book have been included on a companion disk. Ordering details are given at the back of this book, together with details of the Update Service designed to keep you informed of significant changes in SCW.

Janet Swift
March 1994

Chapter 1

Getting Started With Sheets

CA-SuperCalc for Windows (SCW) is an easy to use and yet powerful tool for working with data of all kinds. If you have previously used an MS-DOS spreadsheet, or even another Windows spreadsheet, you will be surprised at just how simple and quick it is to achieve results. However there are some very basic ideas that you need to know before it all makes sense. In particular, you need to know how to make use of the facilities provided by Windows - how to point with a mouse, how to click to select something and how to drag to select a group of objects.

SCW offers two types of spreadsheet - the model and the sheet. The sheet is the simpler of the two and a good place to start. In this book the emphasis is on how sheets work but much of what you discover also applies to models, which are introduced in later chapters.

» The Windows tutorial

If you are already a proficient Windows user then you are ready to proceed straight to SCW. If not then the simplest way to find out how Windows works is to use its own Tutorial which is included as standard with every copy of Windows. To run the Windows Tutorial all you need to do is to select the Help option in the Program Manager's menu bar and then select the Windows Tutorial option.

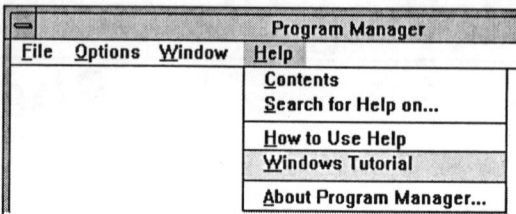

Of course, it is possible that someone might have altered your Windows system and removed the Windows Tutorial to save space. If this is the case then you need to seek help in restoring the tutorial.

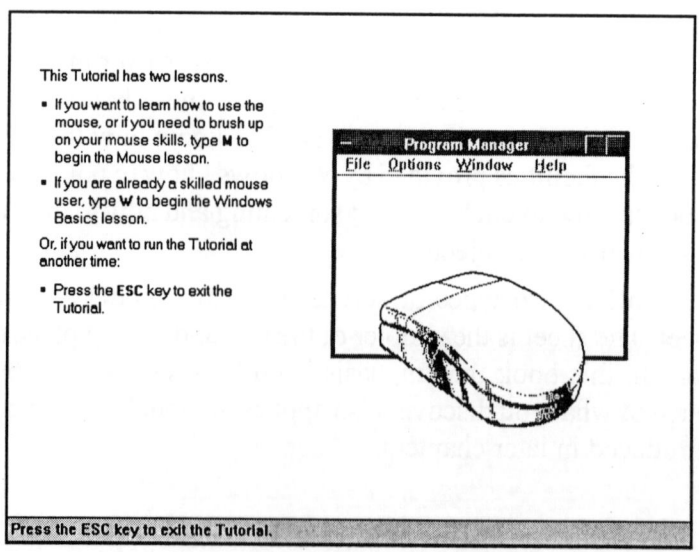

Once into the Windows Tutorial you can opt to learn about how to use the mouse or general principles of how Windows works. Make sure that you know how to:

》 select something by clicking on it

》 select a group of objects or an area by dragging - i.e. moving the mouse while holding down the left-hand button

》 open or activate an object by double clicking on it

» The first five minutes

As long as you know the basics of using Windows then your first 5 minutes with SCW should be enough for you to find your way around. To run SCW you double click on its icon in the Program Manager in the usual way.

CA-SuperCalc

The initial appearance of SCW may at first strike you as being a little sparse, but it has all you need to hand.

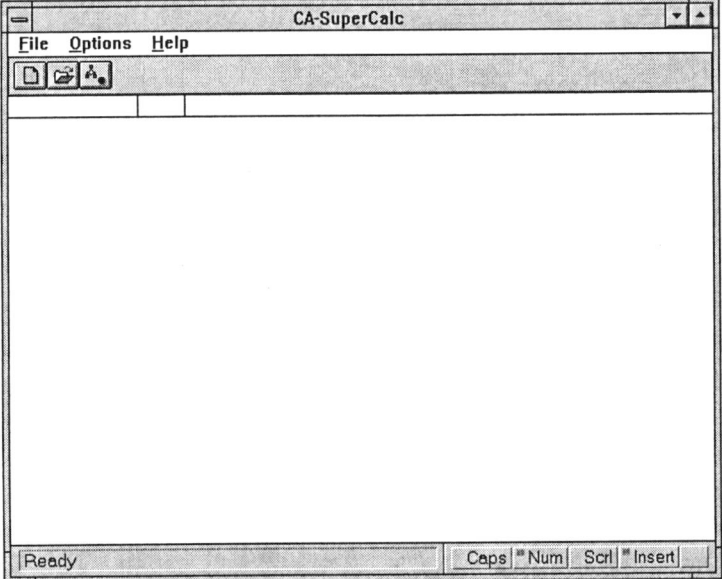

The Menu bar at the top of the window has commands that allow you to open existing documents and create new ones and to modify some aspects of the way that SCW works. At the moment however the two commands that you want to use most frequently are available as the first two icons just below the menu bar.

If you click on the first icon - the one that looks like a sheet of paper - then a new document is opened for you to use. If you click on the second icon - the one that looks like a folder opening - then you can select an existing document to open and work with.

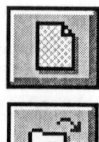

If you do click on the New icon you are next presented with a dialog box which allows you to choose the type of document - Model, Sheet or Macro - that you want to work with. Each of the three types is discussed in later chapters but for the moment we will concentrate on the sheet. The reason is that the sheet is the simplest of the three and the closest to the traditional notion of a spreadsheet. Existing spreadsheet users, and SuperCalc 5 users in particular, will recognise SCW's sheet as a 2D worksheet.

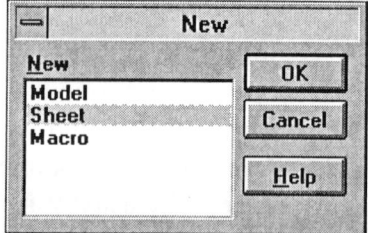

» Inside the Sheet

A SCW sheet is a grid of cells. Each cell can be used to store an individual item of data. To store something in a cell all you have to do is select it and type away. What you type appears in the data entry area and in the cell itself - however the data isn't entered into the cell until you press the Enter key or click on the tick mark to the left of the data entry area. It doesn't matter which you do - sometimes it is easier to use the keyboard; sometimes the mouse. You can change the contents of a cell using any of the standard Windows editing keys until you press enter or click on the tick.

If you press the Insert key you will notice that you can change from typing over what is already on the entry line to inserting new characters. Make sure you select insert or overwrite mode as required.

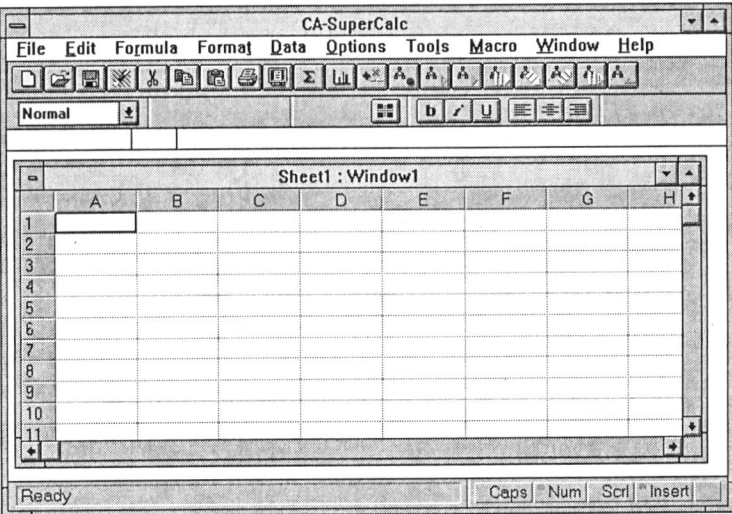

If you are familiar with SC5 you will quickly discover that some of the editing facilities have changed. In particular the down arrow key no longer deletes and the up arrow key no longer inserts. Both of these editing commands would be non-standard in Windows and so they are best forgotten.

» Selecting cells

A basic skill in using any spreadsheet is how to select the cell that you are working with. The currently active cell is marked by a thick box drawn around its borders. This is the spreadsheet cursor and you need to know how to move it around the sheet. The simplest and most direct way is to click on any cell that you want to work with and the cursor will jump to the new location.

The art of double clicking

Many Windows users find "double clicking" a difficult trick. Having failed to select an object they place the pointer over it and jab violently and quickly as if double clicking was a frantic race or a test of reaction times. In fact double clicking is a very easy and relaxed action. First move the pointer over the object you want to activate. Next press the left mouse button so that you feel and hear it go "click". Immediately, and without moving the mouse, press the button again so that you feel and hear a rhythmical "click-click". The trouble is that some users jab at the second click to make sure that it is close enough in time to the first and in consequence move the mouse slightly. This results in the "click-click" being recognised as two single clicks at different locations no matter how close together they are in time. What often happens at this point is that the user, having failed to double click, assumes that it is because the clicks were too slow and tries again - only faster. This makes it even more unlikely that the mouse remains stationary and so the double click is again missed. The solution is to double click at a reasonable speed while keeping the mouse still.

If after following this advice you still cannot master the art of the double click then it might be that you need to tell Windows that you want to double click more slowly. To do this open the Control Panel by double clicking on its icon in the Main program group Once the Control Panel is running double click on the Mouse icon. Finally you will see the Mouse dialog box where you will be able to set the Double Click Speed as slow or as fast as you desire. You can try out your double click skills using the TEST box.

Control Panel

Mouse

This works very well if you want to work with cells that are scattered around the sheet but it isn't it an efficient way of entering a column of figures. You can also move the spreadsheet cursor using the arrow keys. In this case the cursor moves one cell left, right, up or down depending on which key you have pressed.

So you can enter a column of figures by selecting the first cell using the mouse, entering the first value and then pressing Enter followed by the down arrow key and so on.. To make this even easier SCW allows you to press any of the arrow keys to signal that you have finished entering data and the cursor automatically moves in the appropriate direction. In other words, the simplest way to enter a column of figures is to select the first cell and press the down arrow key after each item of data. Moving the cursor using the mouse also has the same effect.

If you can't get out of the habit of pressing the Enter key after each value then see the box *Moving the cursor - /Global,+,Next*. However, you might find the some of the more advanced data entry methods described in the next chapter even more useful.

» Practical - Expenses

As a simple example of how you can enter data into a sheet, and to provide something to build upon in later practicals, we will construct an expenses spreadsheet like the one below.

	A	B	C	D	E
1	Expenses	Record			
2	Week 1				
3		Miles	Lunch	Hotel	
4	Mon	300	10.25	0	
5	Tue	125	11	34.7	
6	Wed	45	12.65	42.2	
7	Thu	88	20.2	29.9	
8	Fri	354	1.5	46	
9					
10					

You should find this very simple but take note of how best to enter the columns of figures. In most cases the simplest method is to press the down arrow key after each entry but if you have selected the "Move Selection after Enter" option - see the box on the next page - then the cursor will move automatically when you press Enter.

At this stage there is no need to worry about clever time saving techniques but it is worth knowing that the list of days of the week can be entered automatically, as can almost any regular series of entries - see Chapter 10. You can also make any sheet look as impressive as you want or need. By selecting typefaces and formats for different entries and altering the widths of rows and columns you could turn your expenses data into a report suitable for any purpose. These aspects of formatting are covered in Chapter 4.

» Edit mode

One of the great advantages of a spreadsheet is that you can change any entry at any time. If you select any cell then its contents automatically appear on the data entry line. To edit this data you have to click on the data entry line or press F2 - the Edit key. Either action places SCW into Edit mode as indicated by the word Edit which appears in the bottom left-hand corner of the window.

While in Edit mode the left and right cursor keys move the editing position within the text on the entry line. What this means is that you cannot complete an edit by pressing an arrow key - only Enter will do.

Moving the cursor -/Global,+,Next

If you just cannot get out of the habit of pressing Enter after each value then the Preferences dialog box will be of interest to you. This is displayed when you select Preferences in the Options menu.

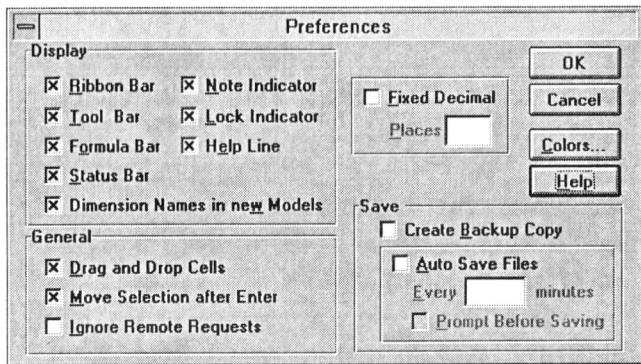

There are a number of choices that you can make using this dialog box to alter the way that SCW works or looks but the one that is of interest at the moment is

Move Selection after Enter

in the General section. If you select this option, by placing a cross in the box beside it, then the cursor will move to a new cell each time you press Enter. The direction of movement is governed by the last arrow key that you pressed. In other words, with this option in force the cursor carries on moving in the same direction after each value you enter.

SC5 users will recognise this as being the equivalent of the /Global,+,Next command which had exactly the same effect on the cursor's behaviour.

» AutoSum

If you have never used a spreadsheet before you will already be impressed by the ability to enter and edit data but this is only just the beginning. You can also perform calculations using any data in the sheet and when you change the data the results are almost instantly recalculated.

The most common calculation that any spreadsheet user needs to perform is to total a column of figures. To make this operation easier SCW has a special AutoSum command. To use it all you have to do it place the spreadsheet cursor in the cell at the bottom of the column of figures that you want totalled and click on the AutoSum icon. The only problem you can possibly have with this operation is working out why the AutoSum icon has a Greek capital Sigma on it. The reason is that Sigma is the mathematical symbol to sum a series of values but you can also think of it as S standing for Sum.

For example, if you place the cursor in the cell just below the last entry in the column of mileage figures in the expenses spreadsheet and then click on the AutoSum icon the total number of miles appears.

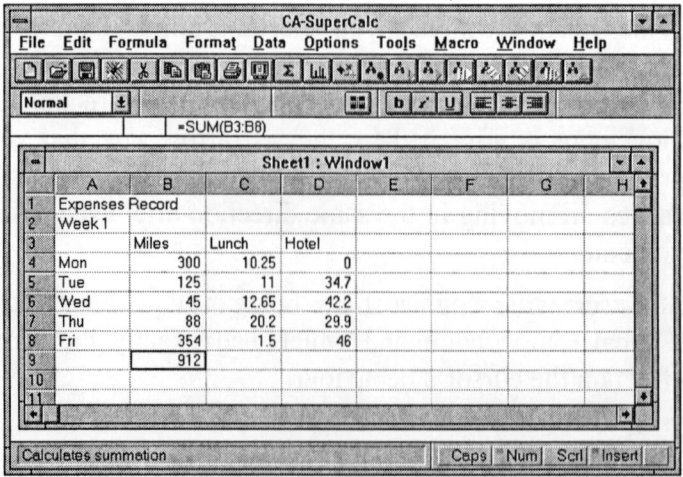

If you change any of the entries in the Miles column then the total is immediately updated. As long as you are working with a colour screen you will also notice that the sum is shown in a different colour. This is a helpful convention - all raw data values are shown in one colour and results calculated using that data are shown in another colour.

If you look at the contents of the cell that displays the total you will find a formula that works out the sum -

=SUM(B3:B8)

If you examine this you should be able to understand exactly what it means - work out the sum of the contents of cells B3 to B8. You could have typed this formula in directly without the help of the AutoSum facility and it would do exactly the same job. In later chapters we look more closely at how functions and formulae work but even then it is still worth clicking on the AutoSum button!

» Cells, formulae and the equals sign

One of the beauties of using a spreadsheet with a mouse is that you can use it to point at the cells that contain the data that interest you. However you still need to know about how cells are referenced in formulae. In SCW columns are lettered starting from A. After column Z the lettering continues with AA, AB, AC and so on to column IV, making 256 columns in all. Rows are numbered 1 to 16,384 and this means that there are 4,194,304 cells in all. If you could see the entire sheet in one go it would need a screen 20 feet wide by 250 feet high! To refer to any cell in this huge sheet all you have to do is give its column letter and its row number as in A1, AB10 or IV16384.

The simplest type of formula that you can enter is one that involves nothing but simple arithmetic. The only difference between spreadsheet arithmetic and normal arithmetic is that you have to use an asterisk * to mean multiply and a slash /

> ## Why do I have to use = ?
>
> Existing SC5 users will find SCW's insistence on starting every formula with an equals sign very puzzling. SC5 automatically recognised formulae without the need for any special indicator. However virtually every other DOS and Windows spreadsheet does insist on the user typing a special symbol to start a formula and so in this respect SCW is no different and no worse. This said, the SC5 method is a better way of working and it is likely that a future revision of SCW will use it. So if you have a version newer than 1.0 it is worth trying out entering a formula without starting it with an equals sign and see if it works! If it doesn't you will have to allow time to acquire the habit of typing an equals sign every time you want something worked out.

to mean divide. For example, 2*2 is 4 and 4/2 is 2. If you enter some arithmetic into a cell then SCW will work it out and show you the result - as long as you remember to start off by typing =, the equals sign. If you don't type the equals sign then SCW assumes that you don't want anything worked out and shows the arithmetic as you typed it in.

The rule is

» anything that starts with an equals sign is stored in the cell but what is displayed is the result of working it out

and

» anything that doesn't start with an equals sign is stored in the cell and displayed exactly as it is.

The only exception is that if you start a formula with + or - SCW will automatically add an = sign for you.

As well as being able to enter simple arithmetic you can also include cell references within calculations. For example, if you enter =A1*2 into a cell then SCW will work out and display the result of multiplying the contents of cell A1 by 2.

» Practical - Expenses II

Now that we know about AutoSum and how to enter formulae it is easy to finish the expenses spreadsheet. The first thing to do is calculate the total mileage and convert this to cash by multiplying by a mileage rate. We have already calculated the mileage total by placing the cursor on cell B9 and clicking on the AutoSum button.

If the mileage rate is 45p per mile then this can be converted into a cash claim by entering the formula

=B9*0.45

into cell B10.

To get the totals spent on lunch and on hotels you can select C10 and click on the AutoSum button and then D10 and again click on the AutoSum button.

Finally to work out a grand total simply enter

=B10+C10+D10

into cell B11 and add some more labels to make the finished result look similar to the sheet below.

	A	B	C	D	E
1	Expenses Record				
2	Week 1				
3		Miles	Lunch	Hotel	
4	Mon	300	10.25	0	
5	Tue	125	11	34.7	
6	Wed	45	12.65	42.2	
7	Thu	88	20.2	29.9	
8	Fri	354	1.5	46	
9	Mileage	912			
10	Claim	410.4	55.6	152.8	
11	Total	618.8			

» Moving around the sheet

Given that a sheet is so huge you clearly can't expect to see all of it at once. The sheet window is exactly that - a window onto the entire sheet. The scroll bars at the side and bottom of the windows are the standard method of altering the portion of the sheet that you are looking at. Think of the scroll bar as representing the entire sheet and the slider shows you the position of the window. You can drag the scroll bar slider to position the window anywhere within the entire sheet. You can also click on the scroll bar to either side of the slider to jump it one whole window.

There are also a range of movement keys but exactly how these work depends on whether or not the scroll lock is on. If the scroll lock is on the movement keys behave like the scroll bars - that is they move the window. If the scroll lock isn't on the movement keys move the position of the currently selected cell. Even with the scroll lock on the movement keys do sometimes move the window to keep the selected cell visible. What is important is that you distinguish between moving the position of the selected cell with scroll lock off and the window with scroll lock on. To turn the scroll lock on or off simply press the Scroll Lock button or click on the scroll lock indicator at the bottom edge of the SCW window.

The most useful movement keys are -

Key	Move
arrow keys	one cell in that direction
PageUp	one window up
PageDown	one window down
Ctrl-PageUp	one window left
Ctrl-PageDown	one window right
Home	A1 (top left of window if scroll lock on)
End	IV16384 (bottom right of window if scroll lock on)

» Saving a sheet

Saving a sheet for later use is very easy. All you have to do is click on the Save button or use the command File,Save. Using the dialog box that appears you can select a suitable directory to save the file in and give it a file name. If you don't know about directories then it is worth finding out - try the Windows Tutorial mentioned earlier.

Saving a sheet is simple enough but to make your work with SCW easier and more reliable over all there are two things you should do. Fortunately both involve settings in the Preferences dialog box. You can get to this dialog box by selecting Preferences in the Options menu.

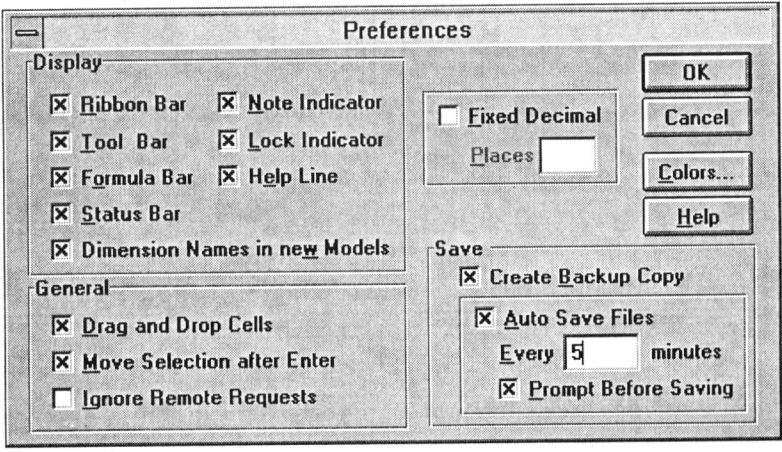

In most cases you should select the Create Backup Copy option - that is this item should have a cross next to it. With this option selected SCW will make a backup of the same name as the sheet but ending in .BAK every time you save a sheet. For example if you save a sheet called EXPENSES then this is stored on disk as a file called EXPENSES.MDS. If the backup option is selected the old copy of the file isn't overwritten but renamed to EXPENSES.BAK. If you should need to return to this older copy you can use the File Manager to rename it. Notice that the Backup option only keeps a single older copy of the sheet that you are working on. It is also stored on the same hard disk drive as the master copy. It is up to you to make more secure long term backups.

Unless you are very short of disk space you should make use of the backup option to increase your security against making silly mistakes. The second option is however not completely without risk of its own. If you select the Auto Save option and enter a time in minutes in the box below then SCW will save all open documents at the stated time interval. This is a way of protecting yourself against the sin of not saving sheets often enough to make sure that a power cut or a machine crash doesn't lose you too much work.

For example, if you set the Auto Save to 5 minutes then your work will be saved at least every 5 minutes and so should the worst happen this is the maximum amount of work you can lose. Now consider what happens if you are just making a few experimental changes to an existing sheet. You could find that the original is overwritten by your temporary changes at the next Auto Save. The only way to guard against this possibility is to also select the Prompt Before Saving option - but this results in you being interrupted at the specified interval to decide if the files should be saved or not.

As long as you are aware of the risks involved in each option you should be able to choose which type of behaviour is most suitable.

» Opening a sheet

Of course once you have saved a sheet you can open it again using the File,Open command or the equivalent icon. This is simple enough. What is usually not so simple is finding the sheet that you have saved! Windows makes it very easy to create and use directories. Before you start any new project you should create a directory to hold the sheets and other documents that you will need to save. Use directories to organise your work and you will never have to search for a sheet again.

If you do lose track of where you stored a sheet then it is worth knowing that you can use the Windows File Manager to search for all of the sheets stored on a disk. Use the command File,Search, specify *.MDS in the Search For box, C:\ in the Start from box and make sure that you check the Search all subdirectories box. After a few minutes you will see a list of all of the sheets and where they are stored.

» If you make a mistake

Perhaps the most important piece of advice that you can be given when working with SCW is that if you make a mistake you should press Ctrl-Z. This will undo the last command you gave. Alternatively you could click on the undo icon in the toolbar. Although the undo command is useful, remember that you can only undo the very last command and not all commands can be undone.

Key points

» Make sure you know how to use general Windows features and mouse operation by running the Windows Tutorial from the Program Manager Help menu.

» Of the three types of document - Model, Sheet and Macro - the Sheet is the most basic and is similar to a traditional 2D spreadsheet.

» You can select a cell by clicking on it. You can move the selection either by using the mouse or any of the movement keys - e.g. the arrow keys.

» When you enter data into the current cell you can press Enter or one of the arrow keys to move to the next cell.

» If you select the Move Selection After Enter option in the Preferences dialog box the current cell will move in the direction of the last arrow key pressed when you press Enter.

» You can find the total of any column of figures by placing the cursor just after the last figure and clicking on the AutoSum button.

» Any arithmetic or formula that you would like SCW to work out has to be entered with a leading equals sign.

» Formulae can involve cell references like A1 and Z13.

» You should select the Backup option in the Preferences dialog box but think carefully before using the Auto Save feature.

» If you make a mistake use the undo command.

Chapter 2

Pointing, Moving and Copying

Once you have used a sheet to enter data and work out some simple results the next stage is to discover how to edit the sheet itself. You often find that a block of data that you entered is in the wrong place and needs to be moved. Equally often you enter a single formula into a cell and then want to make multiple copies of it. Being able to use a mouse to point at the relevant areas of the sheet makes this much easier than a traditional spreadsheet - but if you are familiar with the ways of using a traditional spreadsheet you might find it confusing at first. For example, selecting a range is just a matter of pointing and dragging with the mouse - but how do you select a range that is larger than the window?

» Selecting a range

Selecting a single cell is just a matter of pointing at it with the mouse and clicking. If you want to select a block of cells then the most direct way of doing this is to first select the cell at the top left-hand corner of the block and then drag with the mouse down to the bottom right hand corner. (Dragging is just moving the mouse while holding down the left mouse button.) As you drag the selected area changes to black.

	A	B	C	D	E
1	Expenses Record				
2	Week 1				
3		Miles	Lunch	Hotel	
4	Mon	300	10.25	0	
5	Tue	125	11	34.7	
6	Wed	45	12.65	42.2	
7	Thu	88	20.2	29.9	
8	Fri	354	1.5	46	
9	Mileage	912			
10	Claim	410.4	55.6	152.8	
11	Total	618.8			

EXPENSES.MDS : Window1

Also notice that even though you have selected a range of cells, the first cell you clicked on, i.e. the one in the top left-hand corner, is still shown as the active cell and its contents are displayed on the data entry/editing line.

» Object -> Action

The next question is given that we have selected a range of cells what can we do with it? If you are familiar with an MS-DOS spreadsheet like SC5 you may find this question a little odd. In MS-DOS based spreadsheets you usually select a command, i.e. what you want to do, and then select the range that you want to do it to. In the case of nearly all Windows spreadsheets, and SCW in particular, things are done the other way round. You first select the range and then give the command. You can remember this as

                Object->Action

rather than   Action->Object.

» Range references

It is obvious that to refer to any single cell you simply have to quote its column letter and row number - e.g. C6. This is a cell reference. You can also use the same idea to specify a rectangular range of cells if you quote the cell reference of the top left-hand corner followed by the cell reference of the bottom right. A colon is used to separate the two cell references as in A1:B5 and the result is called a range reference. Most of the time you don't have to type in range references because they will be automatically constructed when you point at a range. However there are times when typing in or editing a range reference is the fastest and most direct way to work.

» Using the clipboard to copy and move

The Windows clipboard and the three editing commands, Cut, Copy and Paste play a key role in working with a spreadsheet. After you have selected a range of cells you can copy their contents to the clipboard. Then you can select another range and paste the contents into the spreadsheet at a new location. The cut operation works in a similar way but it removes the original version of the entries from the spreadsheet. Cut, copy and paste are very versatile tools. To make the best use of SCW you need to make sure that you have mastered cut, copy and paste and all the alternative ways of achieving the same results.

» Cut and Paste = Move

If you have used SC5 or another DOS spreadsheet you will have noticed that SCW does not have a move command. Like other Windows spreadsheets it relies on the combination of cut and paste to lift cell entries from one place and deposit them at another location.

For example, if you want to move the contents of A1 into B1 you select A1 with the mouse and use the command Edit,Cut and press Enter. This copies the contents of A1 to the clipboard. Notice that A1 is now surrounded by a flashing dotted border. When you move the cursor to B1 and press Enter not only do the contents of A1 appear in B1 they also disappear from A1.

You move a range of cells in a similar way. Select all the cells and use Edit, Cut. Then either select the top left-hand cell of the range where you want the data to be moved or select the range that will be occupied. The latter method has pitfalls as SCW follows certain rules about when the Paste range is an appropriate one - this is discussed below with reference to Copy - and when you do not specify it correctly you see the message "Cut and Paste areas do not match" and the move operation will fail - with the data still in its original place. When moving data there is no need to specify all of the destination range so it is better just to select the top left-hand corner.

Note that you can move a range of cells to a new location that overlaps the original range or to a new range that already contains other data. When you use Edit,Cut and Edit,Paste you do not see any warning message about overwriting existing cell entries so do take care when using these commands.

Notice that Edit,Cut cannot be used simply to erase information from a sheet. This is because the contents of the selected cells are only erased from their original location once the Edit,Paste operation has been performed. The command required to get rid of cell contents - the equivalent of /Blank in SC5 - is Edit,Clear (or pressing the Del key). This is discussed in Chapter 4.

» Copying once and many times

If you want to make a single copy of the contents of a cell or range of cells the procedure is similar to that just described. You select the cell or cells, use the command Edit,Copy, then place the cursor in the destination cell (or the top left-hand corner of the destination range) and use Edit,Paste. However, copying is an important technique because it can be used to make multiple copies based on the contents of a single cell and this is the key to much of a spreadsheet's power

For example, suppose you want to copy the contents of cell A1 into the range B1:B10. First select A1 and use the command Edit,Copy. This copies the contents of cell A1 to the clipboard without changing A1 in any way. Next select the range B1:B10 and use the command Edit,Paste. This pastes a copy of the clipboard contents into every cell in the range in a single operation.

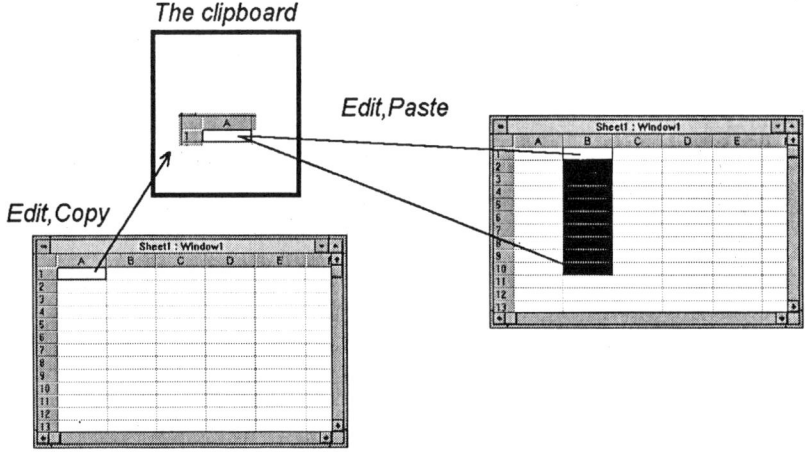

You can see that by selecting a destination range that is bigger than the source range you can create multiple copies. However there are some rules that govern this multiple copying and some convenient short cuts. If you copy a range to the clipboard then you can only paste it to a range that is an exact multiple of its original size. For example, if you copy a 2 by 2 block of cells to the clipboard you can paste this back to a single 2 by 2 block that you select. You can also paste it to any 4 x 2, 2 x 4, 4 x 4, 6 x 2 and so on range. As long as the 2 x 2 block that you copied will fit an exact number of times into the destination range then the paste will work. In this case for example, you couldn't paste the 2 x 2 block into a range 3 cells by 2 cells.

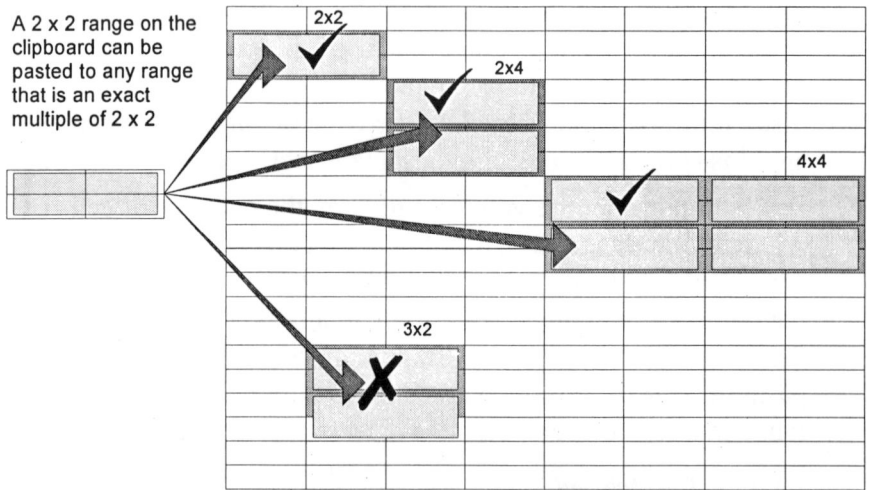

A 2 x 2 range on the clipboard can be pasted to any range that is an exact multiple of 2 x 2

This idea that the destination range must be a multiple of source range is quite easy to understand but it quickly becomes tedious to have to select the entire destination range for the majority of copy operations. To make life easier you can use the short cut of selecting only the top right hand corner, top row or left-hand column of the full destination range. In each case the missing part of the destination range is taken to be the same as the source range.

Copying once and many times **25**

This may sound complicated but in practice it is very natural. For example, if you have copied part of a column, A1:A10 say, to the clipboard then selecting the three cells B1:D1 results in three copies of the column being pasted into B1:D10.

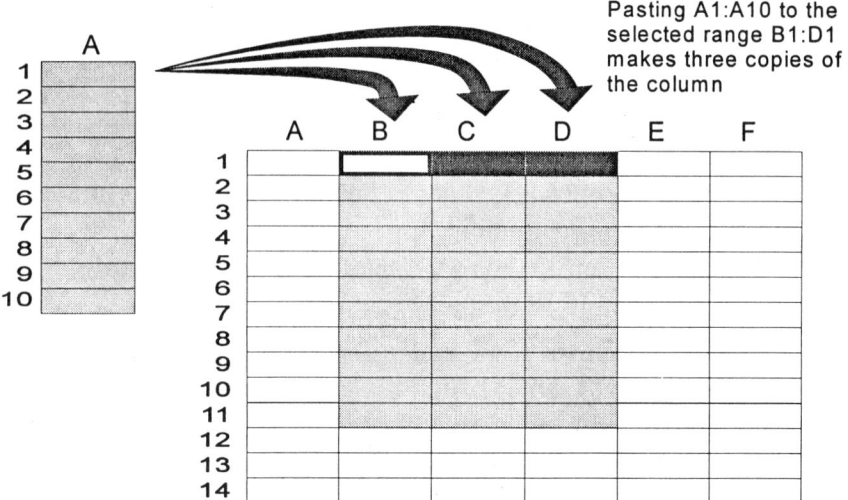

Pasting A1:A10 to the selected range B1:D1 makes three copies of the column

In the same way pasting a row to a part of a column results in multiple copies of the row. Perhaps the most common destination range is the single cell. In this case the source range is pasted in its entirety with its top left hand corner at the selected cell.

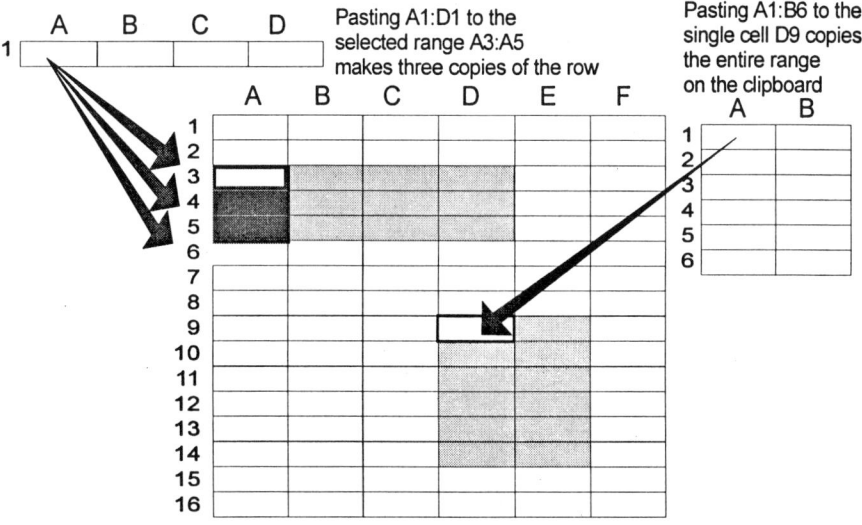

Pasting A1:D1 to the selected range A3:A5 makes three copies of the row

Pasting A1:B6 to the single cell D9 copies the entire range on the clipboard

Once you have practised a little copy and paste seem very natural operations; however there is still a little more to learn. In particular, some multiple copy operations are so common that it is worth adding special commands.

» Using Edit,Fill

Spreadsheets are usually very regular in the sense that the same calculation is often performed on a row or column of data. What this means is that after entering a single formula into a cell the most common copy operation is to copy it down the column or across the row - and this is exactly what Edit Fill Down and Fill Right do.

The Edit, Fill Down command will copy the contents of the top row of a selected area into each of the rows below. Fill Right will copy the column at the left of a selected area into each of the columns to the right. For example, if you want to copy the contents of A1 into A2:A10 you would first select A1:A10 and then use the command Edit, Fill Down. To copy A1 into B1:D1 you would select the range A1:D1 and use the command Edit, Fill Right. Notice that the selection has to include the cell that contains the data that you want to copy.

As well as Edit, Fill Down and Edit, Fill Right there are two other related commands - Edit, Fill Up and Edit, Fill Left. These two operate in the same way but make copies of the bottom row and right hand column of the selected range.

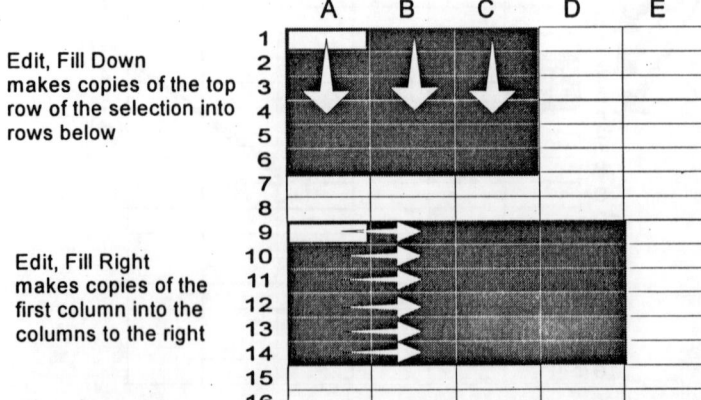

The Edit, Fill commands are so useful that it is worth learning the keypress shortcuts for them -

Fill Down	Ctrl D
Fill Right	Ctrl R
Fill Up	Ctrl U
Fill Left	Ctrl L

It is also important to remember that these Fill commands can be used to make copies of complete rows and columns - not just a single cell.

» Shortcuts for moving and copying

You can give the cut, copy and paste commands in one of three ways - using the Edit menu, using the appropriate icons in the toolbar or using the short cut keypresses - Ctrl-X for cut, Ctrl-C for copy and Ctrl-V for paste. Users can usually remember the first two of these - X looks a bit like scissors for cut, C is for Copy - but why V for paste? It is just because these three keys are next to each other on the keyboard.

» Drag and drop

As long as you are reasonably good with a mouse you might find the alternative drag and drop method of moving and copying faster. For the drag and drop operation to work you must have enabled it using the Options,Preferences command and selecting the Drag and Drop Cells item.

If you move the mouse pointer close to the edge of the selection you will see it change to an open hand. Depending on the screen resolution and the quality of the mouse that you are using this will be more or less difficult. Some users find it easy to make the open hand pointer appear; others seem to find it next to impossible to position the mouse accurately or consistently enough! If you press the mouse left button while the open hand is visible you will see it change to a closed hand pointer.

The closed hand is intended to signify that you have picked up the selected range. Indeed, if you move the closed hand an outline of the select moves with it. If you release the mouse button the selection range is moved to the new location. This is a drag and drop operation and you can use it to move or copy any selection.

If you want to copy the selection simply hold down the Ctrl key while the open hand pointer is showing. When you hold down the mouse button the closed hand will have a plus sign next to it to indicate that a copy operation is being performed. If you don't see the plus let the mouse button go and try again. Once the closed hand and plus pointer are visible you can release the Ctrl key.

If any cells in the drop area already contain data you will see a dialog box asking you if it is OK to overwrite the existing data. In other words, SCW does its best to stop you from making mistakes while using drag and drop.

» What your right mouse button is for

PC mice have a right as well as a left button. While the use of the left button is more or less standardised the right mouse button is used in different ways by different applications. SCW uses the right mouse button to produce a pop-up menu of commonly used commands. The advantage of the pop-up menu is that it appears at the current position of the mouse and so you don't have far to go to select a command. In particular, the quickest way of reaching Cut, Copy and Paste after you have selected an area is via the pop-up menu.

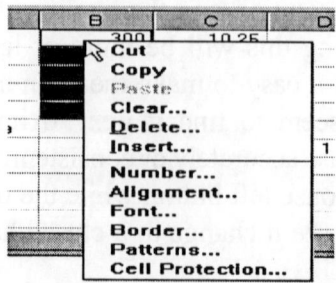

» The toolbar

As well as the main menu, the pop-up menu and their shortcut keys you can also make use of the toolbar at the top of the screen to give commands. Clicking on an icon is a particularly easy way of giving a command - except for the distance that you usually have to move the mouse to reach the toolbar. As in the case of the pop-up menu, it would be less effort to use the toolbar if it was nearer to the position that you were working at. In fact the toolbar's position is flexible and you can move it to any location within the SCW window. If you click on the blank region of the toolbar the cursor changes to an open hand.

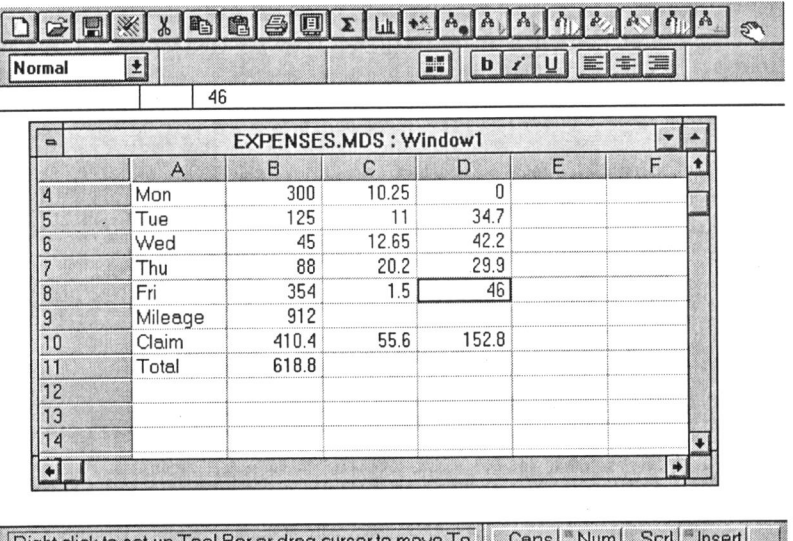

You can then drag the toolbar to either edge or the bottom of the window where it will reshape itself into a strip or drop it anywhere within the main area of the window. If you place the toolbar in the main area of the window it becomes a floating toolbar in the sense that you can drag it to the position closest to the area where you are currently working. If the floating toolbar is too large you can adjust its size by dragging its frame edges - just as you can resize any window.

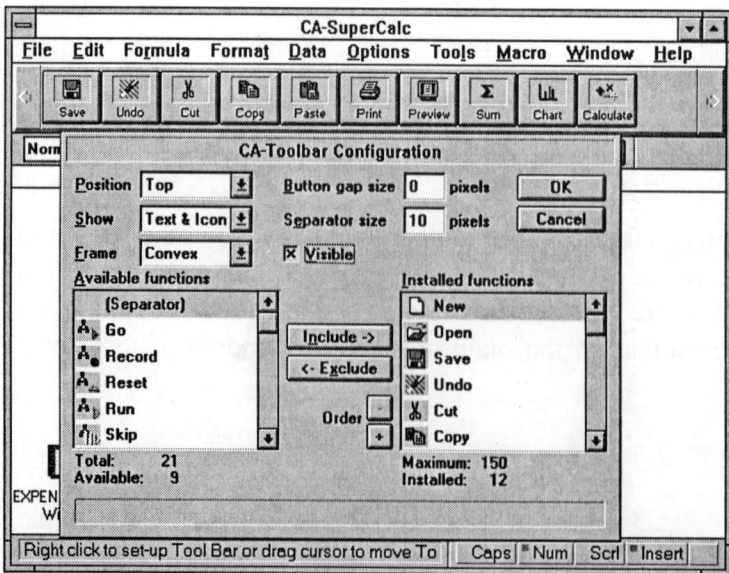

If you want to customise the toolbar to reduce the number of icons or change the way they are displayed you can do so by simply clicking with the right mouse button anywhere on the toolbar or using the Options,Toolbar command. In either case you can use the Toolbar Configuration dialog box to alter the way that it looks and works. In most cases however the basic toolbar is adequate for most purposes.

» Extending ranges

When you first use SCW you will find that pointing and dragging with the mouse is all you need to select ranges. Later you will find that there are times when a little more is needed. In particular, how do you cope with the problem of selecting a range of cells that is bigger than the screen? You can use the drag method because the screen will automatically scroll when you try to drag the selection off the side or bottom of the window but in many cases this can be a frustrating and error prone exercise.

The key to solving this problem is to know that the Shift key is used to signal that you want to add to or extend a selection and not start a new one. If you select a cell and then click on a second cell while holding down the Shift key the range marked out by the two cells is selected. The two cells are taken to be opposite corners of the selected range. If you change your mind and click on a different cell while still holding down the Shift key then the selected range changes accordingly.

» Clicking while holding down the Shift key is known as a "Shift-Click" and it is a standard convention within Windows that a shift-click always extends a selection.

So how does a shift-click help us to select a range that is larger than the screen? The answer is that you can move to the first cell of the range and select it and then you can move to the cell at the opposite corner and Shift-click on it. It doesn't matter if you have to scroll the window to see the second cell or if the first cell moves out of the window, Shift-click will still select the entire range. The only proviso is that you must have the scroll lock off. If the scroll lock is on you cannot alter the selection - only move the position of the window.

You can also extend the range using the movement keys - the arrow keys and PageUp, PageDown, Ctrl-PageUp and Ctrl-Page Down.

» Using Formula,Goto

The Shift-Click method of selecting a large range works as long as you are prepared to use the movement keys to step through the sheet to the required location. A simpler and more direct way of selecting a large area is simply to type in its range reference. If you press the F5 key, or use the Formula,Goto menu command, the Goto dialog box appears. You can enter into this the cell reference of any cell that you would like to make the current selection. You can also enter the range reference of any range that you would like to select.

For example, if you want to select the range B1:Z100 which would be a tedious job using the mouse, you can simply press F5 and enter it into the Goto dialog box.

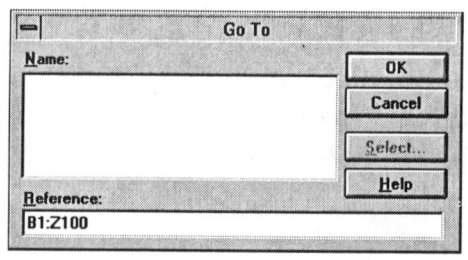

```
┌─────────────────────────────────────┐
│              Go To                  │
│ Name:                    ┌────────┐ │
│ ┌──────────────────────┐ │   OK   │ │
│ │                      │ ├────────┤ │
│ │                      │ │ Cancel │ │
│ │                      │ ├────────┤ │
│ │                      │ │ Select…│ │
│ │                      │ ├────────┤ │
│ │                      │ │  Help  │ │
│ └──────────────────────┘ └────────┘ │
│ Reference:                          │
│ ┌──────────────────────────────────┐│
│ │B1:Z100                           ││
│ └──────────────────────────────────┘│
└─────────────────────────────────────┘
```

When you press return or click on the OK button the entire range will be selected - even though you can't see it all.

Once you have a range selected using Goto you can modify it using the movement keys while holding down the Shift key. If you need to edit a selection in this way you will find it useful to know that pressing Ctrl together with . (dot) changes which corner of the selection is movable. Every selection has a fixed corner, the currently selected cell and a moveable corner - the one diagonally opposite it. Pressing Ctrl-. makes the fixed corner move around the selection in a clockwise direction. Using this and the movement keys in combination with Shift you should be able to modify any selection without having to start from scratch. The only difficulty is in remembering to move from the Ctrl key to the Shift key when you start to alter the selection!

» Practical - Costing a mailshot

The following hands-on exercise is designed to make use of the techniques discussed in this chapter. It is also an example of how a spreadsheet can be used to explore a situation rather than just work out totals and percentages. Its aim is to consider the the idea of using direct advertising to sell a product.

The first task is to enter data which has already been collected on printing costs for the advertising leaflet and the postage costs into a new sheet.

	A	B	C	D
1				
2	Number	Cost	Postage	Total cost
3	1000	95	190	285
4	5000	166	950	1116
5	10000	255	1900	2155
6	15000	345	2850	3195
7	20000	517	3800	4317

You can see that in column A the size of the mailshots under consideration have been entered. Column B contains the estimates of printing that number of leaflets as obtained from a printer.

Column C contains an crude estimate of postage costs assuming 19p per item. The formula to calculate this result for C3 is

=A3*19/100

To copy this into the remaining cells in the column you could use any one of a variety of methods. For example, selecting C3 and then using the Edit,Copy command, clicking on the Copy to clipboard icon or using the Ctrl-C keypress copies the formula to the clipboard.
Once the formula is on the clipboard you can make multiple

copies of it by selecting C4:C7 and pasting it back into the sheet. You can give the paste command either by using the Edit,Paste menu option, clicking on the paste icon or by using the Ctrl-V keypress. Once the formula is pasted into C4:C7 you will see the postage costs for each proposed mailshot size.

Column D contains the total estimated cost of the mailshot and in this case the formula to enter into D3 is simply

=B3+C3

To copy this into the rest of the column we could use the copy and paste operation as before but Fill Down is actually a simpler method. To do this you need to select the range D3:D7 and then use the command Edit,Fill Down or press Ctrl-D. Notice that the selected range has to include the cell being copied - i.e. D3.

So far the spreadsheet gives us the estimated cost for the mailshot but we can also calculate an estimate of the profit. If you assume that 1% of the leaflets stimulate a response and the average profit on each order received is £10, the profit from the mailshot would be

=A3*1%*10-D3

where A3 is the size of the mailshot and D3 is its cost.

To get some feel for how the mailshot performs it is valuable to tabulate the total profit for response rates of 1%, 2% and 5%. To do this you have to enter the formulae

=A3*1%*10-D3   in E3
=A3*2%*10-D3   in F3
=A3*5%*10-D3   in G3

Notice that you can work out a percentage by multiplying by the value followed by a percentage sign. To copy the formulae into the rows below each one the simplest method is to again use the Edit,Fill Down command. Select the range E3:G7 and use the command Edit,Fill Down or press Ctrl-D. The same result could have been obtained by copying the row containing the formulae, i.e. E3:G3, and copying this to the clipboard and then selecting the column E4:E7 and pasting. The moral is that in SCW there is usually more than one way of doing a simple data entry operation but one method will usually be simpler, and therefore better, than the rest.

If you look at the table of results you can see immediately that you need a better than 2% return if you are going to make a profit but if you can get as good as 5% then the return on the entire project is about 100%.

	A	B	C	D	E	F	G
1							
2	Number	Cost	Postage	Total cost	1%	2%	5%
3	1000	95	190	285	-185	-85	215
4	5000	166	950	1116	-616	-116	1384
5	10000	255	1900	2155	-1155	-155	2845
6	15000	345	2850	3195	-1695	-195	4305
7	20000	517	3800	4317	-2317	-317	5683

Key points

» Using SCW involves selecting cells and ranges. The basic action is to select cells and then give a command.

» Three very common operations are cut, copy and paste. These can be used to move and duplicate cell contents.

» The Edit,Fill Down, Fill Right, Fill Left and Fill Up commands are alternative and quicker ways of making duplicate copies of formulae in the row or column at the edge of a range.

» You can drag a selection to a new location using drag and drop and make a copy by dragging while holding down the Ctrl key.

» Pressing the right mouse button displays a pop-up menu which contains commonly used commands including Cut, Copy and Paste.

» There are icon equivalents to many commands in the toolbar and these can often be reached more easily by configuring it as a floating toolbar.

» You can extend a selection using Shift-click or by using the movement keys while holding down the Shift key.

» To select a range that is larger than the window you can drag off the edge of the window, which will then automatically scroll, but this can be tedious. Alternatively you can use the Shift-click method or even better the command Formula,Goto and enter a range reference in the dialog box that appears.

Chapter 3

Calculations

Calculations are the life blood of any spreadsheet. Without them the program is no more than a useful tool to record and edit data. Add the ability to calculate and you have a tool that can analyse, summarise and hypothesise. As you can see it is vital that you understand how a spreadsheet performs its calculations and how to enter formulae that will produce exactly the results you want. Just as poor quality data riddled with errors will ruin your efforts, so just as surely will a mistaken assumption about the way that a formula works.

Fortunately SCW has eliminated the guesswork that used to be associated with entering a formula. It makes it as simple as possible for you to specify any formula correctly and in many cases you can almost avoid typing anything at all.

» Operators

In many cases you can work out exactly what you need to know using simple arithmetic. The four arithmetic operators are *, /, + and -. Any expressions that you write using them will be worked out and the result displayed. The only room for making errors here is in not realising that the order that these operations are carried out in matters. For example, 2+3*4 is not 2+3 (i.e. 5) multiplied by 4 (i.e. 20) but 3*4 (i.e. 12) plus 2 (i.e. 14). The fact that multiplication and division is always done before addition is something that we are taught in school but it is amazing how easy it is to forget when working with a spreadsheet!

SCW and all other spreadsheets will calculate any multiplications and divisions followed by additions and subtractions. If you want to change this order then use brackets to make clear what it is that you are trying to work out. For example, (2+3)*4 is 20 and 2+(3*4) is 14 and even though the brackets are not needed in the second case they do no harm.

If you think that you are unlikely to make such simple mistakes it is worth pointing out that they are easy to make when transcribing a formula written on more than one line to a spreadsheet formula which has to be written on a single line. For example, how should you enter the formula

$$\frac{A1}{A2+1}$$

It is all too easy to transcribe it as

=A1/A2+1

instead of

=A1/(A2+1)

which is correct!

As well as the familiar arithmetic operators there are also a number of less common ones. Whether you will want to use any of these depends on exactly what you are planning to do with your spreadsheet. In later chapters these operators are introduced as needed but it is worth describing the power operator here. To raise any value to a power you use ^ - the caret symbol which is above the 6 key on most keyboards. Raising to a power has a higher priority than any other arithmetic operation and so =A1^2+1 is the same as =(A1^2)+1 and not =A1^(2+1).

» Pointing

When you enter a formula like =A1+B1 there are two ways you can do it. You can type in the cell references or you can point to the cells in question using the mouse. For example, to enter =A1+B1 you could type the equals and then click with the mouse on cell A1. This causes the cell reference to appear on the input line. You can then type the plus sign and click on cell B1. The rule is that anywhere you could type in a cell reference you can point to the cell concerned instead.

» Absolute and relative

You may have noticed that when you copy a formula the result isn't an exact copy. For example, if you enter the formula =A1+1 into B1 and then copy it into B2 the result will read =A2+1. This is so natural a change that it is worth reminding you that an exact copy would read =A1+1. The way that cell references are changed when you make a copy is one of the reasons why spreadsheets are so easy to use. Without this adjustment you would have to enter every formula manually to be correct at its location.

The reason why the automatic formula adjustment works is that when you enter a formula into a cell you usually intend the cell references to be treated as relative to the cell that the formula is stored in. For example, =A1+1 stored in cell B1 usually means "the cell to the left plus one". When you copy this formula into B2 the cell to the left is A2 and so the formula is adjusted to read =A2+1 and so on. Cell references that are adjusted in this way when you copy them are called relative cell references and they are the default.

	A	B	C	D
1		=A1+1		
2		=A2+1		
3		=A3+1		
4		=A4+1		
5				
6				

However there are times when you don't want a cell reference to be relative. For example, suppose you store the current rate of tax in cell A1 and use this in a formula in B2 to work out the tax payable on an amount in A2. In this case the formula would be =A2*A1 but when you copied it down the column to work out the tax on A3, A4 and so on you would not want the reference to A1 to be adjusted. No matter where the formula is copied to the tax rate is still in A1 and the reference is absolute. Notice that the reference to A2 does need to be adjusted as the formula is copied down the column - so a single formula can contain absolute and relative references at the same time.

	A	B	C	D
1	Tax rate			
2		=A2*A1		
3		=A3*A1		
4		=A4*A1		
5		=A5*A1		
6				

To make a reference absolute you have to write it with dollar signs in front of the column letter and the row number. For example, $A$1 is an absolute reference to A1 and will not be adjusted when the formula is copied. Rather than having to type the dollar signs individually it is simpler to enter the cell reference using any of the standard methods and then press F4 which automatically adds the dollar signs to convert a relative reference into an absolute one. So the tax calculation used as an example would have to be entered as =A2*$A$1 if copying is to produce the correct result at each location.

» Mistakes with absolute and relative cell references account for a great many spreadsheet errors.

Whenever you enter a spreadsheet formula you should ask yourself if the each cell reference is relative or absolute and use the F4 key as appropriate. If you are ever unsure if a reference is relative or absolute there is one sure way of finding out. Simply type the formula in again at a different location and see which cell references you have to change and which stay the same to make it correct.

» Moving spreadsheet entries

When you move a spreadsheet entry from one cell to another any cell references it contains remain the same. So for example if A10 contains the formula SUM(A1:A9) and you move it to B10 then B10 will now contain the formula SUM(A1:A9).

In other words, using Cut and Paste results in cells references remaining absolute whereas Copy and Paste treats them as relative unless you specify otherwise. When you think about it this is the logical way for a spreadsheet to work. When you move a cell entry it is usually to make room for some other data or to improve the layout of your sheet and you do not want to make changes to the way that the sheet works. When copying a cell it is usually because you to make the same underlying formula apply to other ranges and so you want automatic adjustment.

» Row and column relative

You should skip this section until you are very confident about the idea of absolute and relative cell references.

Most users quickly come to terms with the idea of relative and absolute cell references. What seems to be more confusing is the fact that a cell reference can be both relative and absolute at the same time. This is a less common situation and can present difficulties when you first come across it. For example, consider a set of discount rates, 5%, 10% and 15%, stored in B1:D1 . Now consider working out the discount on each price in column A2:A7.

	A	B	C	D
1		5%	10%	15%
2	10	=A2*B1		
3	12			
4	22			
5	28			
6	55			
7	88			
8				
9				

The formula to be entered into B2 is simple enough
> =A2*B1

The question is are the cell references absolute or relative. At first sight it looks as if A2 is a relative reference because it needs to change when it is copied down the column into B3, B4 and so on. By the same reasoning B1 looks as if it should be absolute because it shouldn't change as it is copied down the column.

However both of these conclusions ignore the possibility that the formula might be copied in one operation into the other two columns as well as the rows, i.e. into B2:D7. To see what happens consider the correct form of the formula in C2. In this case it should read =A2*C1 and now it looks as if the first reference is absolute and the second relative. The truth is easy to see if you manually write out the correct version of the formula in some of the other cells in the block. As the formula is copied from column to column the reference to column B in A2*B1 changes but the row number stays the same. As the formula is copied down the rows the reference to row 2 in A2*B1 changes but the column letter stays the same. That is the reference to B1 is column relative but row absolute and the reference to A2 is column absolute but row relative. Once you notice this it seems very reasonable. After all, the formula A2*B1 actually means multiply the number on the same row in column A by the number in the same column in row one.

To write mixed absolute and column references all you have to do is use $ signs in front of either the column letter or the row number. So to write the formula A2*B1 correctly it should be

=$A2*B$1

If the formula is entered in this way to cell B2 then it can be copied into the range B2:D7 and SCW will correctly adjust each cell reference. If you don't understand a cell reference that includes a column or row absolute symbol then the only alternative is to enter a correct version of the formula manually in each cell of the top row and copy each one down the column.

	A	B	C	D
1		0.05	0.1	0.15
2	10	=$A2*B$1	=$A2*C$1	=$A2*D$1
3	12	=$A3*B$1	=$A3*C$1	=$A3*D$1
4	22	=$A4*B$1	=$A4*C$1	=$A4*D$1
5	28	=$A5*B$1	=$A5*C$1	=$A5*D$1
6	55	=$A6*B$1	=$A6*C$1	=$A6*D$1
7	88	=$A7*B$1	=$A7*C$1	=$A7*D$1

ABSREL.MDS : Window1

To make life easier you can use the F4 key to cycle through all possible assignments of $ signs within a cell reference. Starting from a completely relative cell reference, A1 say, pressing F4 converts it into a completely absolute reference i.e. $A$1. Pressing F4 again changes this to A$1 and then to $A1 and finally back to A1. You can keep on pressing F4 to cycle through all the possibilities.

Unfortunately pressing F4 cycles every reference in a formula and not just the one that the text cursor is in. The solution to the problem is to select the cell reference you want to change - simply drag across it using the mouse. Pressing F4 only cycles the cell reference you have selected, leaving the rest unaltered.

» Functions

Although you can work out most of the results you are interested in using nothing but simple arithmetic, the real power of a spreadsheet lies in the functions that it provides. SCW has a very wide range of functions and it does its best to make them easy to use.

A function takes the values that you specify and returns a single result. The values that act as inputs to the function are called "arguments" for reasons connected with traditional mathematics. We have already met the sum function, which is perhaps the most used of all spreadsheet functions. This will take the values stored in the cell that you specify and add them up. For example, if you enter

=SUM(A1:A10)

the SUM function will add up the contents of cells A1 to A10 and return the result as the value of the cell it is stored in. The range reference A1:A10 is the function's argument and this will be adjusted if you copy the formula to a new location - that is, the ideas of absolute and relative apply to functions just as much as to simple formulae.

You can also use pointing to enter arguments to functions. If you type

=SUM(

and then select the range to be summed by dragging with the mouse, the range automatically appears on the entry line. All you have to do is type the closing bracket and that's the formula entered.

That's all there is to a function. Of course to make use of them you need to know what is available and what each one does.

» Pasting functions

If you have a good memory you will probably quickly remember the most common functions but there are so many in total that it's impossible to remember details of them all.

The solution to this problem is to use the Formula,Paste Function command or the equivalent keypress - Shift-F3. This displays the Paste Function dialog box which contains an alphabetic list of all of the functions that SCW supports. You can navigate through this list by using the scroll bar at the right hand side or you can use the short cut of pressing the first letter of the function you are looking for.

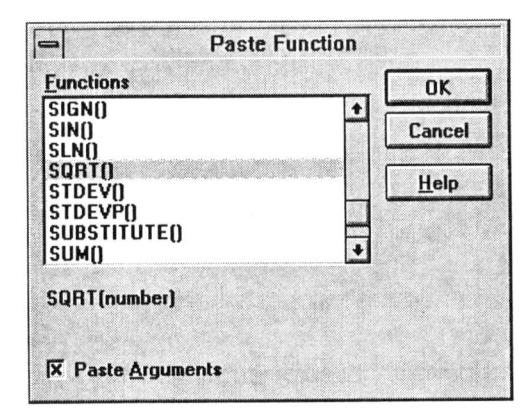

For example, if you are looking for the SUM function pressing the S key takes you to the start of the S section where you can scroll to the exact position required. Just below the list of functions you will see the function that is currently selected and a simple explanation of its arguments.

For example, if you select the SQRT() function you will see SQRT(number) displayed. This is to indicate that this function takes a single argument - the number that you want to know the square root of. If you need more help than this then click on the Help button which takes you directly to a page of on-line help that describes the function in detail.

The Paste Function dialog box isn't just a way of finding the exact spelling of that function you just cannot quite remember - it also allows you to paste a prototype for the function onto the entry line. For example, if you select the SQRT() function and click on the OK button then a prototype for this function is pasted onto the entry line with the dummy argument "number" highlighted.

|X|✓| =SQRT(number)

The reason why the argument is highlighted is that you can now point to the cell, or type in the value, that you would like to work out the square root of. The highlighted argument will be replaced by your next entry, however it is made. In this way the function prototype aids you in entering the function and its arguments.

This raises the question of what happens if a function has more than one argument. For example, the function CAGR will calculate the final worth of a deposit for a given time at a given interest rate. The arguments of the CAGR function are value - the amount deposited; rate - the interest rate per period; and nper - the number of periods. If you paste the CAGR function onto the entry line the value argument is highlighted and you can replace it by a cell reference by pointing.

|X|✓| =CAGR(value,rate,nper)

To replace the second argument you have to use the mouse to highlight it. If you click on a cell its reference will replace that argument. You can continue in this way until all of the arguments have been replaced by cell references. The only problem with this method is that you have to make absolutely sure that you highlight the entire argument and not the commas or the final closing bracket. If you make a mistake then the result can be a function that makes no sense.

If you find this replacement of dummy arguments a chore rather than a help you can opt to paste functions without arguments. Simply click on the Paste Arguments check box to remove the cross. Some functions have such a varied set of arguments that pasting them with arguments is more trouble than usual. The SUM function is one of these. If you paste the SUM function you may be surprised to see that in place of the single argument that you would normally use there are two arguments called number1, number2 and then three dots ...

☒ ☑ =SUM(number1,number2,...)

Although the most commonly used form of the SUM function is SUM(range reference) it can be more complicated than this. You can sum a list of numbers or range references. For example, SUM(A1:A10,B3:Z5,H1:H10) is perfectly valid and will sum the three ranges listed. In other words the SUM function has a variable number of arguments and this is what the three dots signify - that you can carry on the list with number3, number4 and so on. When you use the SUM function as pasted complete with arguments you often have to delete the dummy second argument complete with its dots!

In general when you paste a function it may be supplied with more arguments that you actually want to use - make sure that you delete them.

» Range expressions

We have already seen examples of functions that can use range references as arguments. Not all functions can but in general anywhere you could use a list of values within a function you can use a range reference and vice versa. So for example, SUM(1,2,3,4) is valid as is SUM(A1:A10,3,4). What is less obvious is the fact that you can use range expressions within functions.

A range expression is a piece of arithmetic that you would like to perform on every cell in the range. For example, A1:A10*2 is taken to mean "multiply the value in each cell A1 to A10 by 2". Of course you cannot enter a range expression into a cell because it doesn't return a single value. However you can use a range expression within any formula that reduces the range to a single value. For example,

=SUM(A1:A10*2)

is perfectly valid and will return the sum of each of the cells times two. Of course this is exactly the same as =SUM(A1:A10)*2 but in some cases it isn't possible to reduce a range expression in this way. For example,

=SUM(SQRT(A1:A10))

adds up the square roots of each cell in the range A1:A10. Notice that in normal use you couldn't use a range reference in the SQRT function but in a range expression you can. You can even involve two ranges in a range expression. For example,

=SUM(A1:A10*A1:A10)

multiplies each cell in the range by itself and adds up the result. That is, it works out A1*A1+A2*A2+A3*A3 and so on.

The general principle is that expressions are evaluated for each cell in the range and if there is more than one range then the values are taken in turn.

» Multiple selections

All of the ranges that we have used so far have been rectangular and the range reference has specified the two opposite corners of the range. SCW allows you to use a more general form of range reference composed of an arbitrary collection of rectangular ranges. In this case the range reference simply consists of a list of the range reference for each of the rectangular areas. For example, B4:C6,D7:E9 is a range reference to the two blocks B4:C6 and D7:E9.

You can use a multiple selection anywhere that you would normally be allowed to use a simple range. For example,

=SUM(B4:C6,D7:E9)

would sum all the values in the two blocks.

As well as entering multiple ranges by typing you can also use the mouse to select them. The first range is selected as usual by dragging. The second and subsequent selections have to be made by dragging while holding down the Ctrl key. For example to select B4:C6,D7:E9 you would first select B4:C6 in the usual way and then select D7:E9 while holding down the Ctrl key.

This use of the Ctrl key is a standard Windows convention. Whenever you are making a selection you can add any other selection to it by holding down the Ctrl key. In fact the Shift and Ctrl keys both work to extend an existing selection.

» Holding down the Shift key and making a selection extends the existing selection by adding all of the elements in between to it.

» Holding down the Ctrl key and making a selection extends the existing selection by adding just the new selection to it.

» Names

Range references are perfectly easy to understand but they can often appear cryptic. It may be obvious that a formula such as =SUM(Q13:V15) is the sum of all the profits at the time you write the formula but after a few hours or days it quickly becomes a mystery as to what data Q13:V15 might hold. To avoid this sort of problem it is a good idea to use range names.

To give a range a name you first select the range and then use the Formula,Define Name command or press Ctrl-F3. In either case you will see the Define Name dialog box.

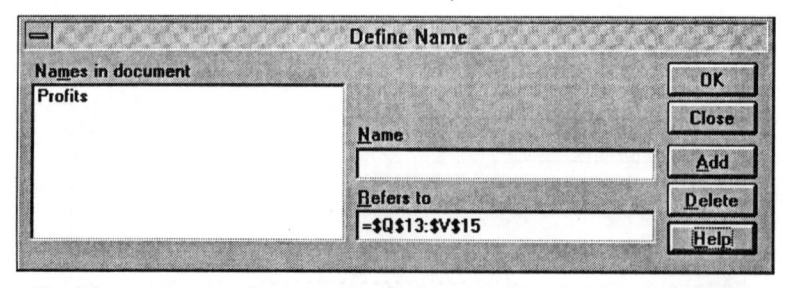

```
┌─ Define Name ─────────────────────────┐
│ Names in document                 OK  │
│ Profits                               │
│                    Name        Close  │
│                                       │
│                                 Add   │
│                    Refers to          │
│                    =$Q$13:$V$15 Delete│
│                                 Help  │
└───────────────────────────────────────┘
```

In this you enter the name and the range to which it refers. If you have selected the range before giving the command then it will already be entered into the Refers to box. However you can edit this or enter any range that you want to give the name to. Once you are satisfied you can click on the Add or OK button. If you click on the Add button you will see the name added to the list of names already defined and you can carry on defining names. If you click on OK then the name will be added and the dialog box closed. Clicking on Close will close the dialog box without adding the current name to the list. Notice that a name can refer to a single cell, a range or a multiple selection. (It can also refer to a particular formula - see later.)

It is worth knowing that you can point to a new range while the Define Name dialog box is open. All you have to do is place the text cursor on the Refers to box as if you were about to type in a reference but instead you click on the sheet behind the box and drag to select an area. Notice that if the Define Name dialog box is in the way you can move it by dragging its title bar.

You can discover what the definition of any particular name is using the Define Name dialog box. If you select a name from the list the range that it stands for is shown in the Refers to box.

When you define a name by typing in a cell reference or range reference you don't have to type the leading equals sign but it is important that you make the references absolute. If you don't make the references absolute the definition of the name will change each time you actually use it - the reason is that SCW will adjust the definition because it is relative. You can use relative references in name definitions but how they are treated can seem a little confusing at first.

Once you have defined a name you can use it anywhere that you would have originally used the cell or range reference. You can do this either by typing in the name directly or by using the Formula,Paste Name command. This displays the Paste Name dialog box from which you can select any of the names that you have defined.

Notice that if you haven't defined any names yet the Formula,Paste Name command is greyed out. Also notice that the names that you define belong to the particular sheet you are working on. If you open another sheet it will have its own set of names.

» Relative names

You can skip this section until you need to know about relative range names.

You can use relative definitions within names but they are a little bit more complicated and it is important that you are clear how they work if you are to avoid mistakes. Fortunately most named ranges are absolute.

The key to understanding relative references in range names is realising what they are taken to be relative to when you enter the definition. All relative cell references entered using the Define Name dialog box are taken to be relative to the currently selected cell. If you later open the Define Name dialog box all of the relative ranges will be adjusted to read correctly relative to the current cell. This means that if you define a name using a relative reference it will seem to change each time you look at it! This may seem disturbing at first but if you think about it this is exactly what you would expect of a relative definition. What the Define Name dialog box shows you as the current definition of any relative name is what it would mean if used in the currently selected cell and again this is exactly what you want to know.

For example, suppose you define a name to refer to A1 and the cell selected while the Define Name dialog box is open is A2. This relative name is then taken to mean "the cell one row above the current cell" as it would be if you entered the reference A1 directly into cell A2. Now if you select another cell, B10 say, and examine the definition of the name you will find that it has changed to be correct for this cell, that is B9. If you were to enter or paste the name into B10 then the name would indeed be taken to be a reference to B9.

» When you define a relative name it is taken to be relative to the current cell and adjusted according to the current cell thereafter.

» Names from labels

It is very often the case that the names that you would like to give to ranges are already in your spreadsheet as text labels - usually as column headings. You can use these labels to define names by selecting the range that contains them and then using the Formula,Create Names command or by pressing Ctrl-Shift-F3. This produces the Create Names dialog box.

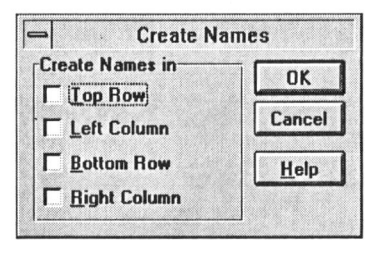

```
┌─                Create Names            ─┐
│ ┌Create Names in─────┐    ┌──────────┐  │
│ │  ☐ Top Row         │    │    OK    │  │
│ │  ☐ Left Column     │    ├──────────┤  │
│ │  ☐ Bottom Row      │    │  Cancel  │  │
│ │  ☐ Right Column    │    ├──────────┤  │
│ └────────────────────┘    │   Help   │  │
│                           └──────────┘  │
└─────────────────────────────────────────┘
```

In this you have to select the row or column that the labels are in - i.e. top row, bottom row, left hand column or right hand column. Once you have done this clicking on the OK button automatically creates one new name for each label. The definition of each name is the part of the row or column in the range that the label is in. See the practical at the end of this chapter for an example of the use of the Formula,Create Names command.

» Converting to names

It often happens that you start a spreadsheet and write formulae that reference cells and ranges before you realise that it would be better to assign names. You can use the Formula,Apply Names command to convert ranges to their corresponding range names.

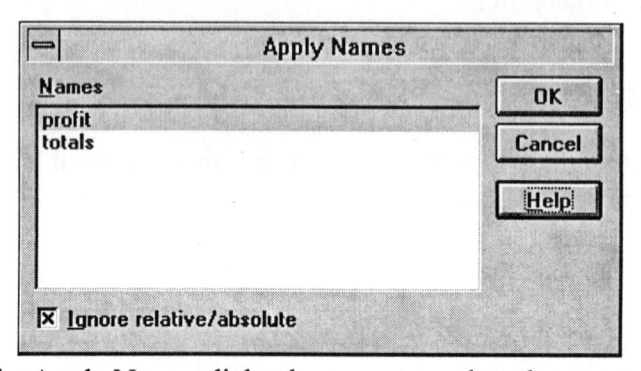

In the Apply Names dialog box you can select the names that you would like to apply and then click on the OK button. After this SCW will search through the currently selected range and replace every occurrence of any named cell or range references with the corresponding name. If you want to perform the conversion to names throughout the sheet simply click on the box where the column names and row numbers meet and the entire sheet will be selected. Always remember to select the range where you want to apply the names before you use the Formula, Apply Names command.

Although the Apply Names command is very useful there are a number of complications that can arise. If you use the default method of applying names then references will be replaced by names even if they don't match the name's definition in terms of absolute and relative references. For example, if you have defined TAX to be $A$1 and apply the name to the whole of the spreadsheet then references such as A1, $A1 and A$1 are replaced by the name TAX even though they don't match exactly. In most cases this is what you require because named ranges tend to be absolute references by their very nature and if you haven't used an absolute reference in the spreadsheet then this is probably laziness!

If however you click on the Ignore relative/absolute box and remove the cross then a reference has to match the name definition exactly before it is replaced.

» Undoing names

If you have used names within a sheet, either by typing them in or by using Apply,Names, then occasionally you will find that you need to convert them back into references. You can remove a name simply by using the Formula,Define Name command, selecting it in the list and then clicking on the Delete button. This certainly removes the name's definition from the list but it doesn't convert formulae that use the name back into their original form by replacing the name by its reference.

If you want to convert a name to a reference before you delete it then you have to use the Formula,Replace command. This can be used to search a selected range for the occurrences of one set of characters and replace them with another. This is a completely general find and replace facility but in particular it can be used to find names and replace them by their references.

In this particular case you first have to lookup the name's definition. For example, if you wanted to replace the name TAX you would need to know that it referred to A1. Once you know the name's definition you next select the range that contains the formulae that you want to replace the name in. If you don't know this range simply select the entire sheet. Next use the menu command Formula,Replace which produces the Replace dialog box.

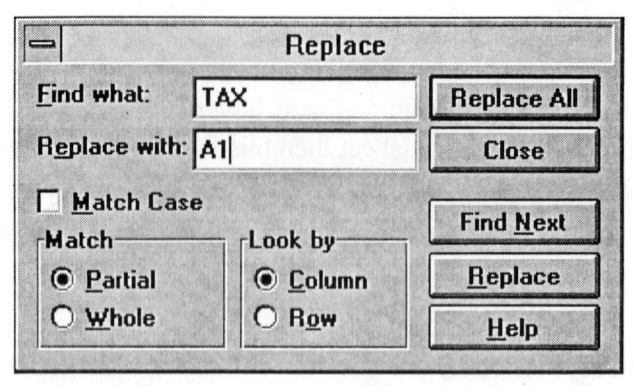

Enter the name into the Find what box and enter the reference into the Replace with box. To make sure that every occurrence of the name is replaced by its reference you need to select the Partial option in the Match Case section of the dialog box. Finally click on the Find Next button and if a valid occurrence of the name is found then click on Replace.

You can carry on using the Find Next button until all of the occurrences of the name have been replaced. If you cannot make the Replace work the chances are that you have forgotten to select the range it is to operate on before using the Formula,Replace command.

In most cases you should not give in to the temptation to click on the Replace All button. The reason is that you will almost certainly incorrectly change text or formulae that contain the name. For example, if you do a Replace All on TAX you will change headings that read "This years TAX" to read "This years A1". Also notice that this method does not work if you try to replace a name with relative cell references in its definition. The reason is that each occurrence of the name has to be replaced by a different cell reference according to its location.

» Formula names

As well as being able to apply names to cell references and ranges you can also apply a name to a formula. To define a name that refers to a formula you simply type in the formula into the Refers to box in the Define Name dialog box.

For example, if you define the name Totals to be

=SUM($A$1:$A$10)

then when you enter or paste the name

=Totals

into a cell it works out the sum of A1:A10. The advantage of this approach is that you can give a formula a meaningful name that hopefully helps explain what the spreadsheet is doing. The disadvantage of the method is that you have to look at the definition of the name in the Define Name dialog box to check that it is correct.

Another advantage of giving a formula a name is that multiple copies of the formula can be entered simply by reusing the name and any changes made to the definition of the name affect all of the copies. This centralised control of formulae is such an attractive idea that you might be tempted to be ambitious. In particular to make the idea work you really have to make use of relative references within the formula and this can be complicated.

Using a relative reference means that the formula can calculate a different result according to where it is stored. The rules for relative references used inside a formula are the same as for simple references. That is, they are taken as relative to the current cell during the definition and automatically adjusted as the current cell changes.

For example, suppose you want to define a formula that will add up the first ten rows of a column. The correct way to do this is to first select the cell that is going to be used to store the result - A11 say. Next type in the formula into the Define Name dialog box as it would be entered into this cell - that is

=SUM(A1:A10). After you have defined the name, Totals, say, you can enter this into cell A11 either using Paste Name or by typing it in. If you now copy this into B11:D11 the formula will be automatically adjusted to sum the column it is stored in. If you change the definition of the formula in the Define Name dialog box, to add up only the first 5 rows say, then every use of the name will change.

All of this may seem complicated at first but it works very well as long as you follow two simple rules:

» When you are defining a named formula involving relative references select the cell that it will be used in and type in the definition as it would be entered into that cell.

» If you want to change the definition of a named formula select a cell that it is or will be used in and edit the definition to be correct for that cell.

What you must never do is enter or edit a named formula when you have just selected an arbitrary cell in the spreadsheet!

» Row and column ranges

As well as specifying cell references and range references you can refer to sets of complete rows and columns. For example, A:C is a column reference to columns A,B and C. Similarly 3:5 refers to rows 3, 4 and 5. You can also make multiple selections as in A:C,F:H. To refer to a single column or row you simply repeat the column letter or row number as in A:A or 1:1.

You can point to row or column ranges by clicking on the row or column header. For example, to select column B you would click on the letter B in the edge of the sheet window. To select a continuous range you can either drag across the columns or rows or use Shift and click. To make a multiple selection you can use Ctrl and click. Notice that the Shift and Ctrl keys add to the selection in the standard way.

You can use row and column references in functions but usually they are more trouble than they are worth. For example, if you enter the formula

=SUM(A:A)

any values in column A will be summed. However, if you store this formula in a cell in column A, which is of course something you are likely to do, it will include itself in the addition!

The main use of row and column references is when you want to apply an operation to a whole row or column. For example, you can cut, copy and paste whole rows and columns.

» Circular references

A circular reference is where a formula either directly or indirectly references itself. Although this self reference can actually be put to good use in most cases it is best regarded as an error. If you enter a formula that references itself you will see the word "Cycle" appear in the bottom edge of the SCW window. In most cases you can easily see what is causing the circular reference and resolve the problem. In situations where you cannot find the cause then you can make use of SCW's auditing facilities - see Chapter 6.

» Controlling calculation

Whenever you enter something into a cell the entire spreadsheet is recalculated. Normally this is exactly what you want but if you are entering a long list of data and you are not interested in seeing intermediate results then you might benefit from turning the calculation off. To do this use the command Options,Calculation and then select the Manual option in the Calculation dialog box.

While manual calculation is selected you can recalculate the sheet by pressing the F9 key, by using the Options, Calculate Now command or by clicking on the recalculate icon. Indeed you can recalculate a spreadsheet at any time but normally this isn't necessary when Automatic calculation is enabled. You can tell that a spreadsheet needs to be recalculated to show the most up-to-date results by the appearance of the word "Calculate" next to the data entry box.

The other options in the Calculation dialog box are relevant to modelling and are discussed in *Multidimensional Modelling with CA-SuperCalc for Windows*.

One useful tip is that pressing F9 while there is a formula on the entry line will evaluate it before you enter it into a cell. For example, if the entry line contains =2*2 and you press F9 this is converted into 4 which can then be entered into the current cell.

» Autosum

The most commonly used function is most definitely the SUM function and SCW makes it very easy to sum any range by simply clicking on the autosum button. What the autosum button actually does depends on what you have selected before you click on it.

» If you select a cell that is at the bottom of a column of data then a SUM function will be constructed that sums from the first data value to the cell just above the one selected.

So if column A contains data in A3:A10 and you select cell A15 the autosum button will create a formula that reads =SUM(A3:A14). Notice that the end of the range is A14 and not A10.

» If you select a range and then click on the autosum button then SUM functions will be inserted into all of the cells in the bottom row and right-hand column of the range - provided they are completely empty.

What this means is that if you select a block with no data in the bottom row SUM functions will be inserted into the bottom row to sum the columns above. For example, if there is data in A1:D10 then selecting A1:D11 will insert SUM functions into A11:D11. Similarly, selecting a block with an empty right-hand column will generate row sums.

If you select a range and the autosum function cannot work out what to do, perhaps because there are entries in both the bottom row and the right hand column, it simply places a =SUM() function on the data entry line ready for you to edit.

» Practical - the mailshot sheet

Although the mailshot example introduced at the end of the previous chapter is complete and fully working it could have been constructed in a more efficient way. For example, the formula to calculate the profit on each mailshot size assuming a given percentage response had to be entered 3 times - once for each percentage. It would have been simpler to enter the original formula in E3 as:

$$=\$A3*E\$2*10-\$D3$$

The use of dollar signs to make the cell references partially absolute enables this formula to be copied correctly into the entire range E3:G7 in a single operation.

You can also use the Formula,Create Names command to convert the column headings into names. Select A2:D7, give the command Formula,Create Names and select Top row in the dialog box. You will then find that A3:A7 is named Number, B3:B7 is named Cost and so on. However these names are of little use in this particular spreadsheet because there is no need to sum or otherwise process these values.

If you want to be a little more adventurous you could define Cost to be $B3 and Postage to be $C3 while the cursor is in cell D3 and then you can enter the formula

=Cost+Postage

in D3 and copy this down the column.

Practical - the mailshot sheet **63**

If you want to take this approach another stage further you could select E3 and define

Number	=$A3
Percentage	=E$2
SaleProfit	=10
TotalCost	=$D3

Notice that it is very important that each of these names is defined while the currently selected cell is E3. Then you can enter into E3 the formula

=Number*Percentage*SaleProfit-TotalCost

and then make a copy of this into the range E3:G7.

As long as you appreciate how these relative range names work this is good way of making sure that a formula is completely understandable.

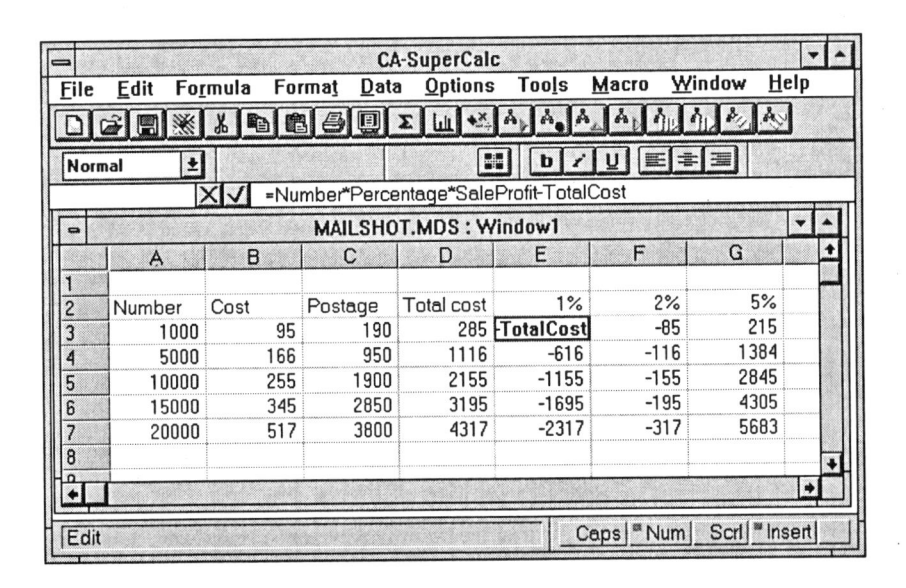

	A	B	C	D	E	F	G
1							
2	Number	Cost	Postage	Total cost	1%	2%	5%
3	1000	95	190	285	TotalCost	-85	215
4	5000	166	950	1116	-616	-116	1384
5	10000	255	1900	2155	-1155	-155	2845
6	15000	345	2850	3195	-1695	-195	4305
7	20000	517	3800	4317	-2317	-317	5683

Key points

» Make sure that you use brackets to force arithmetic to be carried out in the correct order.

» Cell references can be absolute - $A$1, relative - A1 or mixed - $A1 or A$1.

» You can paste a function complete with dummy arguments into the entry line and then replace the arguments by pointing or typing.

» Range expressions are a way of performing the same calculation on every value in a range.

» A range reference can include multiple selections, e.g. A1:B10,F3:H6. You can point to multiple selections by holding down the Ctrl key.

» You can assign a name to any range - including multiple selections. Names can be absolute, relative or mixed.

» Names can be created from labels already in the spreadsheet.

» References can be automatically converted into names but it is more difficult to convert names back into references.

» A name can be assigned to a formula.

» The autosum button can be used to generate more than one SUM function at a time by selecting an appropriate range.

Chapter 4

Formatting

One of the joys of using a Windows spreadsheet is that you can change the way it looks almost instantly and see the result at once. This is the well known What You See Is What You Get (WYSIWYG) facility and it makes formatting almost trivial. However this said, a little organisation goes a long way and the key to organising formats are styles. As long as you have a high enough quality printer available - an inkjet or a laser printer is ideal - you can create presentation quality reports directly in SCW.

As well as the simple WYSIWYG facilities SCW also has hidden power. If you are prepared to find out how to create your own formats then you can obtain even greater control over how data is displayed.

» Format basics

Every cell in a sheet stores a list of format items that control how it displays. Notice that the formatting of a cell never alters what is stored in a cell, only how it looks. For example, if you apply a format that causes numbers to display to only one decimal place then data and results are still stored, and calculations performed, to full precision. If you actually want to work with values rounded or truncated to a given number of decimal places then you have to use formulae to convert the values, see Chapter 9. At the moment what we are discussing is the appearance of the data.

» Applying formatting

A cell's format consists of five attributes:
- Number - a numeric format specification
- Alignment - where data is displayed in a cell
- Font - the font used to display the data
- Border - the style of lines, if any, drawn around the cell
- Patterns - the background pattern of the cell

These five attributes correspond to the first five options in the Format menu. Each one leads on to a dialog box where you can select the details of the format attribute. Also in the format list is an option to set cell protection but this is better discussed in Chapter 6, along with other matters of security and auditing.

To apply a format change to a range of cells you first have to select the cells in question and then use the Format command to modify the aspects of the format that you want to change. You can select multiple ranges and row and column ranges. You can also modify each format attribute on an ad hoc basis for individual cells - but this is not such a good idea. It is much better to organise your formatting in terms of styles. A style is a named collection of format specifications and it provides a way of changing a whole set of attributes in one go. It also provides a way of making sure that format changes are consistent. However before we can go on to learn about using styles we need to look at the way to control the individual attributes.

» Number formatting

If you select the Format,Number option then you will see the Number dialog box.

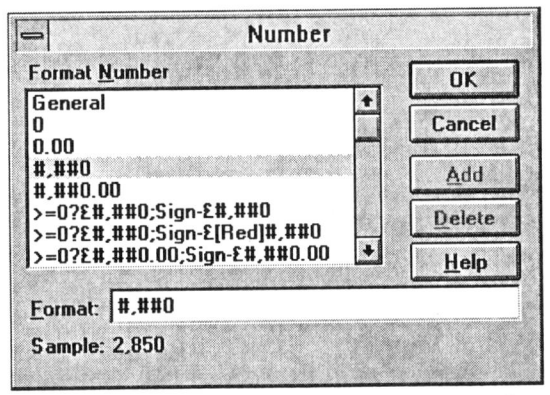

```
Number
Format Number
General
0
0.00
#,##0
#,##0.00
>=0?£#,##0;Sign-£#,##0
>=0?£#,##0;Sign-£[Red]#,##0
>=0?£#,##0.00;Sign-£#,##0.00
Format:  #,##0
Sample: 2,850

OK
Cancel
Add
Delete
Help
```

At first this can look a little off putting because it appears to contain a list of very cryptic items. However, as soon as you appreciate the general principles behind a numeric format their meaning very quickly becomes obvious. Each format specification is a picture of how the number should look. This picture is built up using "place holders" that show how the digits and other symbols that make up the number should be displayed.

You can select any of the predefined formats and edit them in the format box. After editing you can either click on OK to replace the original by the edited version or click on Add to add a new format to the list. You can also delete a format from the list by selecting it and clicking on the Delete button.

In most cases the default format, that is the one called General will work well. This attempts to display a number in a "natural" way - i.e. without a fractional part if at all possible and with as few digits as possible. When you need something a little more precise than this you have to use one of the other supplied formats or create your own.

» Numeric place holders

The two most important place holders are 0 and #. The 0 and the # both show where digits will be displayed so ### and 000 are both pictures of three digit numbers but the difference is that a # is an optional digit and 0 is a mandatory digit. You can think of the # sign as meaning "display a digit here - if there is one" the 0 means "always display a digit here - even if you have to use a 0 that is otherwise unnecessary".

For example, the formats ### and 000 produce the same results as long as there are three digits to display. If there are are only two for example then the ### format will only display two but the 000 format will add a leading 0. For example, 42 displayed using ### will show as 42 but using 000 it will show as 042. The most surprising difference between these two formats is how a zero will show. The 000 format shows zero as 000 but the ### format shows it as a blank - there aren't any digits so ### doesn't show any! There is also the question of what happens if there are more than three digits to display. In both cases the additional digits are displayed - a format using 0 or # never truncates a number.

If you use the place holders after a decimal point then they control how the fractional digits are displayed. Again the same rules apply - a 0 forces a digit in that place and a # shows a digit if there is one to show. For example, ###.## and ###.00 both show at most two digits after the decimal point but the first will sometimes show fewer. That is 123.4 will show as 123.4 using ###.## and as 123.40 using ###.00.

You should be able to see how to use the # and the 0 place holder to control exactly how many digits before and after the decimal point you require. If you want to include thousands separators then all you have to do is include a comma somewhere in the format. It doesn't actually matter where the comma is, SCW will place a comma after every group of three digits before the decimal point. In practice it is usual to place the comma so that it does form a picture of the number. For example, the two formats #,##0.0 and ###,0.0 produce the same results - 12345 displays as 12,345.0 - but the first looks more like a number that has thousands separators.

» Text in formats

As well as controlling how the digits are displayed you can also include other symbols and text. In particular

: - + ( ) space

can be included within a format and will appear exactly where you place them. In addition you can use the currency symbol as defined using the International option in the Windows Control Panel. Any other symbols or text have to be entered either surrounded by double quotes or preceded by a \.

For example, assuming that the Windows currency symbol is £ the format £#,##0.00 would display the value 1234.5 as £1,234.50. If you want to use a currency symbol that is not the Windows currency symbol simply surround it by double quotes or put a slash in front of it. For example, \$#,##0.00 will display 1234.5 as $1,234.50 even if $ isn't the Windows currency symbol.

Notice that by using a preceding slash you can use any character as the currency symbol. The only problem is finding the required symbol on the keyboard. The simplest solution is to use the Character Map Character Map utility which can be found in the Accessories group. If you run this utility you can select any character from any font (see later) and copy it to the clipboard.

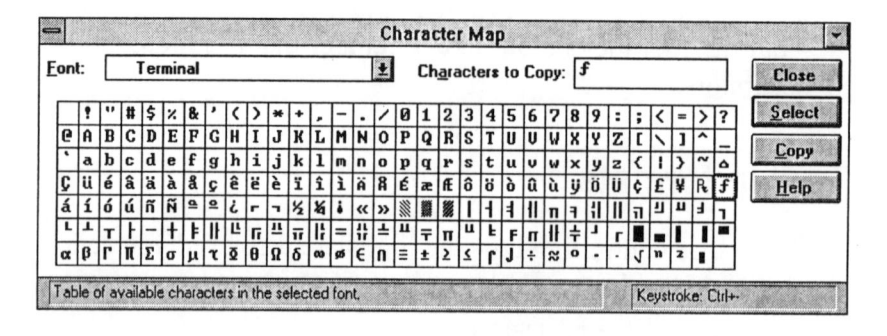

Once the character is copied to the clipboard it can be pasted into the format specification. The only problem is that while the Number dialog box is open you cannot use the Edit,Paste command. The solution is to use the keypress short cut Ctrl-V to paste the symbol. If you do this you may be surprised to see something other than the symbol you selected. The reason for this is that all dialog box entries are displayed using the MS Sans-Serif font and in this font the symbol may look different. When you apply the format to a cell the symbol that you see will also depend on the font that you have selected for its format. Clearly, to be sure of seeing the symbol you selected you also have to select the same font - see later.

This text within a format can be used for more than just adding currency symbols. For example, the format

##0.### "μ A"

will add the unit symbol for microamps to the end of any value. The format ##0 "Km" will show values as kilometers and so on. You can even include explanatory text within a format as in "The total profit is "£#,##0.00. This has the advantage over placing the text in the cell next to the result in that the text and value remain close together irrespective of the size of the value.

If the cell's content is text you can include this in the format specification by using the @ symbol. For example,

"The answer is "@

would show the message 'The answer is yes' if the cell contained the text 'yes'. The @ symbol is useful for advanced formats and special effects.

» Advanced numeric formats

SCW's format specifications are very powerful. As well as the basic numeric formatting you can control colour and set up conditional formats that cause values to display according to their value or type.

One format control that you will use very rarely is the asterisk. Any character in a format specification that follows an asterisk is repeated until it fills the available space. SCW actually fills a cell with repeated # (hash) symbols if a column is too narrow to display the data. You can use the asterisk to construct formulae that draw attention to incorrect data types or out of range values - but to do this you need the conditional form of the format described later in the this section.

To set the colour of the value displayed in a cell you can use any of the following format commands:

    [BLACK]   [WHITE]
    [RED]   [GREEN]
    [BLUE]   [YELLOW]
    [CYAN]   [MAGENTA]

For example, the format [RED]£###0.00 will display monetary values in red.

As well as the colour commands you can also remove any sign from the displayed value using the command NOSIGN. For example, to display a negative value using the bracket notation used in accounting you would use the format

    [RED]NOSIGN (###0.##)

However, this would display positive values in exactly the same way as negative values. What we really need is a format that will use [BLACK] + ###0.## for positive values and [RED]NOSIGN (###0.00) for negative values. You can do this by way of a conditional format which will apply one of two formats depending on whether a condition is true or false. In general a conditional format is specified by:

    condition ? true format; false format

where the condition is either true or false for the value being formatted. If the condition is true then the true format is used if it is false the false format is used. For example, to format negative numbers differently the condition would be <0 and the conditional format might be something like

    <0?[RED]NOSIGN (###0.##);[BLACK] + ###0.##

You can see that this looks very complicated but it is composed of two formats that are simple enough and a test to see which one of them should be used. You should now be in a position to at least understand the conditional formats that are supplied as standard.

» Practical - See when you are overdrawn

As an example of applying formatting, consider the following simple example. All the values in the Debit, Credit and Balance columns need to show in a monetary format but you want to be able to notice immediately if

	A	B	C	D
		BALANCE.MDS : Window1		
2	Month:	January 1994		
3	Details	Debit	Credit	Balance
4	Balance brought forward			£780.89
5	Mortgage	£320.50		£460.39
6	Salary		£1,256.43	£1,716.82
7	Phone	£100.35		£1,616.47
8	Electricity	£300.00		£1,316.47
9	Deposit	£1,500.00		-£183.53

you go 'into the red'. SCW has anticipated this and if you look in the list of supplied Number formats you will find the one selected here:

>=0?£#,##0.00;Sign-£[Red]#,##0.00

This is a conditional format with the condition being that the cell entry is greater than zero. When the condition is true a format is used that includes the currency symbol currently set up in the Windows Control Panel, one mandatory digit before the decimal point and two mandatory digits beyond it. Thousands separators will also be included as appropriate. In the event of the condition proving false a negative sign will be included and the cell entry will be made in red. In all other respects the number format will be the same.

The formula to keep the running balance is simply

=D4-B5+C5

This is entered into D5 and copied down the column. If you load or type in this example you will see that three colours are shown on the screen. Blue for data entry - both text and numbers, black for the positive results of the formula and red when the formula results in a negative number.

> **Warning!**
> **Don't ignore the E**
>
> If a number becomes too large or too small to display the required number of zeros in the space provided SCW, and indeed nearly all spreadsheets, will automatically change to scientific or exponential format. You can recognise a number in scientific format because
>
> | 1.2E+09 |
> |---------|
>
> it has an E in it. If you don't understand this way of writing numbers then it is vital that you either find out or alter the format or column width so that you can read the number in a format that you do understand. Don't make the mistake of thinking that the E has no meaning and ignoring it. For example, in the example shown in this box the value isn't 1.2 but a very large number indeed!

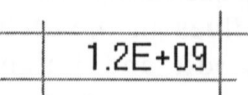

To go on and make more creative use of conditional formats you need to discover what sorts of conditions it is possible to write. This topic is covered more fully in Chapter 8 in connection with the IF function. However, it is worth saying that you can use any of the logical functions and in particular the large list of IS functions. For example, if you want a cell to show in red if it contains text and green otherwise you would use the format

    IsText?[Red]@;[Green]

Using similar methods you can easily create formats that change according to the type of data or the value in a cell.

» Scientific format

If you are a scientist or an engineer then SCW's scientific, or exponential, format will require no further explanation but if not then it will appear very cryptic. Scientific format is useful because it allows very large and very small numbers to be displayed in a narrow column width. Indeed if a column width is too small for a value to be displayed using general format then it automatically selects exponential format. Because of this it is advisable to at least recognise this format when you see it!

To understand the how and why of scientific format, consider the wastefulness of printing so many zeros in the value 1230000. Scientific format reduces the number of digits needed to represent this number by displaying it with a single digit before the decimal point and a count of how many places the decimal point has to be moved to give the correct magnitude of the value.

For example, 1230000 would be written in exponential format as 1.23E6 - the 'E' serves as punctuation between the value and the number indicating the shift needed in the decimal point. In this case the exponent, as it is called, is 6 and so the decimal point has to be moved 6 places to the right to give the value its correct magnitude.

E6 = move the decimal point 6 places to the right:

move	1	2	3	4	5	6
value	12.3	123	1230	12300	123000	1230000

A negative exponent indicates that the decimal point has to be moved to the left and this is how numbers smaller than one are represented. For example, 1.23E-6 is scientific notation for 0.00000123, i.e.

E-6 = move the decimal point 6 places to the left:

move	1	2	3	4	5	6
value	.123	.0123	.00123	.000123	.0000123	.00000123

As well as displaying numbers in scientific format SCW can also accept values typed in using it.

For the mathematically inclined it might be interesting to know that a number in exponential format nnnnnEee is equivalent to the value nnnnn $*10^{ee}$.

To define a scientific format you need to include the symbol E+ . How many digits are displayed for the exponent depend on how many place holders you write following the E+. You can also alter the number of digits displayed before the E. For example, 0.##E+0000 will display 1234567 as 1.23E0006

» Other formats

As well as the purely numeric formats there are also a range of format symbols that apply to dates and times. These are best described together with the details of how dates and times in general work - see Chapter 9.

The percentage format is a numeric format but its use fits into the wider issue of how to deal with percentages within SCW and this is also described in Chapter 9.

» Alignment

You can control the way data positions itself using the Alignment option in the Format menu. You can select Left, Center or Right alignment by clicking on the appropriate option in the Alignment dialog box. The only puzzle might be what General alignment and Wrap Text are for?

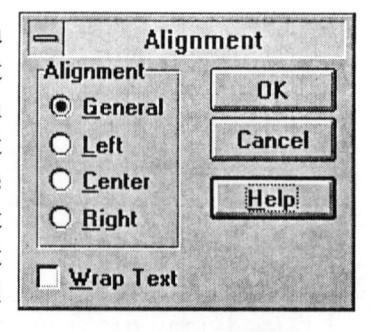

General alignment is the default and this causes text to align to the right and numbers to the left. In most cases this provides a reasonable choice for columns of figures and their headings.

Normally text entered into a cell will be displayed on a single line and spill across the neighbouring cells - as long as they are blank. If you apply a Wrap Text alignment text does not spill over but is contained within the cell. The text lines are broken to stop them crossing the cell boundaries and so to see all of the text you may need to alter the row height - see later. You can think of Wrap Text as forcing the text into multiple lines so that it fits into the cell. You can use this facility to add explanatory text to spreadsheet reports - see the practical at the end of this chapter.

Notice that Left, Center and Right alignment are also available as icons just below the Toolbar.

» Fonts

The Format,Fonts command allows you to display any value, text or formula in any of the fonts that are available in Windows. You can select the font type, size, style and colour using the Font dialog box.

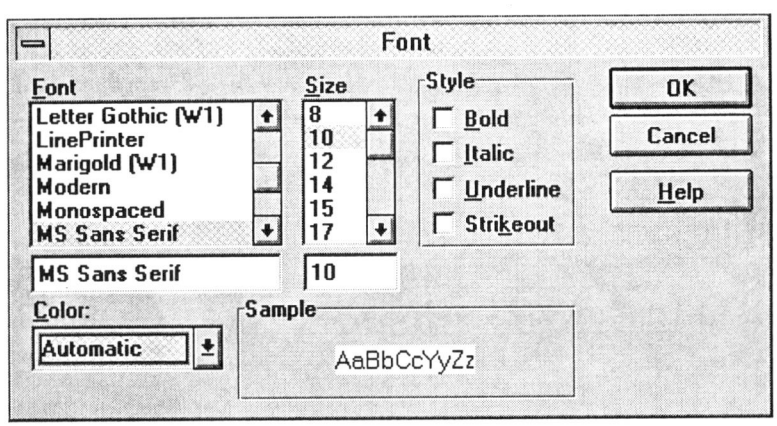

```
┌─────────────────────────── Font ───────────────────────────┐
│ Font                    Size     ┌Style──────┐   ┌──────┐  │
│ Letter Gothic (W1)  ↑   8    ↑   │ ☐ Bold    │   │  OK  │  │
│ LinePrinter             10       │           │   └──────┘  │
│ Marigold (W1)           12       │ ☐ Italic  │   ┌──────┐  │
│ Modern                  14       │           │   │Cancel│  │
│ Monospaced              15       │ ☐ Underline│  └──────┘  │
│ MS Sans Serif      ↓    17   ↓   │ ☐ Strikeout│  ┌──────┐  │
│                                  └───────────┘   │ Help │  │
│ MS Sans Serif           10                       └──────┘  │
│ Color:               ┌Sample─────────────────────┐         │
│ Automatic       ↓    │   AaBbCcYyZz              │         │
│                      └───────────────────────────┘         │
└────────────────────────────────────────────────────────────┘
```

This is simple enough but the effects that selecting a particular font produces can vary according to the type of output device you are using. Indeed the fonts that you can choose from may vary according to the output device you select - see Chapter 7. In principle it is preferable to restrict your choices to TrueType fonts and perhaps Adobe Type I fonts if you have Adobe Type Manager (ATM) installed. Only these two types of font can be scaled to any size without loss of quality. You can control the fonts installed on your system using the Fonts utility in the Windows Control panel.

Notice that you can select font styles Bold, Italic and Underline using the icons just below the Toolbar.

The only other difficulty you may have is in knowing what a point is! The answer is that one point is roughly 1/72nd of an inch. What is more important is that 10 point type is large enough for the body of a table and 12-16 is large enough for titles.

» Borders

You can add a border to any area of the spreadsheet to construct rulings and tables. The Border dialog box, summoned by the Format,Borders command, is very easy to understand. The four boxes Left, Right, Top and Bottom draw lines on the specified edge of every cell in a selection.

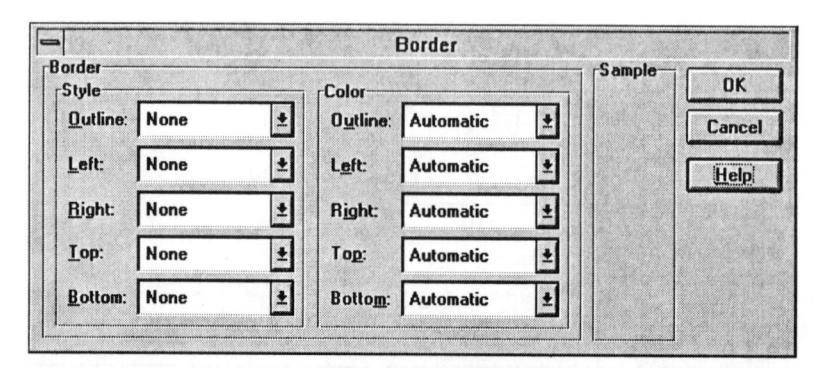

Border				
Style		**Color**		**Sample**
Outline:	None	Outline:	Automatic	OK
Left:	None	Left:	Automatic	Cancel
Right:	None	Right:	Automatic	Help
Top:	None	Top:	Automatic	
Bottom:	None	Bottom:	Automatic	

The Outline option is different in that it does not affect every cell in the selection, only the cells at the edge. It adds lines right round the outside edge of the selection. You could achieve the same result by selecting each edge in turn and selecting an appropriate border - top, right, bottom and left.

» Using borders

The only tricky part of using borders is what happens when you apply a border to a range that contains cells with borders already set? The key to understanding the way that the borders command can be used to create complicated rulings is to realise that each cell draws its four borders independently of the rest. That is, when you see an outline around a group of cells this is not a box or even four lines arranged to form a box but the individual lines that are the appropriate edges of each cell. You could select any cell in the outline and alter how it is displaying its edge lines.

Remember

» each cell has four edge lines which can be set in groups to particular line styles to create the illusion of longer lines and boxes as required.

It is obvious how you put a frame around a set of cells but how do you create a set of table rulings? When you see a table of data the first impulse is always to draw an outline around it as a first step.

	A	B	C	D	E	F	G
1							
2	Number	Cost	Postage	Total cost	1%	2%	5%
3	1000	95	190	285	-185	-85	215
4	5000	166	950	1116	-616	-116	1384
5	10000	255	1900	2155	-1155	-155	2845
6	15000	345	2850	3195	-1695	-195	4305
7	20000	517	3800	4317	-2317	-317	5683
8							
9							

MAILSHOT.MDS : Window1

However, if you do this the next step is to create the rulings in the body of the table by setting all of the cells in the same selection to have a line on the right and bottom edges. If you do this you will find that you have now ruined the outline at the bottom and right hand edge.

This isn't unreasonable as you told the cells in this selection to set their right and bottom edges to a new line style.

The solutions to this problem are either to set the right and bottom lines in the body of the table using two selections that

	A	B	C	D	E	F	G
1							
2	Number	Cost	Postage	Total cost	1%	2%	5%
3	1000	95	190	285	-185	-85	215
4	5000	166	950	1116	-616	-116	1384
5	10000	255	1900	2155	-1155	-155	2845
6	15000	345	2850	3195	-1695	-195	4305
7	20000	517	3800	4317	-2317	-317	5683
8							

leave out the cells in the outline or you could just set the outline for a second time! A much better idea is not to bother setting the outline first but to do it after the rulings in the table.

Another tip is that because of the way that individual lines are drawn around individual cells it is difficult to produce a good looking table body that uses double rulings.

If you want to produce more complicated rulings within the body of a table then it is worth noticing that you can combine two horizontal and two vertical rulings. For example, if you select one line style for the left hand side of a cell and another line style for the right then where cells meet in the body of the table the two line styles will be drawn. There is a bit of overlap between the right side and left side of adjacent cells so you will have to experiment with the technique. For example, by setting a double line on the left and double line on the right you will see a three line vertical ruling on the screen.

» Patterns

As well as drawing borders around each cell you can also determine the way it is filled with colour or a pattern. The Patterns dialog box appears in response to the Format,Patterns command. You can select a fill pattern from the drop down edit box and then select two colours from the Foreground and Background boxes.

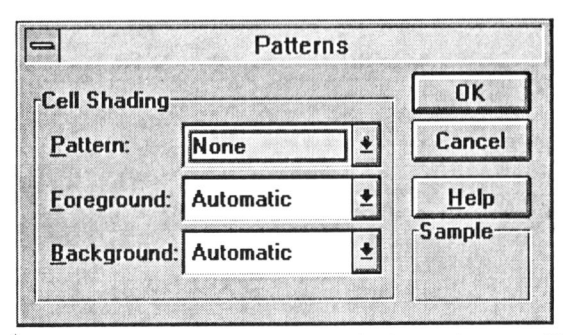

The only difficulty you might have is in understanding what the two colours refer to. Each pattern that you select has two colours associated with it - a foreground colour which is shown as black in the Patterns box and a background colour which is shown as white in the Patterns box. The actual colours that the pattern is displayed in when used on the sheet depends on the foreground and background colours you have selected.

The most common mistake in using the Patterns dialog box is to select a foreground colour and then wonder why the cell hasn't changed colour at all. The reason is that you also have to select a pattern. If you want to set a cell to a solid colour then select the solid black pattern that is the next option after None in the list. It may look black in the list but it is actually solid foreground colour.

» Pop-up

It is worth mentioning that all of the format commands are available on the pop-up menu that appears when you click the right mouse button. This is very convenient as the menu appears right next to the mouse position after you have selected the range of cells to format. Unfortunately it doesn't have the Style command as one of its options and this is likely to encourage the use of ad hoc formatting. Styles are a better way - see later.

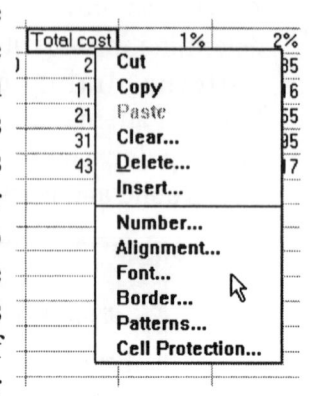

» Controlling the display

One of the difficulties of judging how rulings and other formatting effects will look on paper is that the spreadsheet grid tends to interfere. You can remove the grid display and modify a range of other display options using the command Options,Display. If you click on the Gridlines option the gridlines vanish. Clicking on the Row & Column Headings option makes the row and column headings vanish. Notice that selecting these options only affects the way that the sheet is displayed on the screen and not how it prints out.

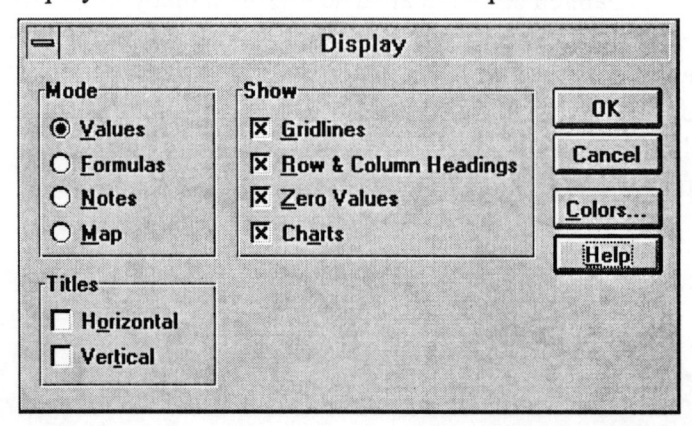

By clicking on the Zero Values option zeros will no longer be displayed and clicking on the Charts option causes charts - see the next chapter - not to appear. The two other sections in the Display dialog - Mode, useful in debugging a sheet, and Titles - are both covered in Chapter 6.

» Clearing formats

Although the Edit,Clear command is a simple one some of its options don't make much sense until you have looked at formatting. The Clear dialog box, which can be displayed by using the Edit,Clear command; by pressing Del; or from the pop-up menu, will clear the current selection. However what it clears from the current selection depends on the Clear dialog box. If you select Formulas then all data and formulae will be cleared from the range but formats will be left unaltered. Similarly if you select Formats then all data and formulae are left and only the formats are reset to their defaults - i.e. General and None as appropriate. The Notes option clears cell notes which are discussed in Chapter 6. If you want to clear everything - values, formulae and formats then select All.

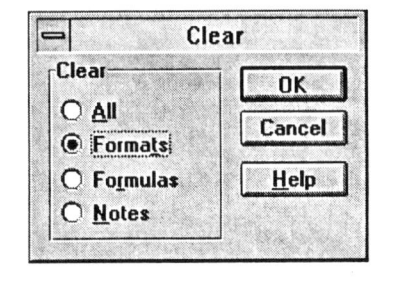

The reason for the different clear options is that you might want to re-use a spreadsheet complete with formatting but with new data. This involves the idea of a spreadsheet template which is discussed in Chapter 6.

You will also find options that affect the whole SCW display in the Preferences dialog box.

» Controlling colour

There are a number of places where you can set colours within SCW and this can be confusing at first. The master colour control is the Color Overrides dialog box that appears when you click on the Colors button in the Preferences dialog box.

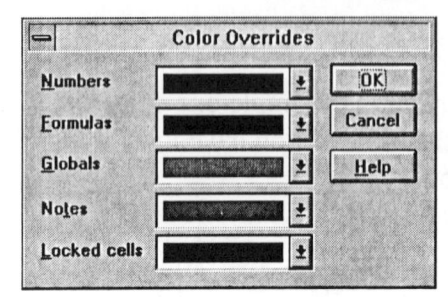

Using this you can set default colours for Numbers, Formulas, Globals, Notes and Locked cells. (Globals apply to models.) To set the default colours for each sheet window use the Options,Display command and click on the Colors button. The colours that you select override the defaults set by the Preferences dialog box.

You may be wondering about the Automatic colour that is listed in most of the colour control dialog boxes. The answer is that it is the default colour appropriate to the object as set by Windows. To change the defaults use the Color utility in the Control Panel and then select the colours that you want to apply in the Color dialog box. Notice that this changes everything in Windows not just SCW's colours.

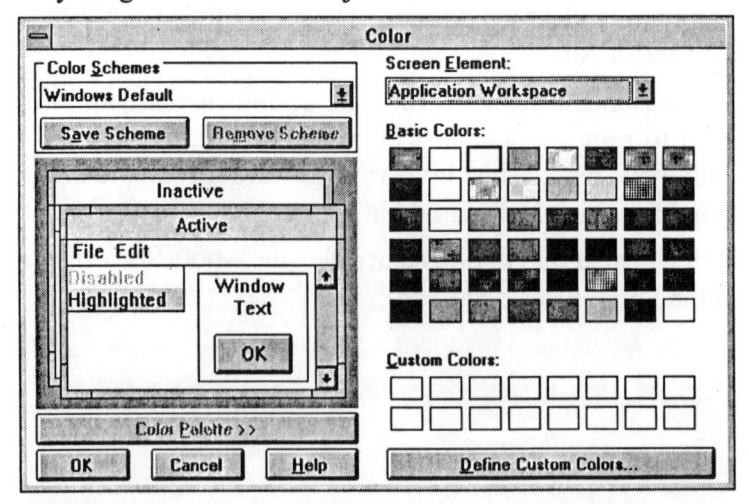

» Column width and row height

Although we have already met formats which alter the amount of space needed to display a value, so far we haven't looked at ways of altering the space available to it. In principle, altering the column width or row heights is a simple business. If you move the mouse pointer close to the crack between column or row headings it changes to a cursor that indicates that you can change the size of something. If you now drag while this cursor is displayed you will find that the column width or row height changes.

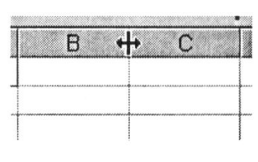

If you want to change the width or height of a set of columns or rows you can select them before you drag one of their separators. It doesn't matter which separator you drag and it works for multiple selections.

The main problem with dragging column widths and row heights in this way is that you quickly end up with a spreadsheet with a variety of cell sizes. This often looks messy when a small number of regular sizes would actually do. The best way to control column width accurately is to use the Format,Column Width command which displays the Column Width dialog box. In this you can enter the exact column width that you want to set the currently selected columns to. You can also set a default width for columns and reset the selection back to this default. The width is measured in terms of characters in the default font, 10 point MS Sans Serif. If you change to another font then the number of characters that fit into the column will also change.

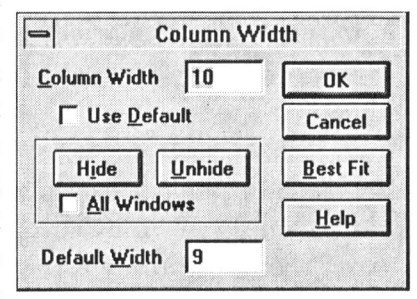

The Best Fit button is also worth knowing about. If you click on this then each of the selected columns is scanned in turn for the entry that needs the largest column width and the column adjusted so that it just fits. Clearly if you just want to make sure that everything is visible then all you have to do is select the entire spreadsheet and click on the Best Fit button.

By using the Format,Row Height command you can set the height of the currently selected rows on a similar fashion. In this case the height is measured in points - with an initial default of 13.

When you check the box Fit largest font the row widths will be adjusted to fit the largest font that you have used in the row. Notice that this is different to the Best Fit column option because it works all the time it is selected. It is also selected on a row by row basis - that is some rows can be self adjusting and others fixed. If you change the size of a font then the row will automatically re-size without the need for you to use the Row Height dialog box again. If you manually set the row height then this will disable the Fit largest font option for that row.

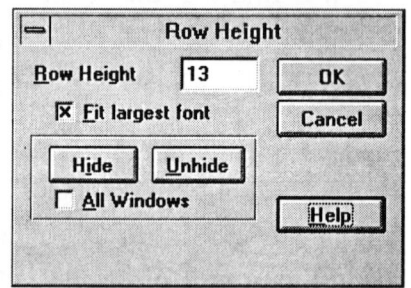

Notice that in both the Row Height and Column Width dialog boxes there are buttons concerned with hiding and unhiding rows and columns respectively. Hidden rows and columns are often useful to avoid the mechanics of a spreadsheet overwhelming the importance of its result and the use and purpose of these buttons is obvious.

» Styles

Although you can produce a reasonably formatted spreadsheet using nothing but the format commands introduced so far, this ad hoc approach makes it difficult to be consistent. A much better method is to define styles. A style is a named collection of formatting attributes. You can apply a style to a range of cells and all of the cells are set according to the specification in the style. Each cell also remembers which style it is controlled by and if you make a change to the specification of a style all of the cells that it controls are updated. However any ad hoc formatting changes you make after applying a style are honoured and take precedence until the style is re-applied or changed.

To apply a style you first select the range and then use the command Format,Style. The Style dialog box that appears contains a list of all of the styles that have been defined. As you select each style a short description of the formatting attributes that it alters is given in the Description box.

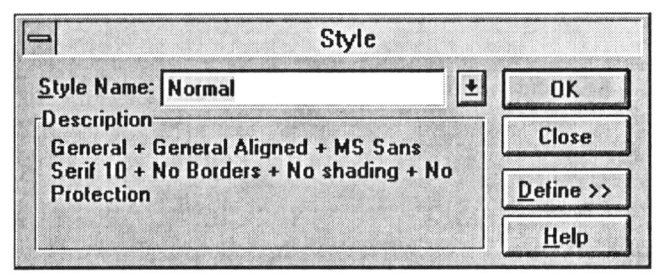

```
┌─────────────────────── Style ───────────────────────┐
│ Style Name: │Normal              │ ▼ │    OK       │
│ ┌Description──────────────────────┐   ┌──────────┐ │
│ │ General + General Aligned + MS Sans│   │  Close   │ │
│ │ Serif 10 + No Borders + No shading + No│ ┌──────────┐│
│ │ Protection                      │   │ Define >>│ │
│ │                                 │   ┌──────────┐│
│ └─────────────────────────────────┘   │   Help   │ │
└─────────────────────────────────────────────────────┘
```

A faster way of applying a style, assuming you don't need to see its description, is to use the drop down list of styles that appears just below the toolbar's normal position. To apply a style simply select from the pull down list of style names. Also notice that the style box shows you the current style applied to any cell that you select.

Only a few styles are defined as standard. The Normal style is the default which is applied to all cells. Apart from the normal style there are only three others which are simple numeric formats. To see what styles can really do you have to define some of your own.

To define a new style you click on the Define button which "unfolds" the Style dialog box to reveal a new set of buttons and check boxes.

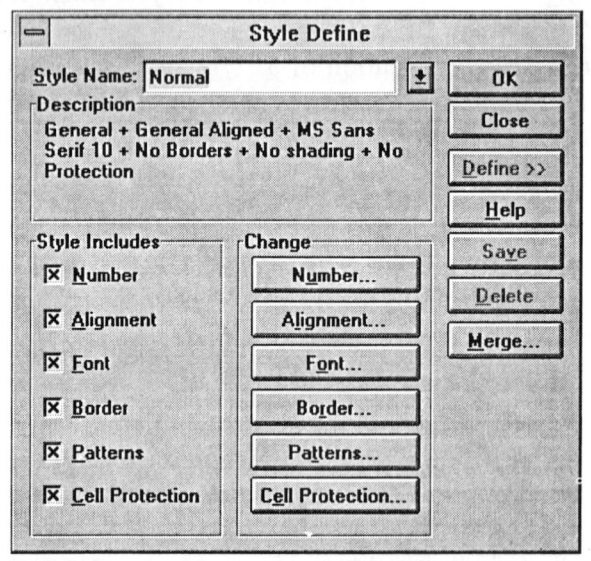

```
┌─────────────────── Style Define ───────────────────┐
│ Style Name: Normal                    OK           │
│ Description                           Close        │
│ General + General Aligned + MS Sans                │
│ Serif 10 + No Borders + No shading + No  Define >> │
│ Protection                                         │
│                                       Help         │
│ ┌Style Includes─┐ ┌Change─┐           Save         │
│  [X] Number       Number...                        │
│                                       Delete       │
│  [X] Alignment    Alignment...                     │
│                                       Merge...     │
│  [X] Font         Font...                          │
│  [X] Border       Border...                        │
│  [X] Patterns     Patterns...                      │
│  [X] Cell Protection  Cell Protection...           │
└────────────────────────────────────────────────────┘
```

The first step is to type in a new style name or select a style that you want to modify. Next you have to decide which aspects of formatting the style is going to affect. You can choose to control any or all of the formatting attributes that we have discussed - including cell protection which is discussed in Chapter 6. Any attribute that you choose to define as part of a style will be controlled by the style. Any attribute that you don't include will be unaffected by applying the style. For example, if you choose to define a style that includes only Number and Alignment then applying this will only alter the Number and Alignment attributes of a cell - its font, border etc. will remain as you set them.

» Practical - Formatting the mailshot

The best way to appreciate how styles can be used is via a simple example - the Mailshot table. The first thing to do is to define a new style called Heading which can be used to format the table headings. Using the Style Define dialog box it seems reasonable to set the Number format to General, Alignment to Center and Font to Arial 14 point. Once the style is defined the next step is to apply it to the headings in the top row of the table. This is most easily done by selecting the headings and then using the drop down list of styles at the top left.

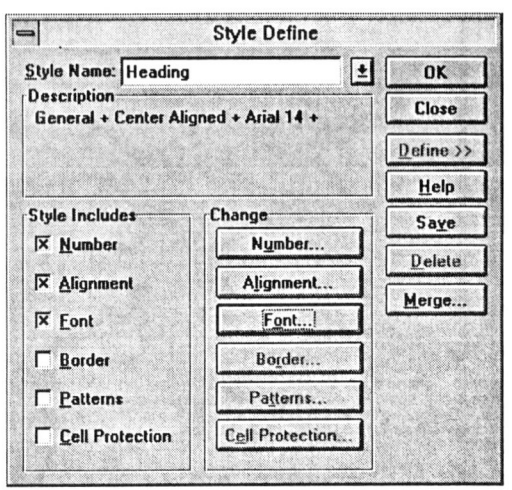

Once the new style is applied to the spreadsheet you can see a number of things. The most obvious is that the row height has been automatically adjusted but the column widths need attention. Less obviously the use of the Heading style has changed the formatting of the percentages from Percent to General and so spoiled the look of the table.

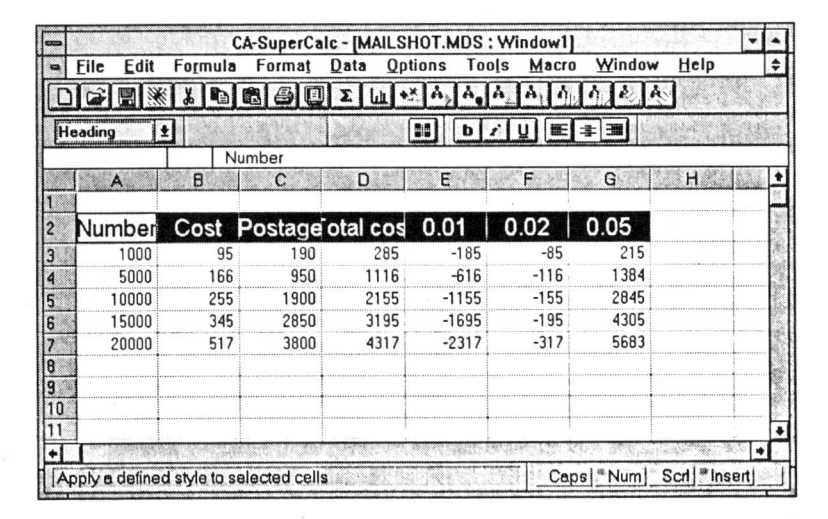

Number	Cost	Postage	Total cost	0.01	0.02	0.05
1000	95	190	285	-185	-85	215
5000	166	950	1116	-616	-116	1384
10000	255	1900	2155	-1155	-155	2845
15000	345	2850	3195	-1695	-195	4305
20000	517	3800	4317	-2317	-317	5683

The solution to the column width problem is to select columns A through G and use the Column Width Best Fit option. The solution to the number format is to change the Heading style so that it doesn't modify the formatting of numbers when it is applied in the future and set an ad-hoc percentage number format to E2:G2. Notice that it is better to do this than apply the percent style to E2:G2 because while this produces the same result and doesn't alter the font set by Heading, it breaks the connection with the Heading style. What this means is that if you were to change the heading style in the future E2:G2 would not change their format.

	A	B	C	D	E	F	G
1							
2	Number	Cost	Postage	Total cost	1%	2%	5%
3	1000	95	190	285	-185	-85	215
4	5000	166	950	1116	-616	-116	1384
5	10000	255	1900	2155	-1155	-155	2845
6	15000	345	2850	3195	-1695	-195	4305
7	20000	517	3800	4317	-2317	-317	5683

In general you should create styles which only control the formatting attributes that are common to all of the data types to which it might be applied. For example, when Heading was defined it seemed reasonable to set the numeric format to general - partly because there was the assumption that headings are mostly text items! In practice of course table headings can be a range of different data types including text, percentages, currency and dates and in each case a different numeric format is need. The solution to the problem is to define the Heading style so that it controls the font and alignment say and leave the numeric formatting to be resolved on a cell by cell basis.

Practical - Formatting the mailshot **91**

The next style that we need is something to control the look of the body of the table. In this case a style that controls the alignment, font and colour of the font seems reasonable. The colour of the font is included because there is no need to make any distinction between formulae and values in the table. (By default formulae are shown in black and values in blue.)

```
┌─────────────────── Style ───────────────────┐
│ Style Name: body                      [±]   │   OK
│ ┌Description─────────────────────────┐      │   Close
│ │ General Aligned + Times New Roman 12,│    │   Define >>
│ │ Black +                             │    │   Help
│ └─────────────────────────────────────┘    │
```

The font has been selected to be Times New Roman. This is a serifed font as opposed to Arial which is used in the heading which is a sans-serifed font. It is often the case that a serifed and sans-serif font work together in pairs in this way - one for the headings and one for the bulk of the text.

Applying the body style to the figures in the table produces a pleasing result but it would be nice to see the costs and profits in currency format and to highlight the negative values by showing them in red. To avoid breaking the association between the table and the body style this is done by selecting B3:G7 and applying the numeric format shown below. Note that this displays whole pounds and no pence.

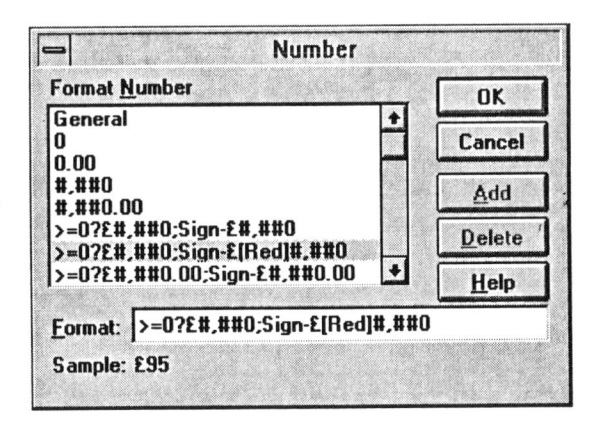

```
┌─────────────────── Number ──────────────────┐
│ Format Number                               │   OK
│ ┌──────────────────────────────┐ [±]        │   Cancel
│ │ General                      │            │   Add
│ │ 0                            │            │   Delete
│ │ 0.00                         │            │   Help
│ │ #,##0                        │            │
│ │ #,##0.00                     │            │
│ │ >=0?£#,##0;Sign-£#,##0       │            │
│ │ >=0?£#,##0;Sign-£[Red]#,##0  │            │
│ │ >=0?£#,##0.00;Sign-£#,##0.00 │[±]         │
│ └──────────────────────────────┘            │
│ Format: >=0?£#,##0;Sign-£[Red]#,##0         │
│ Sample: £95                                 │
```

With this format in use some of the currency values are too large to fit into the column widths so the Column Width Best Fit button has to be used again.

The next step is to add some rulings to the table. Usually it is better to start by adding the rulings in the body of the table. This is achieved by selecting the entire table and setting the right and bottom edges of each cell to the lightest ruling. It is very easy to produce a table that is dominated by heavy lines so it is a good idea to always start with the lightest ruling for the body. It is also a good idea to turn off the display of the sheet grid so that you can see the effect of the ruling more clearly.

	A	B	C	D	E	F	G
1							
2	Number	Cost	Postage	Total cost	1%	2%	5%
3	1000	£95	£190	£285	-£185	-£85	£215
4	5000	£166	£950	£1,116	-£616	-£116	£1,384
5	10000	£255	£1,900	£2,155	-£1,155	-£155	£2,845
6	15000	£345	£2,850	£3,195	-£1,695	-£195	£4,305
7	20000	£517	£3,800	£4,317	-£2,317	-£317	£5,683
8							

The rulings to divide the headings from the rest of the table can be applied by selecting the headings row A2:G2 and setting the bottom edge of each cell to a double line. The alternative of selecting the row below the headings and setting the top edge to a line style isn't as good because it leaves the lines set on the bottom edge of the heading cells still showing. Selecting the entire table and placing a double line outline around it almost completes the rulings needed but it is worth adding a heavy ruling to separate the table input data from its conclusions - the profits for each response rate. To do this simply select the range D2:D7 and set the right

Practical - Formatting the mailshot

hand edge to a heavy line. Again the alternative of setting the left edge of E2:E7 isn't advisable because it would double up with the existing line on the right hand edge of the adjacent column.

Number	Cost	Postage	Total cost	1%	2%	5%
1000	£95	£190	£285	-£185	-£85	£215
5000	£166	£950	£1,116	-£616	-£116	£1,384
10000	£255	£1,900	£2,155	-£1,155	-£155	£2,845
15000	£345	£2,850	£3,195	-£1,695	-£195	£4,305
20000	£517	£3,800	£4,317	-£2,317	-£317	£5,683

The result looks quite good but it does demonstrate the problems of using the Best Fit option. Now that the table has rulings the Best Fit option looks a bit tight. In most cases you should only rely on the automatic sizing of columns to get you started, manual adjustment is usually necessary. The same is true of the row heights - notice the way the "g" of Postage touches the ruling line. Again the solution is manual adjustment. Finally adding a title, formatted using the MainHead style - Arial 20 point - Centered - and adjusting the height of row 1 gives us the final table.

Proposed Direct Mail Profits

Number	Cost	Postage	Total cost	1%	2%	5%
1000	£95	£190	£285	-£185	-£85	£215
5000	£166	£950	£1,116	-£616	-£116	£1,384
10000	£255	£1,900	£2,155	-£1,155	-£155	£2,845
15000	£345	£2,850	£3,195	-£1,695	-£195	£4,305
20000	£517	£3,800	£4,317	-£2,317	-£317	£5,683

Key points

» Formatting only alters the way a value is displayed by a cell - never the value itself.

» You can construct quite sophisticated numeric formats that change according to the type of data or its value.

» Formatting attributes - numeric format, alignment, font, border and fill can be assigned to ranges on an ad-hoc basis.

» Colour can be controlled from within SCW and using the Windows Color control.

» Row height and column width can be adjusted manually or automatically.

» Styles are named groups of format attribute settings. Applying or editing a style changes all of the attributes that the style controls.

Chapter 5

Charts

SuperCalc for Windows charts are easy to use and sophisticated but you almost certainly need some guidance on how to use them. The reason is that there are so many simple and direct ways of achieving something that you can waste time looking for a more traditional and round about method. This is particularly true if you have grown accustomed to the way that DOS spreadsheets, and SC5 in particular approach charting. At first you may find the new approach strange, limiting even, but in practice it is quite the reverse.

» Basic principles

SCW's charting facilities follow the standard "select a range then give a command" way of doing things. First you select a range that contains the data. The data has to be arranged in columns but it doesn't have to be stored in a single rectangular block. Once you have selected the data to plot you next click on the Chart button in the Toolbar. Oddly there is no menu or keyboard short cut for this Toolbar button. After you have clicked on the chart button the cursor changes to a crosshair and you have to drag to define the area where the chart is to appear. All charts are embedded with in a sheet but there are ways to look at and print them on their own. As soon as you release the mouse button the the chart will be drawn in the area that you have indicated.

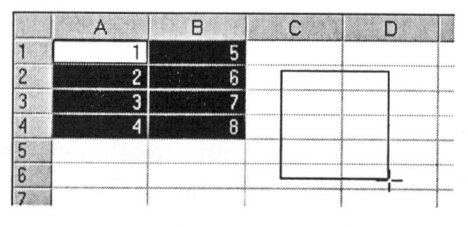

When you first see the chart you may be worried that it isn't what you expected. Don't worry because this is just a default chart that you can quite easily modify into the chart that you really wanted.

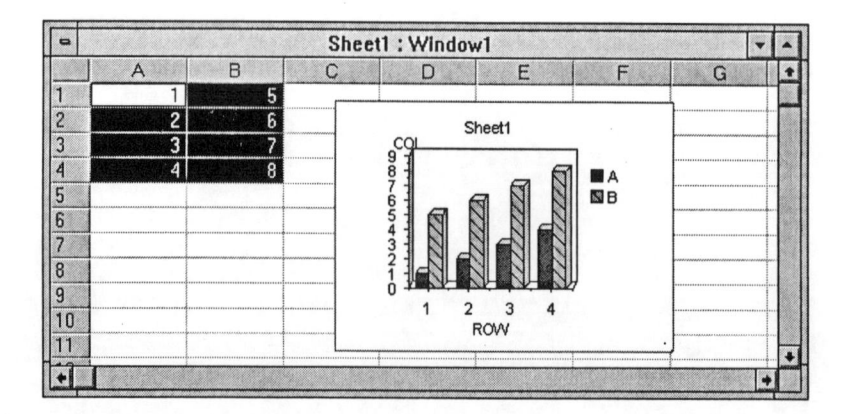

» Editing charts

Any chart that you create is embedded in the spreadsheet that contains the data on which it is based. You can move the chart within the sheet by clicking on it to select it and then dragging it to its new location. Similarly you can re-size it by dragging the edges of the frame that appears when the chart is selected. You can also delete a chart while it is selected.

If you want to edit the chart any more than a simple move or resize you need to double click on the chart to open its edit window. A chart edit window is independent of the sheet window that contains the chart but any changes you make to the chart in the edit window are visible in the chart window. The chart edit window has its own particular set of menu commands and its own Toolbar.

Most of the commands in the chart menu and toolbar are obvious but a key idea is the way that data series work.

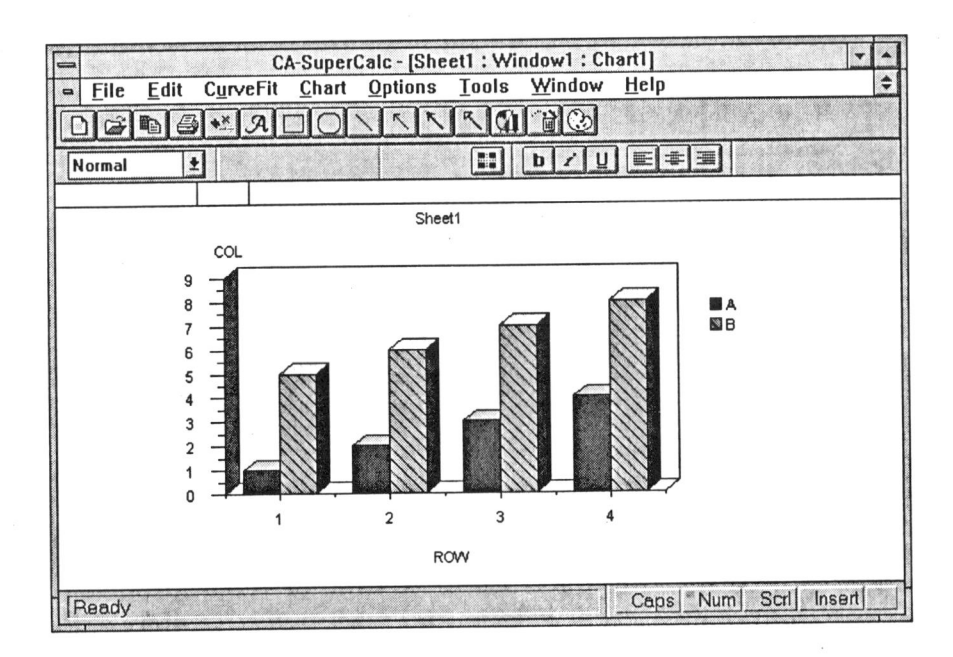

» Data series

A chart displays a number of data series - roughly speaking a set of measurements on the same thing. Some charts, such as the pie chart only display a single series but the majority of charts need at least two series. The first series is plotted on the horizontal or X axis the second and subsequent series are plotted on the vertical or Y axis. How you assign data series to the X or Y axis affects the chart you product.

For example, if there are only two data series then the first might be assigned to the X axis and the second to the Y axis. Points would then be plotted on the chart corresponding to pairs of values - one from X and one from Y. In the case of a SCW chart these pairs are always taken from the same row in a pair of columns. So what we are interested in is assigning columns of data to either the X or Y axis. This is achieved using the command Chart,Assign Data. The dialog box that appears in response to this command varies according to the the type of chart you are editing but its general features remain the same.

For a column chart the dialog box is called "Category Selection".

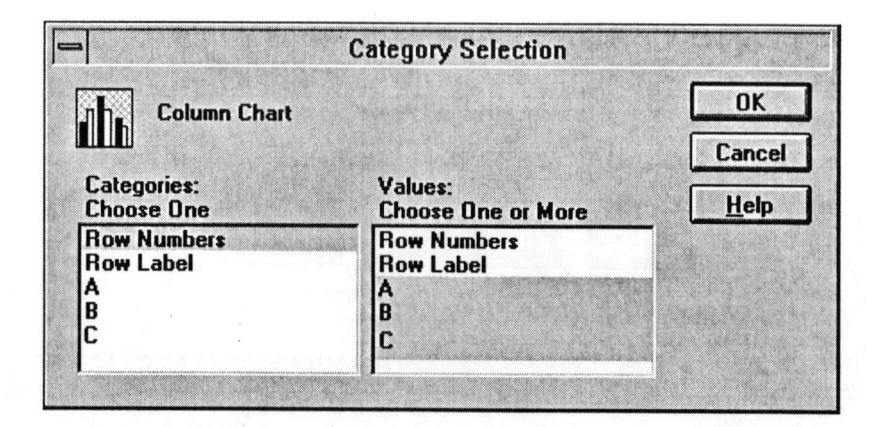

```
┌─────────────────────── Category Selection ───────────────────────┐
│                                                                    │
│  ▁▂▄  Column Chart                                      ┌─ OK ─┐  │
│                                                         └──────┘  │
│                                                         ┌ Cancel ┐│
│  Categories:               Values:                      └────────┘│
│  Choose One                Choose One or More           ┌─ Help ─┐│
│  ┌──────────────┐          ┌──────────────┐             └────────┘│
│  │Row Numbers   │          │Row Numbers   │                        │
│  │Row Label     │          │Row Label     │                        │
│  │A             │          │A             │                        │
│  │B             │          │B             │                        │
│  │C             │          │C             │                        │
│  └──────────────┘          └──────────────┘                        │
└────────────────────────────────────────────────────────────────────┘
```

In all cases, except for the Pie chart, the dialog box allows you to make two selections. You can pick one of the data series to be the horizontal, or X axis, series and any number of the remaining series to be plotted on the Y axis. The data series that are listed will include all of the columns of data that you selected before clicking on the chart button and two that you didn't.

The two series Row Numbers and Row Labels are always included as possible selections. The Row Numbers series is just the sequential number of each data item starting from the top of the selection. The Row Labels series is similar but it is the actual row number that each data item is stored in. For example, if the data area selected is A10:C15 the Row Numbers data series would be 1,2,3,4,5,6 and the Row Labels data series would be 10,11,12,13,14,15. You can think of these two as forming two extra, "phantom" data series in any selection you make. They are actually more useful when working with Models than Sheets. In our example, the other data series listed would of course be the data in columns, A, B and C, making a total of five data series to choose from.

SCW always chooses the Row Numbers data series to plot on the X axis and the remaining column data series to plot on the Y axis. In many cases this isn't what you require because one of the columns of data will represent the X axis data. All you have to do to put this right is select the column series to use on the X axis and the remaining column series are automatically used for the the Y axis.

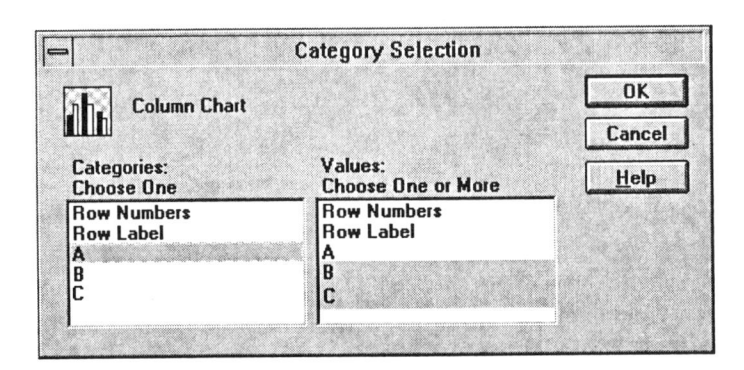

» A five minute chart

To emphasise how easy it is to create charts, and to indicate some to the things that might confuse, it is worth creating a simple chart. Starting from a blank sheet enter some numeric data into three columns A10:C15 say. Any values will do but make sure that you do not repeat any values in the first column. Next select the range, click on the Chart button and select the area where you would like the chart to appear. The chart that results will plot all three data series i.e. Columns A, B and C against the Row Number as the X axis. You should be able to see that the X axis is marked out as row 1, 2, 3, 4, 5 and 6.

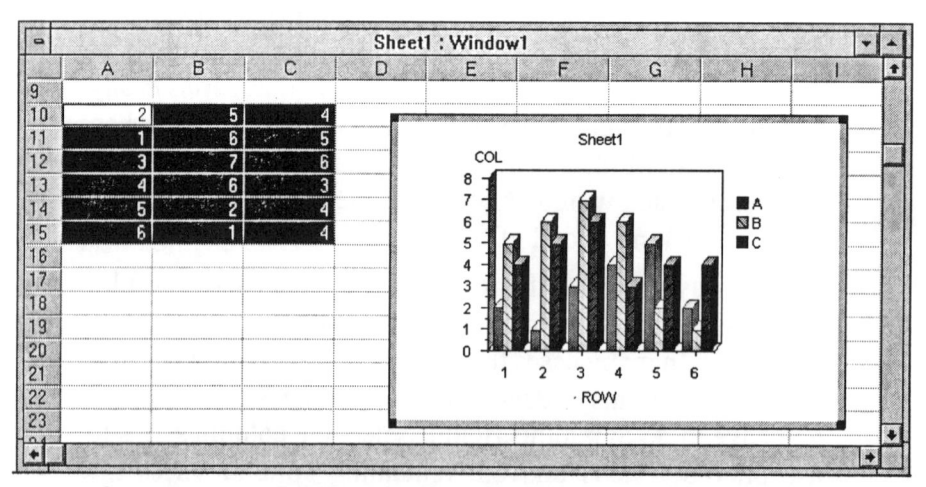

If you want to change this double click on the chart and then select the Chart,Assign Data command. If you choose the Row Labels as the X axis then the chart stays the same but the values are the actual row numbers i.e. 10 to 15. If you select the data in column A as the X axis then you can only sensibly plot the B and C data series on the Y axis.

» Categorical and non-categorical data

The next step in understanding how SCW's charts work is to make the distinction between categorical and non-categorical data clear. Categorical data, as its name suggests consists of a number of category labels which carry no numeric significance. For example, if you have a table of sales data for lines of sweets

Product	Number
Zippy bars	1000
Zappy bars	1500
Chocologic chews	5000

then the names of each sales item represent categorical data. The names carry no numeric significance and this is obvious. Categorical data is often used as the X axis data series in a bar or column chart because the heights of the bars allow you to compare the number sold in each category. However, now consider the situation where the product names are replaced by a product code - as in product 1, 2 and 3. In this case the table of data looks more as if both data series are non-categorical.

Product	Number
1	1000
2	1500
3	5000

It is also clear from the previous example that they are not! The product code may be numeric but it carries no numerical significance. For example, there is no sense in which a Zappy bar is twice a Zippy bar! However now when you plot a bar chart you might be tempted to interpret the X axis is this way!

In practice it is vital that you distinguish between categorical and non-categorical data and recognise the fact that even when numbers are used the data can still be categorical.

» Chart types

There are a range of different chart types available but exactly how these chart types behave and when they are appropriate depends on the type of data you are working with.
To change the chart type all you have to do is click on the Chart Type icon in the Toolbar or use the Chart,Chart Type command - both are only available while you are editing a chart.

There are eleven types of chart that you can select from but it is actually more helpful to think of them as variations on three fundamental types:

>   Bar
>   XY
>   and   Pie

The **bar chart** always assumes a categorical X axis. The distances between the bars means nothing - only their relative heights are meaningful. SCW supports four varieties of bar charts. There are two trivial variations - the column chart which has vertical bars and the bar chart which has horizontal bars. If you plot multiple data series on the same bar or column chart multiple bars are drawn for each category. This is often called a "clustered bar chart".

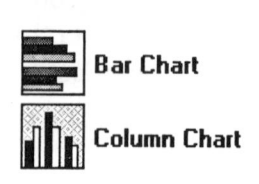

Bar Chart

Column Chart

An alternative way of showing multiple series on the same bar chart is to stack the bars of each series one on top of the other. Not surprisingly this is called a stacked bar chart! SCW supports stacked versions of both the column and bar chart and again the only difference is that one has horizontal bars and the other vertical bars.

Stacked Bar Chart

Stacked Column Chart

The **XY chart** is superficially like the bar chart. Its main purpose, however, is to give an indication of how fast a change is occurring. In the case of a bar chart you can compare the relative heights of the bars but you shouldn't try to interpret the rate at which the bars are increasing or decreasing. The reason is simply that the horizontal scale is categorical and so the distances between the bars is arbitrary. This means that you can change a steep slope into a negligible slope by moving the bars further apart. An XY chart, on the other hand, is used where the horizontal data series is non-categorical and the numeric distance between plotted points is meaningful. In other words, you can interpret the slope of a line drawn between the points plotted on an XY chart.

SCW supports six varieties of XY chart. The **Line chart** and the **Scatter chart** are the basic types and they only differ in that the line chart joins the plotted points and the scatter chart doesn't. In other words a line chart is a scatter chart with connecting lines!

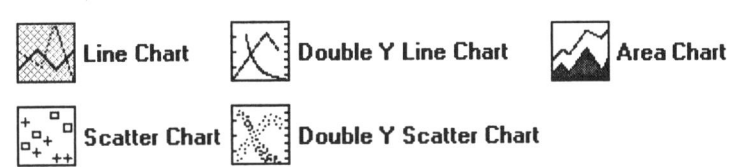

⬚ Line Chart	⬚ Double Y Line Chart	⬚ Area Chart
⬚ Scatter Chart	⬚ Double Y Scatter Chart	

If you plot multiple series on either a line chart or a scatter chart they will be drawn using the same Y axis. This is fine as long as all of the data series are composed of values in the same sort of numeric range. If they are not you need to use either a Double Y Line chart or a Double Y Scatter chart which offer two different Y axis scales - one shown on the left and one on the right. Again the only difference between the scatter and line version of the charts is that the line chart connects the plotted points.

The line chart also has one variant that the scatter chart doesn't - the **Area Chart**. If you plot a single data series an area chart is just a line chart with the area under the line shaded in. It is only when you plot multiple series that the difference becomes more than cosmetic. Each series is added to the previous series in the manner of a stacked bar char.

Polar Chart The **Polar Chart** is essentially a scatter chart where the X data series is plotted as an angle and the Y data series is plotted as a radius. A polar chart is specifically designed for plotting data that involves measurements made at particular angles.

Pie Chart The third main chart type - the **Pie chart** - is available in only one variant but that is really all you need! The pie chart is different from the rest in that it plots only a single series. Each data value is shown as a percentage of the total corresponding to the area of its pie slice. Pie charts are only ever used for showing how a total breaks down into percentages.

» Categorical data and XY charts

There is one additional feature of the XY chart family that, while it is practically very useful, might serve to confuse the issue. In theory an XY chart should always be plotted using a non-categorical variable on the X axis. The reason is, as already explained, is that you cannot read any meaning into the slope of a line drawn between two plotted points if the X axis is categorical - and if you cannot read any meaning into it why bother doing it!

Practice is never as simple as theory and the fact of the matter is that there are lots of occasions when the distinction between categorical and non-categorical data is slightly blurred. For example, if you want to plot data corresponding to measurements made at the start of each month - is the X axis categorical or not? Clearly it isn't categorical because the start of each month is so many days after the preceding month and if you plot a line chart you could interpret the rate or change i.e. the slope of the line. However if you enter the months as text - Jan, Feb and so on - they cannot be plotted on a strict XY chart because the X axis has to be numeric. In most cases, and SCW is no exception, spreadsheets allow you to use categorical data on the X axis in an XY chart. What happens is that the data is plotted as if the first category corresponded to 1, the second to 2 and so on.

In other words,

» XY charts can use both categorical and non-categorical data as the X data series.

This may be true but you still have to be aware of problems that might arise if you forget or ignore the simple fact that this is only possible because the categories are assumed to be equally spaced. For example, to return to the measurements made at the start of each month it is clear that there is a small, and usually negligible, error introduced in treating all of the months as being the same length.

It isn't difficult to construct an example that really is misleading. For example, if sales data is available for three months you might be tempted to plot a line chart like the one below and draw from it the conclusion that sales increased faster in the second half of the year.

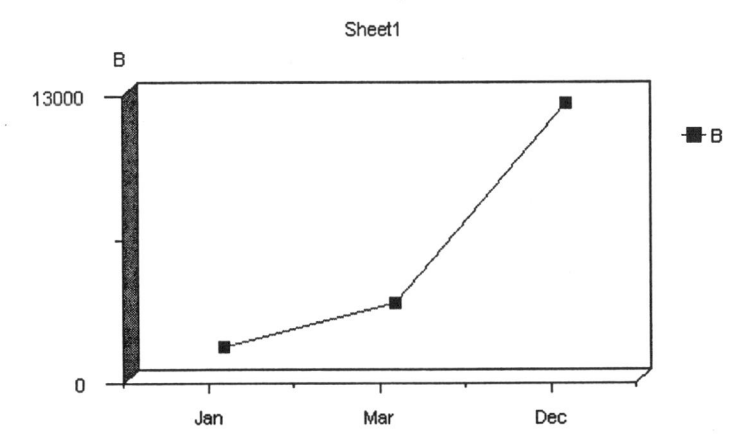

Of course this conclusion ignores the fact that there are more days between March and December than January and March. In this case the assumption of equal spacing between the categories is clearly wrong.

If you change the data so that the month numbers are used in place of month names a more accurate line chart is produced showing the truth of the matter - sales are increasing at a steady rate.

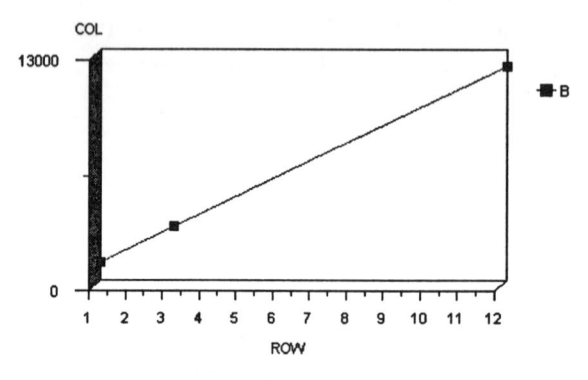

» Selecting a chart type

If you already know the type of chart that you want you may be irritated by always having to start off from a default type - you don't! If you press the Shift key while you drag to define where you want the chart to be placed then you will see the Chart Selection dialog box from which you can select the appropriate chart type. After this you will see the appropriate Assign Data dialog box. If one of the columns of data contains text data then you will go through this selection routine even if you did not press Shift.

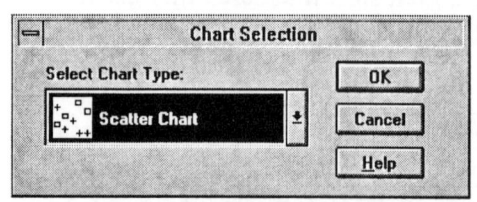

You can set the default chart type to the last type used by using the command Save Preferences while in the chart editing window.

> **Help for SC5 users**
> **How do I draw a scatter diagram with lines?**
>
> If you are an SC5 user you will find some aspects of SCW's charts puzzling at first. For example, there is still a line chart and a scatter chart (XY chart in SC5 terms) but how can you draw a scatter diagram with connecting lines? The answer is that in SCW there is no difference between a scatter chart and a line chart other than the connecting lines. In SC5 a line chart could only work with categorical data but in SCW a line chart can work with any type of data. In addition there is no need to sort the data values into order on the X data series to plot a sensible connected scatter diagram - SCW will do this for you automatically.

» Customising charts

In the main customising charts is one of the easiest of tasks and needs little further comment. You can add a range of different types of graphics objects to a chart using the buttons in the Chart Toolbar.

You can add text, rectangles, rounded rectangles, lines, and three types of arrow. Also on the toolbar is a button to select the chart type, to delete the currently selected object and to set the colours in use.

Once you have inserted an object into the chart it can be edited by double clicking on it or by selecting the equivalent menu command - Edit,Attributes. You can also edit the predefined objects such as titles and axes in the same way. In each case an appropriate dialog box appears. These are:

» Text - the text dialog box allows you to select the font, point size, style, alignment and orientation. You cannot use styles and you cannot use the shortcut buttons on the ribbon bar. Notice that all text values have to be entered into this dialog box - you cannot use cell references to text in the sheet.

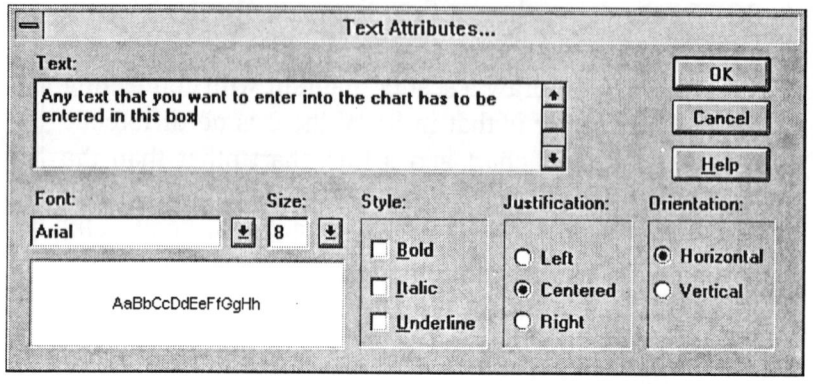

» Lines - the line dialog box allows you to select line width and style - dotted or solid. Notice that you cannot convert one arrow format to another using this dialog box.

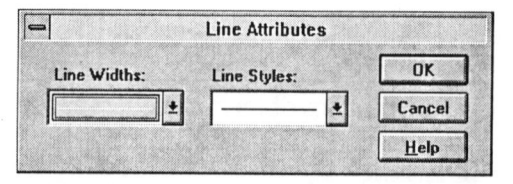

» Rectangles -- the fill and border dialog box allows you to select border style and fill pattern.

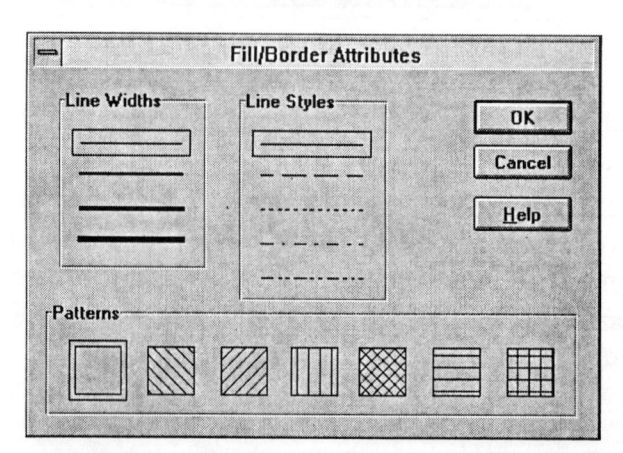

As well as being able to edit the objects that you have added you can also edit the ones supplied as standard when a chart is created such as the axis labels, titles etc.

» Axis control

The principle of double clicking on an object to edit it also extends to the more technical aspects of the chart. In particular if you double click on either of the axes - the axis lines not the numbers or labels below - you will see either the X or Y axis dialog box. The two dialog boxes are identical apart from which axis they control.

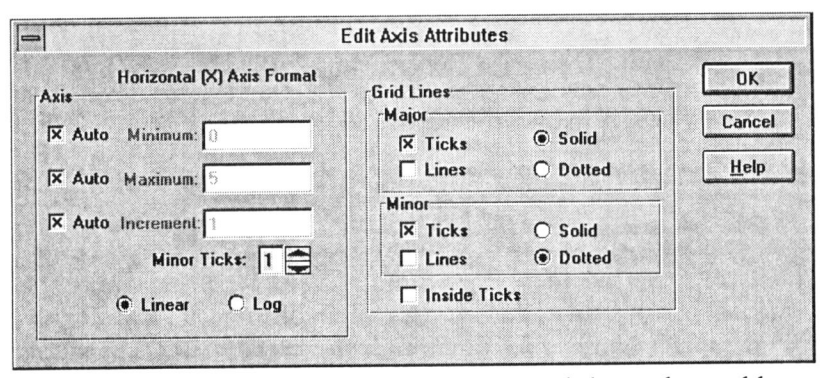

For a non-categorical axis you can control the scale used by setting the maximum and minimum value and the number of divisions or increments to be shown between the two values. Normally you can leave these set to Auto so that SCW selects them by examining the data but sometimes you can make a neater scale by setting them yourself. Each of the increments between the maximum and the minimum is marked by a "major tick" on the axis. You can also indicate divisions between the major ticks by setting the number of minor ticks that should be displayed.

The Grid Lines section of the dialog box controls the drawing of grid lines in place of either the major, minor or both types of tick. You can also opt for the tick marks to be on the inside of the axis.

Finally you can select a linear or log axis. In most cases you will want to use a linear axis but for qualities where doubling or other non-linear behaviour is natural a log axis is more suitable.

For a categorical axis you can only alter the look of the ticks used and their placement.

If you want to format the axis labels, i.e. the text or numbers that line up with the ticks, you have to double click on them. This produces the Plot Axis Attributes dialog box.

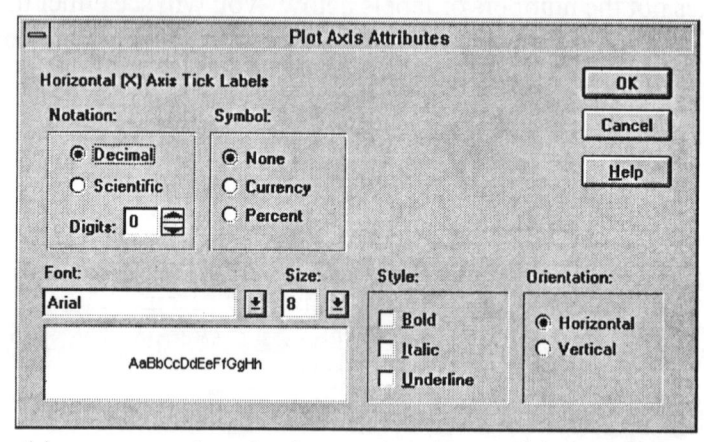

In this you can select the font, point size used, orientation and choose between a fixed number of digits after the decimal point or scientific notation. You can even prefix the values with a currency symbol or postfix with a percentage sign. Notice that you cannot control the formatting of the labels as flexibly as you can values in a spreadsheet. In particular there are no facilities for using anything other than the Windows default currency symbol and there is no way of handling dates, but see Chapter 9.

In the case of a categorical axis you can only change the font, point size and style.

» Legends

The legend is the key to identifying each of the data series in a multi-series plot. In the case of a bar chart it shows the colour and pattern used for each series and for an XY chart it shows the line colour and plot symbol. If you double click on the legend frame you can alter the font and style using the Legend Attributes dialog box.

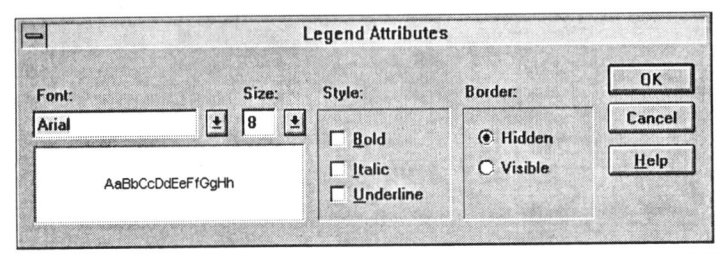

If you double click on the individual legend symbols used for a particular series you can customise the line and plot symbol used for that series. If you find it difficult to double click on the individual legend symbols use the command Edit,Series and click on the Attribute button in the dialog box that appears.

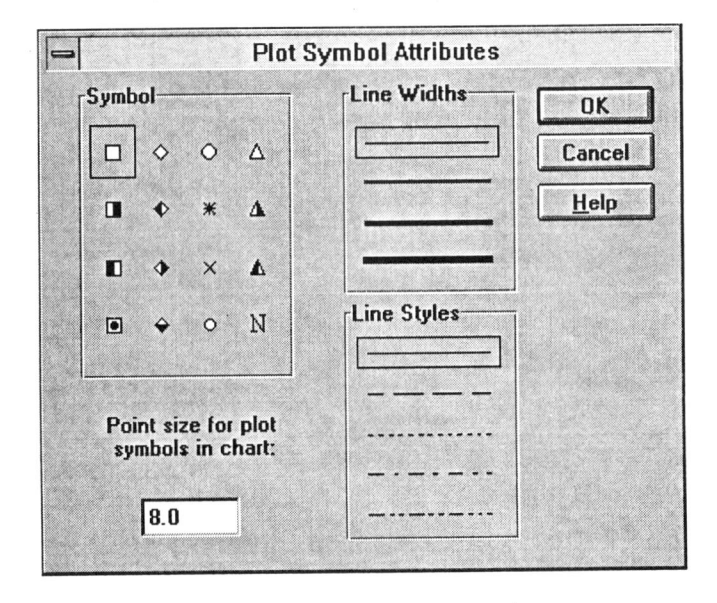

The Plot Symbol Attributes dialog box only allows you to change the plot symbol for a line and scatter chart, the line style for a line chart and the fill for a bar and area chart. In other words, you cannot turn a scatter chart into a line chart by selecting a line width.

You can also edit the legend box to make it larger or smaller and move it to any location. If you want to separate the elements of the legend so that they can be positioned independently then use the Chart,Ungroup Legend command. If you then want to bring all of the separate elements of the legend into alignment use the Chart,Align Legend command. To regroup a legend use the Chart, Group Legend command. Finally if you don't want to see the legend at all use the Chart, Hide Legend command.

» Controlling colour

You can change the colour of any object simply by selecting it and then using either the Edit, Line Color, Edit, Fill Color or Edit,Text Color commands. A quicker way of reaching the same dialog box is to click on the colour button in the Chart Toolbar. Depending on the type of object selected you will either be able to set the colour for the text and border or fill and border.

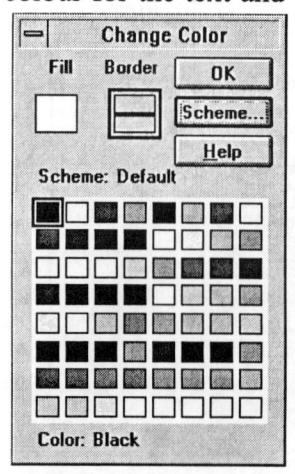

To select a colour simply click on the colour you want to assign to the currently selected object and then click on the OK button.

SCW uses a colour scheme, i.e. a predefined set of colours, to allocate colour to objects as they are drawn. The current scheme is shown in the dialog box and you can select a different one by clicking on the Scheme button. Only two schemes are provided as standard - Default and Gray. Use the default if you are mainly viewing charts on the screen and black and white printing is a secondary consideration. Use Gray when you are primarily concerned with printing charts. Notice that when you select a new scheme all of the colours are changed in one go.

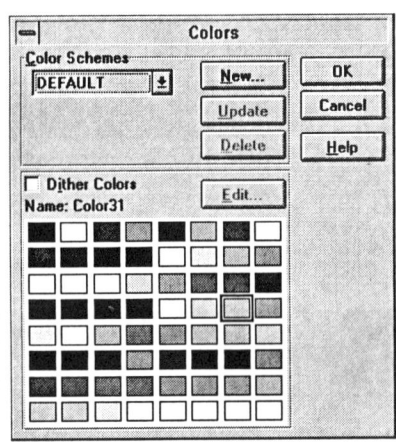

You can define new colour schemes by clicking on the Scheme button and then clicking on New - or directly from the Edit menu via the Color Scheme option. You cannot change the colour assignments in the two standard schemes - Default and Grey. The new colour scheme inherits the colours of the currently selected scheme. Once you have a new scheme you can then edit any of the colours by double clicking on the the colour squares in the palette. This displays a colour mixer where you can select the new colour or type in its specification as RGB or HLS values. Notice that you cannot redefine the first two colours in any scheme - they are always black and white. Colours are assigned to data series in sequence. If you are planning to print the chart on a printer that has a low colour resolution then the dithered colour display will be closer to the printed result.

» Front and back

If you draw two graphics objects then the one that you draw last appears to be on top of the earlier object. This is a natural way to build up an annotated chart. However, sometimes the order of drawing isn't the order in which the objects should be displayed. To move one object in front of another use the command Edit,Bring to Front. This brings the selected object to the front of all other objects. In the same way Edit, Send to Back puts the selected object behind all other objects. To achieve the ordering that you want you may have to use both commands a number of times.

» Chart editing

As well as being able to edit the individual components of the chart there are a small number of commands that directly alter its look. The Edit,Remove Depth and Edit,Add Depth commands control the 3D look of the chart. Edit,Remove Plot Frame takes away the rectangular box around the chart and the Edit,Switch Axis command turns the chart through 90 degrees. If you think about this it is obvious that this turns a bar chart into a column chart and vice versa. Finally the Edit,Add Value Labels command labels each bar chart column with the corresponding Y value.

» Chart templates

We have already examined the idea that the area you select before you click on the chart button determines the columns of data that you can select a chart's data series from. Correct and efficient use of charts depends on understanding data series a little more clearly. For example, it is important to realise that you cannot edit or change the range that is being charted in any way. This even extends to modifications that you may make to the spreadsheet such as inserting rows or columns into the range. You have to select the entire data range that you want to chart and then give the charting command - after this the only way to change the data range used for the series is to rebuild the chart from scratch. This means that there is no simple method of creating chart templates. You should keep this in mind when you are considering spending a lot of time customising a chart.

» Duplicate categories

Normally when you plot a bar chart or a line chart with categorical data there is exactly one occurrence of each category. The reason is simply that there should be one bar or plotted point per category so what is the program to make of multiple occurrences of the same category? In practice there are various ways of dealing with this problem. You can assume that the categories are in fact distinct and not duplicate measurements for the same category. You can assume that the second occurrence of the category is a mistake and so should be ignored. You can assume that the data really does represent multiple measurements from the same category and combine them into one - either by summing or averaging.

Most spreadsheets expect you to deal with multiple occurrences of the same category before you try to chart the data. In other words, it is up to you to process the data into the correct format but SCW will handle the processing automatically for you. When it detects multiple occurrences of the same category it automatically displays the Duplicated Category names dialog box.

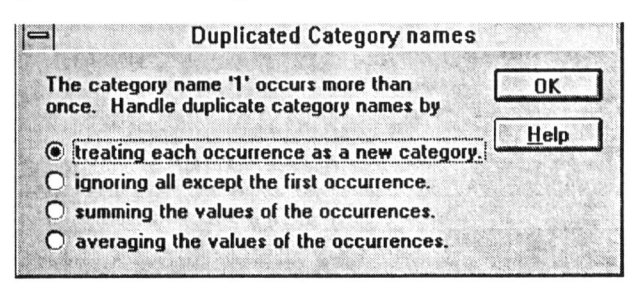

```
┌─────────────────────────────────────────────────────┐
│ ═  │           Duplicated Category names            │
├─────────────────────────────────────────────────────┤
│ The category name '1' occurs more than      ┌────┐  │
│ once. Handle duplicate category names by    │ OK │  │
│                                             └────┘  │
│                                             ┌──────┐│
│ ⦿ treating each occurrence as a new category.│ Help ││
│ ○ ignoring all except the first occurrence. └──────┘│
│ ○ summing the values of the occurrences.            │
│ ○ averaging the values of the occurrences.          │
└─────────────────────────────────────────────────────┘
```

From this you can select the most appropriate way of handling the multiple occurrences. In many cases this situation arises because you have not considered the nature of the data sufficiently in the first place and more fundamental processing is usually the cure.

» Mixed chart types

It is sometimes useful to overlay a line chart on a bar chart so that you can see more clearly the relationship between different types of data. SCW allows you to overlay different types of chart but not all pairings are possible. Essentially a bar chart can be overlaid by a scatter or line chart or you can overlay a bar, line or scatter chart by another of the same type. You cannot overlay pie charts, line charts or stacked bar charts.

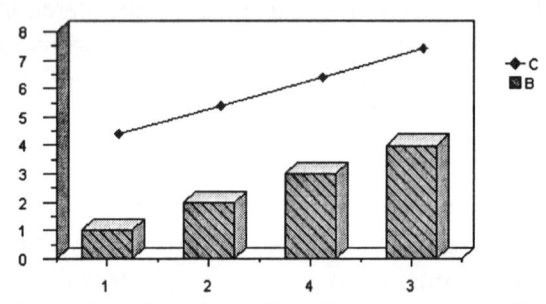

To overlay a bar chart by a line chart, say, you first need to create a bar chart that includes all of the data you want to use. It is better to include too much rather than too little because while you can delete a data series you cannot add one. Once you have the bar chart use the Assign Data command to select just the data series that you want to show on the bar chart. Next use the Chart Type command and select a line or scatter chart. When the Assign Data dialog box appears select the data that you want to show on the line chart and make sure that you select the Overlay option. If you select the Replace option then the first chart will be lost. Notice that you have to create the bar chart before the line chart.

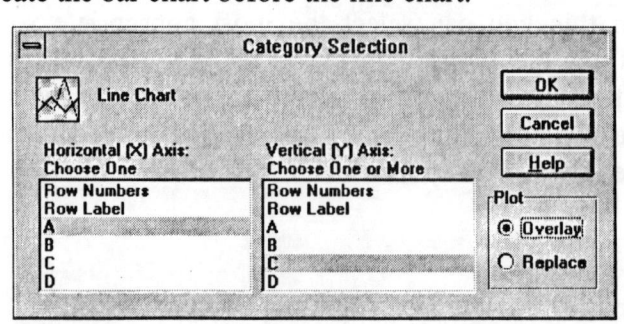

You can carry on overlaying charts in this way but you cannot return to an earlier chart to change the data series assignments. If you make a mistake and want to remove one of the earlier charts you can do so using the Edit,Series command. This produces the Series Attributes dialog box which can be used as an alternative method of setting the series colour, fill and plot symbol. However it can also be used to remove a series from a chart.

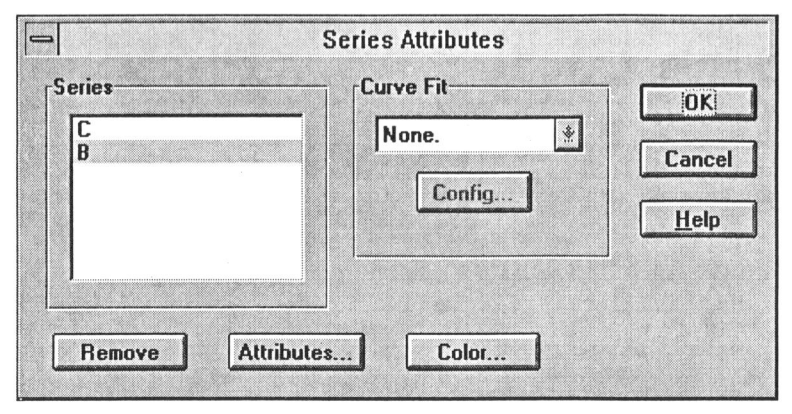

If you select a series and click on the Remove button then that series will be removed from the chart but not from the list of data series that you can use to create a chart. If you remove all of the series plotted on a given chart then that chart is also removed. So, if you have constructed a bar chart overlaid by a line chart and you want to remove the line chart simply remove the data series that it plots.

There is a difficulty if you have used the same series more than once because you will not be able to tell which occurrence of the data series corresponds to which chart. The solution is to select the series and then use the Attributes or Color button to identify which chart it belongs to by its plot symbol or colour.

Once you have removed a chart you can of course use the data series again to overlay another chart.

» More than one X series

Chart overlaying has one specific use that you may not realise is a solution to a problem that you might encounter. If you plot one of the XY charts - scatter or line - then you can only select one X data series against which the other data series are plotted. This is fine as long as you have multiple measurements on each of the data series for the same X values - but this isn't always the case. The solution is to overlay two scatter or line charts each one using a different data series for the X axis.

For example, suppose measurements have been made on the internal temperatures of two enclosures at different cooling air speeds. As long as you could obtain measurements of temperature at the same air speed in each enclosure then a simple line chart will do to display the relationships.

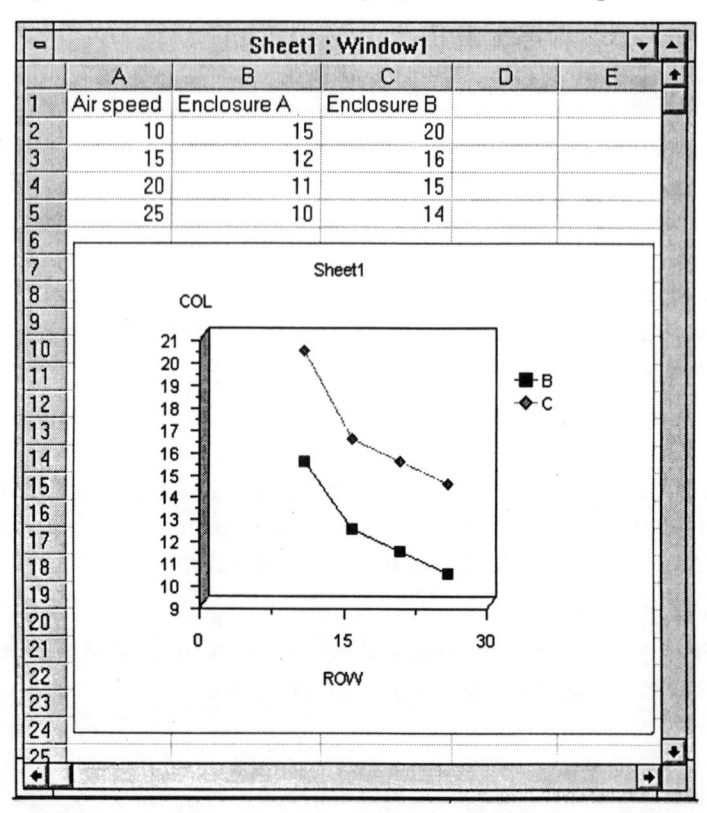

Air speed	Enclosure A	Enclosure B
10	15	20
15	12	16
20	11	15
25	10	14

However suppose it wasn't possible to obtain the temperature readings on enclosure B for the same air flows as enclosure A. In this case there would be four data series two X series and two Y series. To construct a line chart using these you would first select all four columns of data and then click on the chart button in the usual way. However instead of constructing a line chart involving all four series you would select series A to be plotted on the X axis and B on the Y axis - leaving C and D unused. Next you would select the line chart type for a second time and this time use C as the X axis and D as the Y axis - remembering to click on the Overlay box so as not to remove the first chart. The result is a pair of line plots on the same chart but using different X data series. You can repeat the overlay for other pairs of XY series.

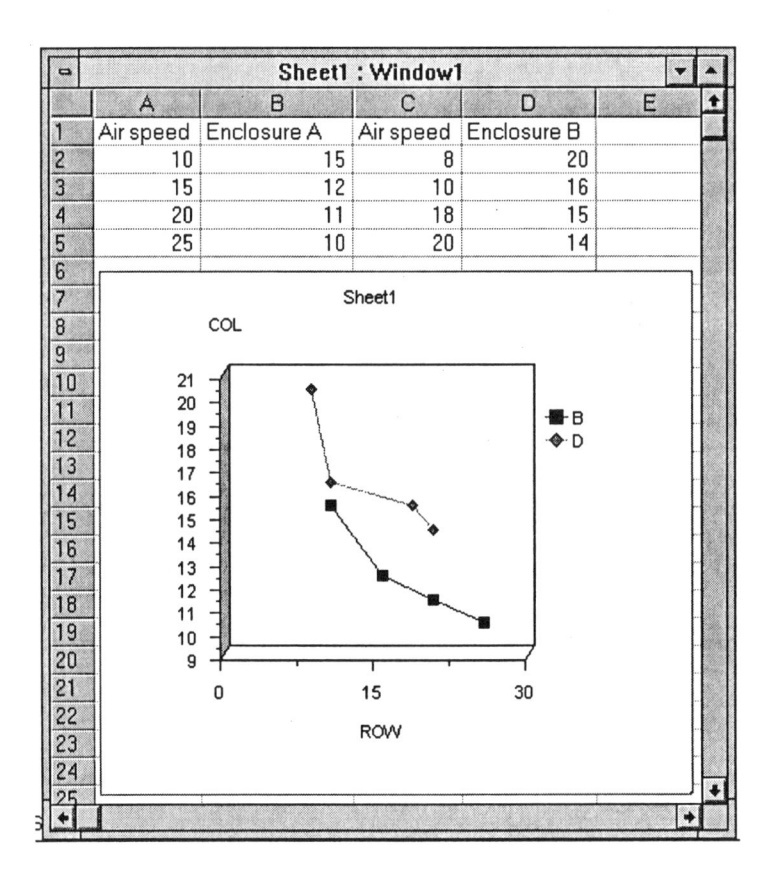

	A	B	C	D	E
1	Air speed	Enclosure A	Air speed	Enclosure B	
2	10	15	8	20	
3	15	12	10	16	
4	20	11	18	15	
5	25	10	20	14	

» Error bars

Often the data values plotted on a chart are known to contain random errors of measurement. In such cases it is a good idea to show error bars around each plotted point to give the viewer a better chance of interpreting the chart. More usually error bars stop a viewer from over interpreting the data! SCW allows you to place error bars around each plotted point on a line, scatter or bar chart using the commands Chart,X Error Bars and Chart,Y Error Bars. In either case the Error Bar Options dialog box appears.

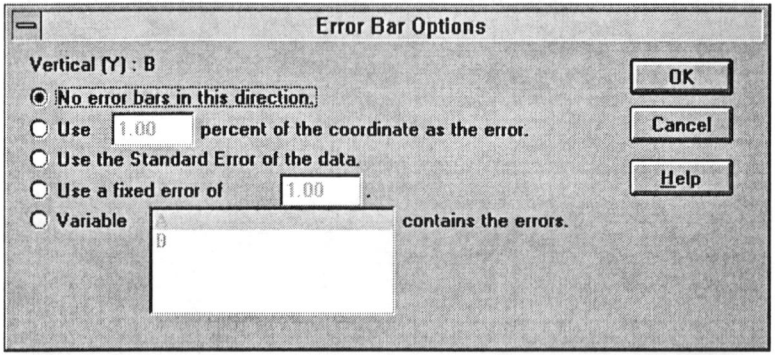

```
┌─────────────────────── Error Bar Options ───────────────────────┐
│ Vertical (Y) : B                                                │
│ ● No error bars in this direction.              ┌────OK────┐    │
│ ○ Use  1.00   percent of the coordinate as the error. ┌──Cancel──┐│
│ ○ Use the Standard Error of the data.                           │
│ ○ Use a fixed error of   1.00  .               ┌───Help───┐     │
│ ○ Variable   A              contains the errors.                │
│              B                                                  │
└─────────────────────────────────────────────────────────────────┘
```

The default option is not to plot error bars at all. The other options are for four ways of determining the size of the error bars.

The first method is to use a fixed percentage of the measurement. It is often the case that a measurement is claimed to be accurate to plus or minus so many percent of the reading. For example, if a measuring instrument is accurate to + or - 10% then you should select this option and enter 10 as the percentage. Notice that the error bars are 10% above and below the plotted value making total error range 20% of the measurement.

The second method is to use the standard error of the data. The standard error is actually an estimate of the variability of the mean of a set of data. That is, if you compute the mean or average from the data you can say that it is plus or minus the standard error. In this case we are using the standard error of the mean as an estimate of the error on each of the measurements.

The third method is to specify a fixed value for the error. Many instruments claim a fixed error either as plus or minus some value or as a percentage of the maximum reading.

The final method is to use a data series that gives the error in each of the measurements. The values in this data series are treated as specifying the plus and minus error in the value. If you want to make use of a data series to specify the error make sure to include it in the range that you select before you draw the chart.

If there are multiple Y data series you can set error bars on each one individually. Simply select the plot symbol in the legend for the series before you use the Chart,Y Error Bars command.

As a simple example of using error bars, consider the airflow versus temperature chart constructed earlier. In this case the measuring instrument - a thermometer - claimed an accuracy of plus or minus 0.5 degrees. Clearly the correct option is the fixed error with a value of 0.5. The only complication is the fact that two Y series are involved. The error bars can be set for each in turn by selecting the appropriate plot symbol in the legend and then using the Chart, Y Error Bars command.

» A Hi-Lo chart

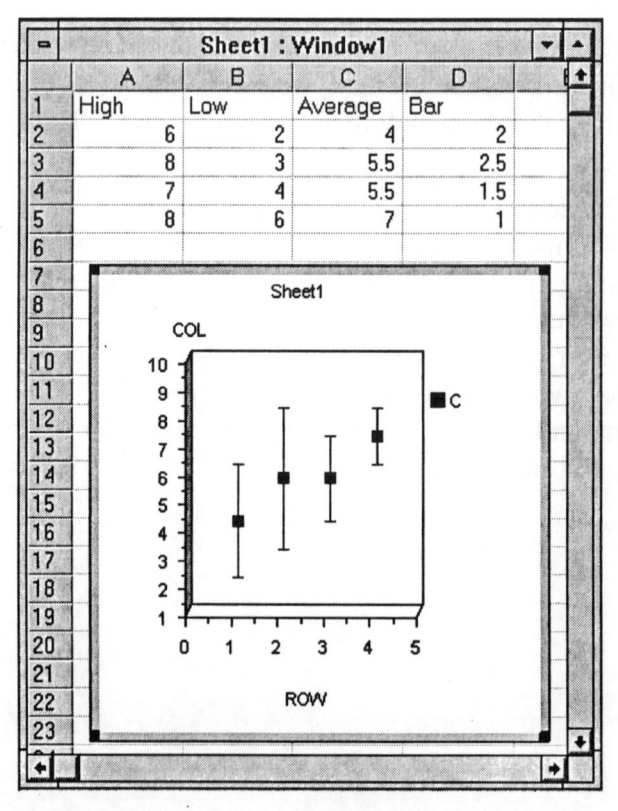

Hi-Lo charts are very frequently used to plot financial data and although SCW doesn't have a Hi-Lo chart option it isn't difficult to construct one. The basic idea is to use the error bars on a series that represents the average of the high and low values. The best way of explaining this is by way of an example. If the High data is stored in A2:A5 and the Low data in B2:B5 then to plot this as the top and bottom end of a set of error bars we need to calculate the average of the High and Low values and halve the difference. The average can be calculated by entering =AVERAGE(A2:B2) in C2 and using Fill Down into C3:C5. The difference can be calculated by entering =(A2-B2)/2 into D2 and using Fill Down into D3:D5. Now if we draw a scatter chart of C2:D5 and select C as the plotted Y values and D as the source of the error bars the result is a Hi-Lo chart with the top of each error bar at the High value and the bottom at the low value. In most cases you will have to adjust the Y axis scaling because this isn't guaranteed to keep the error bars in view. If you don't want to see the average plotted then simply select N (i.e. none) as a plot symbol. You can also plot other data series as symbols on the scatter plot to simulate Hi-lo-open-close charts.

» Curve fitting

As long as you are working with non-categorical data on both the X and Y axis you can use SCW's curve fitting to try to find an equation that best fits the data. The subject of curve fitting is a matter of statistical theory and therefore beyond the scope of this book, but it is worth indicating what is possible. Each Y series can have a separate curve fitted and you can select the type of fit either by using the Edit,Series dialog box or by selecting the series in the legend and using the CurveFit menu. You choices are:

» Simple - a straight line.

» Polynomial - with a variable number of terms up to the fifth power. Simple corresponds to fitting a polynomial of degree 1.

» Logarithmic - equivalent to fitting a straight line to data plotted on a log Y axis.

» Exponential - suitable for data that exhibits exponential growth or decay.

» Interpolate - fits a curve that is guaranteed to go through the plotted points.

If you select one of these options the equation of the curve is calculated using regression (also known as least squares) and the curve is plotted on the chart. The equation of the curve is also inserted as text into the chart. In each case you can specify the accuracy to which you would like the coefficients of the equation to be calculated. In most cases two or three digits is sufficient.

You should be careful when using curve fitting not to read more into the fit than is justified. For example, if you have only three points then a cubic polynomial can be created to fit exactly. Whenever you fit a curve to limited data a good fit is likely. SCW also reports a quantity called R^2 along with the equation of the curve. This measures the goodness of fit as a proportion of the variation that the curve accounts for. For example, if you fit a curve to the data and find a value of R^2 of .9 this means that 90% of the variation in the data is accounted for by the curve and only 10% remains unexplained or due to random effects. Again you should be cautious in interpreting such results when small quantities of data are involved.

If you really want to see how well a curve fit works on limited data then you need to resort to proper statistical procedures, see *Multidimensional Modelling with CA-SuperCalc for Windows* for more on curve fitting.

As an example of curve fitting consider again the air flow and temperature data. It is good practice to try to fit as simple a curve as possible first i.e. a straight line and this is especially true when there is so little data. As you can see a straight line does seem to fit quite well with an R^2 of .91, i.e. 91% of the variation is explained by the fitted line. However if you also add the .5 degree error bars you can see that not all of the variation from the line can be due to the inaccuracy of the measuring instrument.

$y = 17.60 - 0.32x \quad r^2 = 0.91$

Temperature vs Air flow

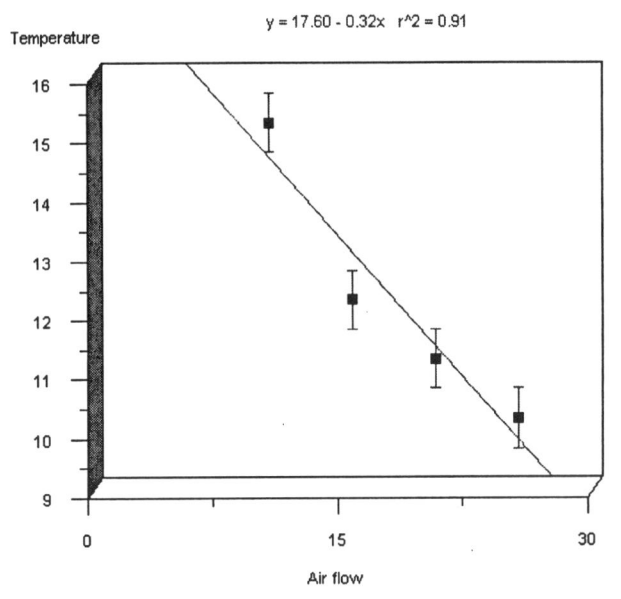

» Practical - A pie chart of sales data

The pie chart is probably the simplest of all charts but even it can pose unexpected problems. Consider the sales figures shown below. What is required is a pie chart of the total sales showing the proportion sold at each outlet. In other words, we need a pie chart of the data in column G but the pie segments should be labelled by the text in column A. The solution to this problem is to make a multiple selection, A5:A8 and

	A	B	C	D	E	F	G
2							
3		Bordeaux	Bordeaux	Burgundy	Rioja	Rioja	Total
4		'78	'83	'86	'86	'87	
5	High Street	850	2230	873	639	1175	5767
6	Market Place	552	1046	587	933	1342	4460
7	Long Lane	203	399	272	116	200	1190
8	Back Avenue	133	197	424	151	82	987
9	Total	1738	3872	2156	1839	2799	12404

G5:G8 before clicking on the chart button. As column A contains text you will automatically be asked to choose the chart type - Pie in this case - and you should assign data series A to the categories and G to the values. The result can be seen below.

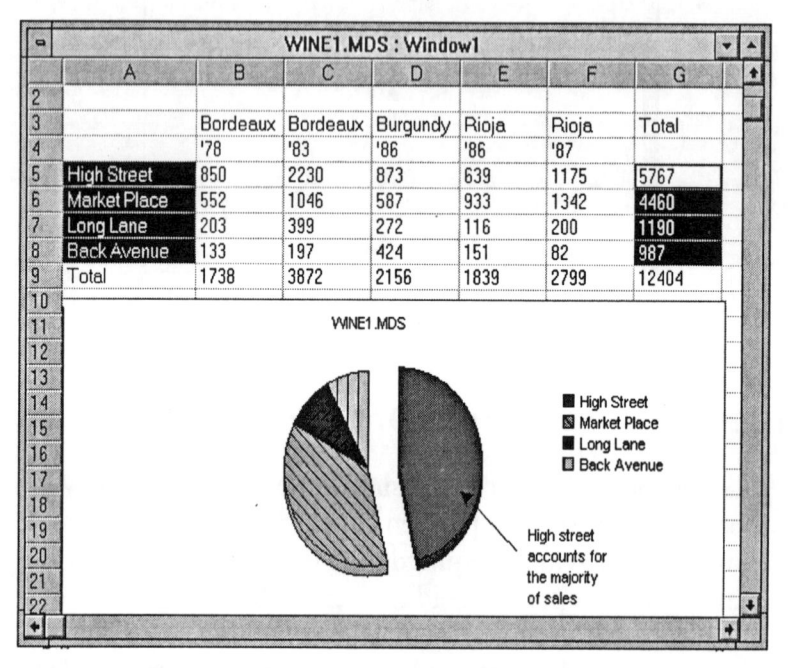

	A	B	C	D	E	F	G
2							
3		Bordeaux	Bordeaux	Burgundy	Rioja	Rioja	Total
4		'78	'83	'86	'86	'87	
5	High Street	850	2230	873	639	1175	5767
6	Market Place	552	1046	587	933	1342	4460
7	Long Lane	203	399	272	116	200	1190
8	Back Avenue	133	197	424	151	82	987
9	Total	1738	3872	2156	1839	2799	12404

The only other modification made to the basic chart is to drag out the segment corresponding to High Street. All of the pie segments can be dragged from the centre to produce an exploded pie. The addition of an arrow and some explanatory text completes the chart.

» Transposing a range

It is worth pointing out that the task of drawing the previous chart would have been more difficult if a pie chart of sales by wine type was required. The reason is simply that this is arranged in a row and you can only chart a data series arranged as a column.

The solution is obviously to make up an additional copy of the data as a column. There are a number of ways of doing this but the simplest is to use the Edit,Paste Special command. This displays the Paste Special dialog box which you can use to set up a number of variations on pasting data into a range.

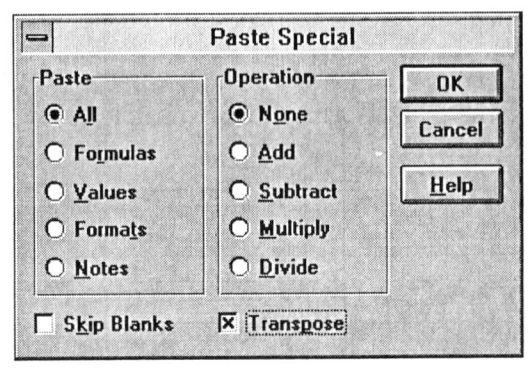

```
┌─────────────────────────────────────────────┐
│ ═│            Paste Special                 │
│ ┌─Paste─────────┐ ┌─Operation──┐  ┌──────┐  │
│ │ ⦿ All         │ │ ⦿ None     │  │  OK  │  │
│ │ ○ Formulas    │ │ ○ Add      │  └──────┘  │
│ │ ○ Values      │ │ ○ Subtract │  ┌──────┐  │
│ │ ○ Formats     │ │ ○ Multiply │  │ Help │  │
│ │ ○ Notes       │ │ ○ Divide   │  └──────┘  │
│ └───────────────┘ └────────────┘ ┌────────┐ │
│   □ Skip Blanks    ☒ Transpose             │
└─────────────────────────────────────────────┘
```

In this case the option of interest is the Transpose box which will paste a column as a row and a row as a column. Using this the data in the pie chart sheet can be copied as a column and charted. The only problem is that if the original data changes the pasted transposed data will not. The obvious solution to this is to use a column of formulae that reference the original data in the row. However there is no easy way to write a formula that can be entered into a single cell and then copied down a column so that it automatically adjusts to give each value in the corresponding row. There is a way of doing this but it isn't simple. It depends on using the COMPREF(r,c) function which provides a computed cell reference to the cell at row r and column c. For example, COMPREF(2,1) is a reference to cell A2. The formula

=COMPREF(1,ROW())

copied into a column H1:H10 say will automatically refer to the cells in A1, B1, C1 and so on. The reason is that ROW() returns the current row number and this is used to generate the column number in COMPREF so transposing the data.

Key points

» Charts are embedded in sheets by first selecting the data, clicking on the chart button and dragging to define the area of the sheet to be used.

» You can edit a chart by double clicking on it. This takes you to the chart editing window which has a range of special tools and menu commands.

» The type of chart plotted can be selected from a range of bar, line, scatter charts and pie charts.

» It is important to distinguish between categorical and non-categorical data when constructing a chart.

» Bar charts plot categorical data on the X-axis. Scatter and line charts can plot categorical or non-categorical data on the X-axis.

» Multiple occurrences of the same category is dealt with automatically.

» The only difference between a line chart and a scatter chart is that connecting lines are drawn between the plotted points.

» You can edit all of the graphical objects within a chart and add boxes, lines and arrows.

» Some combinations of charts can be overlaid to produce a mix of chart types within the same frame.

» Overlaying charts is a way of dealing with multiple X-axis data series.

» You can include error bars and fit a variety of curves to data in scatter and line charts.

Chapter 6

Audit
Making Sheets Work

In this chapter we take a look at some of the practicalities of working with spreadsheets. Often a spreadsheet starts out small and easy to cope with but quickly grows into a large but valuable monster. To keep your sheets under control you need to organise how they are constructed and how they are used. However, even the best of us make mistakes and this brings us to the topic of spreadsheet auditing and the answer to the question "how was that calculated?"

» Windows and workspaces

In the previous chapter we discovered that double clicking on a chart takes us to the chart editing window. In fact you can create any number of windows onto a sheet - simply select the Window,New Window menu command. Each window provides you with an independent view of the entire sheet. So for example, you could use one window to examine data at the top of the sheet and another to look at results further down the sheet. You can switch between windows using the Window menu command which displays a list of all of the available windows. Alternatively you can use Ctrl-F6 to move to the next window and Shift-Ctrl-F6 to move back to the previous window.

Each window can have its own set of display options and the window settings and positions are saved when you save the sheet. That is, when you open a sheet the windows that you were using when you saved it are also re-opened.

Chart windows behave in the same way as sheet windows apart from the fact that you can name them. Use the command Window,Name command and type in an appropriate name. A window's name appears on its title bar.

While on the subject of charts it is worth mentioning that a chart is only visible in windows that were created after it was. If you create a new window and then create a chart in the original window you will not see the new chart in both windows. Similarly if you delete a chart in one window it doesn't vanish in any other windows.

As well as multiple windows into the same sheet you can, of course, open multiple sheets. When you are working with Windows applications this is so standard a feature that it can almost be taken for granted - but it is a powerful feature that allows you to work with multiple sheets and cut and paste between them. You can also write formulae that reference data and even ranges in other sheets. Links between sheets and indeed other Windows applications, are described later in this chapter.

The only problem with multiple windows is that you can quickly become swamped by their number! To make best used of windows it is important that you know the basic commands. The Window,Tile command will show you all of the windows tiled in rectangular portions of the screen in the available screen space. The Window, Cascade command will order your windows one behind another like a stack of cards. Both of these commands are really only useful when you have a small number of windows in use. In most cases it is better to resize each window independently and minimise those that are not in current use.

To move a window simply drag its title bar. To resize a window drag its boundary. If you click on the up arrow in the right-hand corner of a window you will maximise it. To minimise it to an icon click on the down arrow. To restore the window to its previous size click on the double headed arrow - all of these are standard Windows operations. What often puzzles users is how to close a window when it is maximised? The solution is to double click on the close box at the far left hand end of the menu bar. Although this looks as if it belongs to the whole application it actually belongs to the current window.

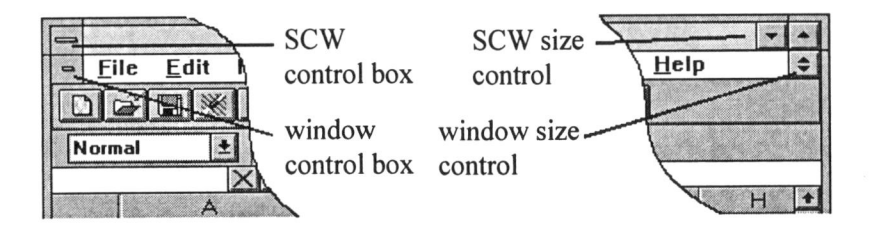

If you have a lot of windows minimised as icons then you can use the Window,Arrange Icons command to move then into rows and columns but if you need to use this command you probably have too many windows open for your own good!

You can always close a window, either by using the Close command in the menu that appears when you click on its control box or by using Alt-F4.

If you need a sheet or window available but you don't actually want to use it - for example, if it is linked to a sheet you are using or if it is a macro sheet - then you can use the Window,Hide command to make it invisible. To make any sheet visible use the Window,Unhide command and select it from the list presented.

A collection of sheets and windows is known as a workspace and you can save and load entire workspaces. The command File,Save Workspace will save the details of all of the open sheets and windows. You have to supply a workspace name and a name for any unnamed sheets that are in use. You will also be asked if it is OK to save each of the open sheets. Saving a workspace does not save new copies of the existing sheets it simply remembers which sheets and windows (and models) are open at the time and the position of each window. If you open a workspace all the sheets and windows are restored to their positions when you saved the workspace. You can open a workspace using the standard File Open command but in this case look for files ending in .MDW.

» Spreadsheet surgery - inserting and deleting

As you create a spreadsheet you are almost sure to want to rearrange the rows and columns of data and formulae that you have entered. In some cases it is enough to drag the data and formulae to new locations but often it is easier to insert and delete rows and columns.

The easiest way of doing this is to select a row or column range and then use the command Edit,Insert which is also available on the pop-up right mouse button menu. This will insert the number of rows or columns that you have selected. The new rows and columns are blank and are default formatted. They replace the rows and columns that you had selected which are moved to the right or down the sheet. In fact all of the rows below the insertion point and columns to the right of the insertion point are moved and cell references are adjusted accordingly. Notice that all cell references - both absolute and relative are adjusted when rows or columns are moved by an insert operation. The rationale is that the formulae should be adjusted to use the data that they were using before the insert. For example, if the formula =$B$1 is stored in C1 and a new column B is inserted the formula, now in D1, is adjusted to read $C$1.

The opposite of inserting a row or column is deleting. This works in more or less the same way. You select a column or row range and use the command Edit,Delete and the columns or rows selected are removed, complete with any data they may have contained. All of the rows below the deleted rows and all of the columns to the right of the deleted columns are moved up to take their place. Again cell references are adjusted so that they refer to the same data that they did before the deletion. However in this case it is possible to delete a row or column that contains a cell that a formula is using. In this case the cell reference is not adjusted but replaced by the warning indicator #REF! When you see #REF! you know that a formula has been damaged by a row or column deletion.

When you insert a new row or column all of the rows below and columns to the right move down by one or to the right to make room for it. Of course at the bottom and far edge of the spreadsheet this causes a problem. The reason is that the spreadsheet cannot get any bigger and so the bottom row and far right hand "fall off" the edge. This isn't a problem as long as there is nothing stored there. If there is the insert will not be performed and you will see the error message "cannot shift non-blank cells off sheet". This is a perfectly reasonable and meaningful error message as long as you remember that inserting does move at least one row or column off the edge of the sheet.

As well as being able to insert or delete an entire row or column you can also insert or delete a block of cells. If you select a block and then use the Edit,Insert or Edit,Delete commands the appropriate Edit dialog box appears. If you are inserting or deleting a block of cells SCW needs to know what to do with the contents of the cells. You can opt for the cells to be shifted to the right or down on an insert, or up or to the left on a delete. You can also select Entire Row or Entire Column but this simply reduces the insert or delete to a column or row operation which we have already looked at. The cell references in cells that are moved as a result of an insert or delete are adjusted so that they still reference the same data. Notice that using Edit,Clear on a range isn't the same as using Edit,Delete. Edit,Clear deletes the contents of the cells in the block where Edit,Delete deletes the cells and moves the contents up or to the left. You should think about Edit,Insert and Edit,Delete as operating on the structure of the sheet and not the data and formulae.

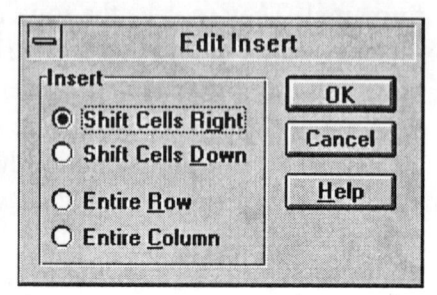

Chart ranges are not adjusted when you insert or delete rows, columns or blocks. This can lead to results you didn't anticipate!

» Organising sheets

One of the problems in working with 2D sheets is that you often need to use different areas for specific purposes. For example, you might use the top left hand corner for the first quarter's financial results and the rows below that for the second quarter's. This is fine as long as you keep in mind that the sheet is being used in this way at all times.

The problems usually start when you first forget about the use of other parts of the sheet and insert and delete columns. For example, if you are working on the second quarter's results you will only see this area of the sheet in the current window. As a result it is very easy to forget about the first quarter's results being directly above and so insert a new column, or worse delete an existing column without thinking about its wider effects.

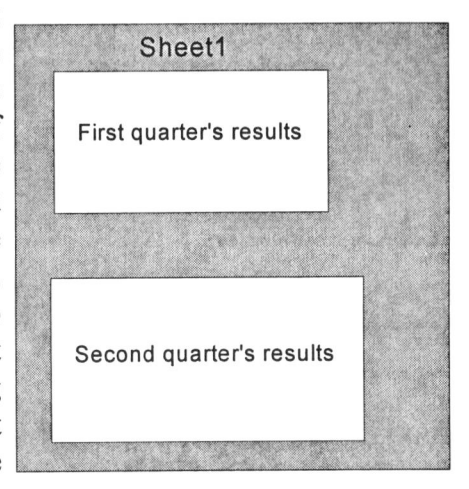

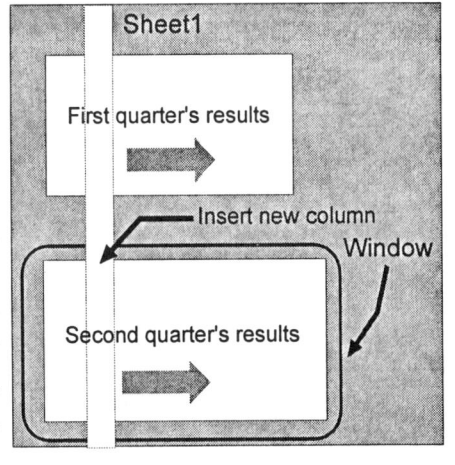

This problem of unwanted interactions between different areas of the sheet used for different purposes is often more subtle than this. You are safe to insert rows in the one above the other arrangement but if the areas are next to each other then this too becomes a problem. You can also find that adjusting the width of a column produces unwanted effects, as does changing formatting and even moving data.

One solution is to use areas that do not share rows or columns. Such an arrangement works until one of the areas is expanded to the point where it overlaps with another. Still this is the best that can be achieved using a single 2D sheet and this is the preferred layout if you are planning to use different areas for different purposes.

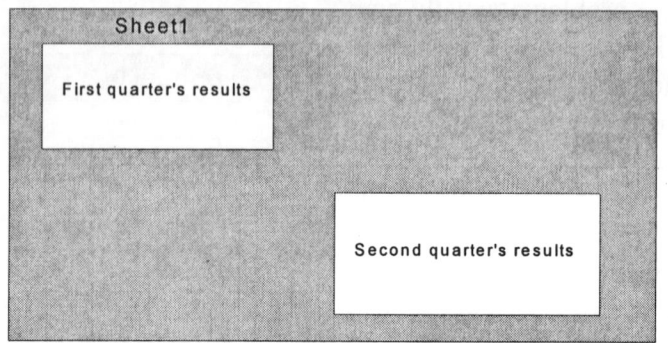

```
                    Sheet1
    ┌─────────────────────┐
    │ First quarter's results │
    └─────────────────────┘
                              ┌─────────────────────┐
                              │ Second quarter's results │
                              └─────────────────────┘
```

It is worth saying that sometimes the sharing of rows or columns can be an advantage. If tables share the same structure and you can guarantee never to need to insert or delete columns then the "one above the other" layout has the advantage that the tables can share the same pattern of column widths.

Of course one way of avoiding trouble caused by using different areas for different purposes is not to do it at all! You could use a multidimensional model for the same purpose and use the "quarter number" as a dimension or you could use separate sheets for each quarter's results. If you use separate sheets you can still gather data together across the quarters using linked formulae - see later.

» Title locks

A title lock is a surprisingly simple idea but it can make the difference between making a large spreadsheet usable or impossible. A very common arrangement in a spreadsheet is to have text at the top of each column or at the left of each row that indicates what the data is. These headings not only allow someone to view the sheet and interpret the figures they provide essential guidance on what data should be entered where. A very common cause of data entry errors is the need to look at a column heading and then scroll down to the first free row to actually enter the data. It only takes a moments loss of concentration or a wrong keypress to ensure that the data is entered into the wrong column!

This is quite unnecessary as it is very simple to arrange for the column or row headings to remain visible on the screen at all times. All you have to do is place the cursor just below the column headings and to the right of any row headings and use the command Options,Display - which is also available on the pop-up menu if you click with the right mouse button on the window's title bar.

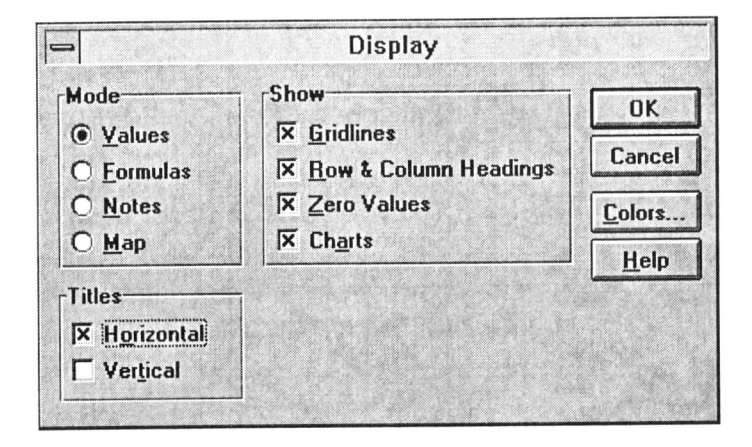

If you select either or both of the Titles Horizontal or Titles Vertical options that appear in the Display dialog box then the relevant titles will be locked into place. If you select Horizontal then all rows above the current cursor's position will always be visible in the window. If you select Vertical then all of the columns to the left of the cursor's position will also remain fixed on the screen.

For example, if the titles in a sheet are in row 1 placing the cursor anywhere within row 2 and using the command Options,Display and selecting Horizontal locks row 1 so that it is visible even if row 2,3, etc. have scrolled off the top of the screen.

Of course you can't move the cursor into the title lock area using the cursor keys - but you can by clicking with the mouse in the title area. To undo a title lock simply repeat the Options,Display command and uncheck the appropriate Horizontal or Vertical box.

Titles are also useful when you print out a large spreadsheet, see the next chapter.

	A	B	C	D	E	F	G
1	NAME	DEPARTURE	DESTINATION	DATE	TIME	DAYS	PRICE
9	Flight Sales	Gatwick	Alicante	20-Dec	04:30:00 PM	14	£174.00
10	Flight Sales	Gatwick	Murcia	20-Dec	03:10:00 PM	21	£128.00
11	Owners Abroad	Gatwick	Murcia	20-Dec	03:10:00 PM	14	£128.00
12	Owners Abroad	Gatwick	Murcia	24-Dec	03:00:00 PM	14	£132.00
13	Owners Abroad	Gatwick	Alicante	17-Dec	08:10:00 AM	14	£129.00
14	Monarch	Gatwick	Alicante	24-Dec	04:40:00 PM	21	£129.00
15	Monarch	Manchester	Alicante	17-Dec	08:40:00 AM	21	£149.00
16	Beach Villas	Gatwick	Alicante	17-Dec	08:10:00 AM	21	£144.00
17	Falcon	Gatwick	Murcia	17-Dec	03:00:00 PM	21	£157.00
18	Tarleton	Gatwick	Almeria	21-Dec	10:30:00 AM	14	£130.00
19							

» Sheet merging

One way of minimising the problems with large spreadsheets is to split them up into separate sheets to keep them small. This is clearly a possibility for data such as the four quarters financial results described earlier. Each sheet has the same sort of structure but different data. This makes it an ideal candidate for a spreadsheet template - see later - but what happens when it is necessary to form totals for the year end?

If each of the quarters results were stored in the same spreadsheet it would be possible to write formulae that reference them all to form a total.

The traditional solution to this problem is to use spreadsheet consolidation. This is where individual spreadsheets are read in and merged to form a new combined spreadsheet. SCW does have a merge operation which is useful but not as flexible as a traditional consolidate option. The reason for this is that SCW offers better ways of solving the problem! If you still want to try to merge files for consolidation then you can use the File,Merge command and then click on the Options button. Using the Merge Options dialog box that appears you can control the way that the merge works. In most cases you will want to merge only values from the sheet on disk. If you perform a simple merge then the contents of each cell in the sheet on disk are read in and are stored in the corresponding cells of the current sheet.

If you select the Overwrite existing data option then the data from the sheet on disk will replace any data already in the current sheet. If you do not select this option the data from the sheet on disk will only appear in the blank cells of the current sheet.

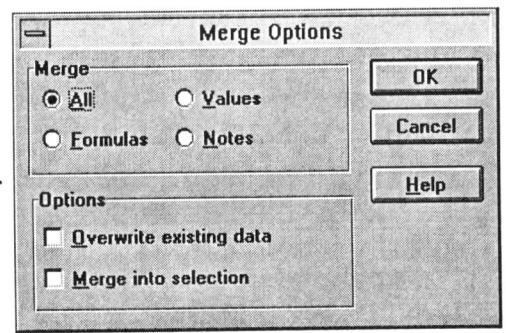

It is more useful to check the option Merge into selection. If you do this the contents of the cells of the sheet on disk are stored in the range selected in the current sheet. The merge is performed in such a way that cell A1 of the sheet on disk is stored in the top left hand corner of the selected range. This makes it possible to merge a number of sheets that have data stored in the same area into different areas of the current sheet. Using merge in this way isn't difficult but it is error prone. One single mistake - forgetting to check the read into selection option or selecting the wrong file - and the result is a mess that is difficult to sort out.

» Sheet links

A much better method of working with data contained in multiple sheets is to use sheet links. You can write a reference to a different sheet simply by including its name. For example, to refer to cell A1 in the sheet Q1 you would use the reference 'Q1.MDS'!$A$1. In general to refer to a cell in another sheet you would use:

'sheetname'!cellref

The sheet name has to be enclosed in single quotes and the cell reference, which is preceded by !, is usually absolute. If the sheet referred to is loaded into memory then the link is an active one in the sense that changing data in it automatically updates the sheet that refers to it. If the sheet is stored on disk then links are updated when first made and whenever the sheet containing the link is loaded. You can also refresh links manually using the command File,Links which is described later.

You can use a link within a formula just as you would a cell reference. You can also link to a range, as long as this is within a function that can operate on the range. For example, =SUM('Q1.MDS'!'$A$1:$D$10') will sum the range A1:D10 in the sheet Q1. Notice that you have to enclose the range in single quotes.

If you find typing in links too error prone you can enter them by pointing with the mouse just as you would enter a cell reference. The only difference is that you need to have the second sheet open and visible. You can also use Edit,Copy and Paste,Link to paste a single or a set of links into a sheet.

You can see how links would be the solution to the four quarters problem. You would simply create a fifth sheet called totals and write linked formula something like

=' Q1.MDS' !A1+' Q2.MDS' !A1+
    ' Q3.MDS' !A1+' Q4.MDS' !A1

This is easy enough but there are a few problems. The main one is that when you copy a link using Edit,Copy and Edit,Paste or Fill Down etc. the cell references are not adjusted. This means that you could find that you have to manually enter multiple copies of a formula. It also isn't easy to link to a large number of sheets for the same reason - you have to enter the name of each one. In practice it isn't a good idea to use a great many links because it slows everything down to have to get data from disk.

You can use the clipboard to copy single and multiple links between sheets. If you copy a range from one sheet then to paste the data as values or formulae into another simply use the Edit,Paste command. To paste the range as a set of links use the Edit,Paste Special command.

Pasting links from the clipboard is a way to create a copy of a range in one sheet in another but it doesn't help with constructing ranges of linked formulae that refer to more than one sheet. There is a way to create formulae that auto-adjust as you copy them but it makes use of some advanced techniques and it best introduced as part of an example.

Also notice that saving a set of linked sheets as a workspace provides the ideal way of organising a set of closely co-operating sheets.

» Practical - Links in action

The sales of different types of wine at each of three outlets are recorded monthly. The three sheets that make up a quarter's results are stored as WAPRIL.MDS, WMAY.MDS and WJUNE.MDS. The problem is to build up a TOTALS sheet that summarises all of the data. The difficulty is that while it would be easy to construct a single formula totalling each of the subtotals, what is required are totals for each of the wine types and each of the outlets. Using a simple manual method this would require entering a formula like

=' WAPRIL.MDS' !$B$5+' WMAY.MDS' !$B$5+
' WJUNE.MDS' !$B$5

This is not a problem but it only calculates the totals for Bordeaux sold in the High Street over the three month period. There are another 19 formulae to be entered like this one and they only differ in the change from B5 to B6, B7 and so on. Unfortunately you cannot create this set of regular formulae simply by copying because cell references in links are not adjusted.

	A	B	C	D	E	F	G
				WAPRIL.MDS : Window1			
1	Sales of Red Wine						
2	April 1994						
3		Bordeaux	Bordeaux	Burgundy	Rioja	Rioja	Total
4		78	83	86	86	87	
5	High Street	406	789	343	376	256	2170
6	Market Place	236	348	204	340	503	1631
7	Long Lane	68	134	172	38	143	555
8	Back Avenue	55	76	160	52	26	369
9							
10	Total	765	1347	879	806	928	4725
11							
12							

However it is possible to write a link formula that does self adjust as it is copied - but it relies on the use of three obscure functions. As we saw earlier the COMPREF function is included in SCW as a way of translating SC5's computed cell references but it turns

Practical - Links in action **143**

out to have lots of uses within SCW itself! The function COMPREF(row,col) generates a standard cell reference to the cell at the given row and column numbers. For example, COMPREF(1,1) is the same as A1. You can use COMPREF within a link formulae to generate the cell reference as long as you enclose it in single quotes. The other two functions needed to complete the method are ROW() which returns the row number of the cell it is stored in and COLUMN which returns the column number of the cell it is stored in. Putting these three functions together you should be able to see that

$$\text{COMPREF(ROW(),COLUMN())}$$

is a reference to the cell in which the formula itself is stored.

This isn't much use on its own but in a link formula it can be used to refer to the same cell in another sheet. For example:
=' WAPRIL.MDS'!' COMPREF(ROW(),COLUMN())'
is a link to the same cell in the sheet WAPRIL.MDS as the formula is stored in. That is, if the formula is stored in B5 the link is to ' WAPRIL.MDS' !B5 and so on. You can see that by copying this formula into a range you can automatically link to the same range in another sheet. Of course you could have achieved the same effect by copying the range onto the

	WTOTAL.MDS : Window1						
	A	B	C	D	E	F	G
1	Sales of Red Wine						
2	Totals						
3		Bordeaux	Bordeaux	Burgundy	Rioja	Rioja	Total
4							
5	High Street	850	2230	873	639	1175	5767
6	Market Place	552	1046	587	933	1342	4460
7	Long Lane	203	399	272	116	200	1190
8	Back Avenue	133	197	424	151	82	987
9							
10	Total	1738	3872	2156	1839	2799	12404
11							

clipboard and then using Edit,Paste Special to paste the links into the totals sheet. However the COMPREF method is a good deal more flexible than this. If you enter the, admittedly complex looking, formula:

=' WAPRIL.MDS' ! ' COMPREF(ROW(),COLUMN())' +
 ' WMAY.MDS' ! ' COMPREF(ROW(),COLUMN())' +
  ' WJUNE.MDS' ! ' COMPREF(ROW(),COLUMN())'

into B5 and then copy this into B5:F8 all of the subtotals will be automatically generated.

You can use COMPREF(ROW(), COLUMN()) even when the ranges in the sheets are not the same. All you have to do is add or subtract an offset by which the rows and columns are shifted relative to one another.

This method of writing link formulae works well but there is one side effect. You must have the sheets referenced open and in memory. Also if you make changes to them then the links will not be automatically updated. The reason is probably because the link formula is too complicated for SCW to work out that an update is necessary. Unfortunately you cannot use the manual update method provided by the File,Links command because it too doesn't recognise that there is anything to update! If you close the linked sheets and reload them then the formula will be updated. To make things simpler define a workspace that includes all of the sheets involved.

» Links to other documents - DDE

Sheet links are just a special case of the general linking facility provided by Windows - DDE or Dynamic Data Exchange. You can create dynamic links between SCW and other applications and types of document in much the same way that you create inter-sheet links. It is obvious that you can link sheets to models and this topic is discussed in detail in *Multidimensional Modelling with CA-SuperCalc for*

Windows. To make a link to another application you do need to know a little about the structure of the documents it uses. The simplest way of making a link is to select the data item that you want to link to, copy it to the clipboard, change to the other application and then use the Edit,Paste Special or Edit,Paste Link command. Which command is available varies according to the application.

For example, if you select a section of text in a word processor such as Microsoft Word for Windows, copy this to the clipboard and then paste it into a cell in SCW using Edit,Paste Link then the text will appear in the cell. However, unlike a simple paste operation a link has been created and the text will be updated if it is changed in the word processor. If you examine what has been pasted into the cell then you will see that the paste operation has in fact created a link formula.

		=WinWord|Document1!DDE_LINK1[1,1]		
	A	B	C	D	E
1	sample of text				
2					

All link formulae follow the same general form,

    Application|'Topic'!'item'[R,C]

where Application is the name of the application to which the document referred to as Topic belongs; item specifies the precise item in the document and the optional [R,C] notation picks out the exact row and column of the item to be retrieved. In the case of the link to Word, the application's DDE name is WinWord, the topic is called Document1, i.e. its filename, and the item is DDE_LINK1. The way that the item determines which data is linked varies according to the particular application. In the case of Word, the item is in fact a bookmark called DDE_LINK1 automatically inserted by the linking operation. (The single quotes around the topic and item are not needed if their names do not contain spaces or special characters.)

You can construct a link formula manually but in this case you need to know the details of the application's name and how it names its topics and items. For example, if you manually create a bookmark in a Word document then you can write a link formula to it. SCW's application name is SCW or SCW.EXE, its topic are sheet or model names and its items are ranges. For example, you can paste a link to a range of cells into Word and a link formula - called a field code in Word terminology - is inserted into the document. Notice that SCW can be on the receiving end of a link - a DDE client - or on the transmitting end - a DDE server.

» Managing links

If you want to see what links exist in a given sheet then use the command File,Links. This displays the Links dialog box which not only lists the sheets and other applications that the current sheet is linked to but allows you to modify the links.

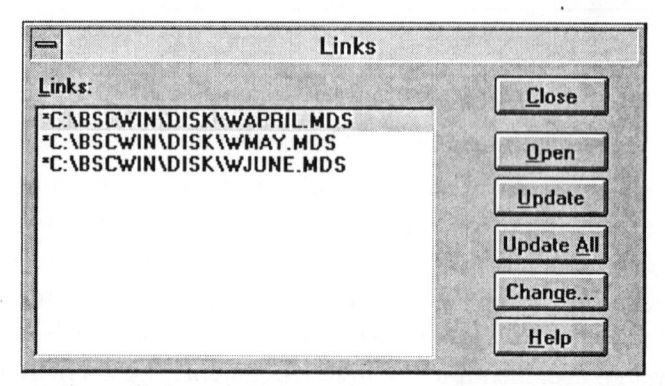

```
Links
Links:
*C:\BSCWIN\DISK\WAPRIL.MDS          Close
*C:\BSCWIN\DISK\WMAY.MDS
*C:\BSCWIN\DISK\WJUNE.MDS           Open

                                    Update

                                    Update All

                                    Change...

                                    Help
```

If you select a link and click on the Open button then the sheet involved in the link is loaded into memory. Clicking on the Update button updates the selected link and, of course, clicking on Update All does just that. If you want to change the file that the link is to then you can click on the Change button and pick the file from the standard File dialog box. Notice that this only changes the file that the link is to and not the item, i.e. the cell or range.

» Templates and protection

A template is the working core of a spreadsheet ready to receive data and provide results. Often a spreadsheet starts out its existence as a one-off quick calculation of some result. However if a spreadsheet is useful once it tends to be useful again and so they tend to linger on. If you discover that you are making use of a temporary spreadsheet on a regular basis then you need to take a careful look at it to make sure that it is accurate and robust.

The best way to make a spreadsheet robust is to convert it into a template. That is, leave all its formulae and formatting intact and remove all of the data. Save the spreadsheet as a blank template and when you want to use it load it, enter new data and save it under a different name.

For example, the monthly wine sales spreadsheet used in the linking examples is the same sheet with different data. Ideally this should be saved as a template, i.e. without data, for use in recording each month's figures. If the first spreadsheet of its type had been constructed as a one-off, complete with data, then to convert it into a template all that is necessary is to select the data area B5:F8 and use the Edit,Clear command being careful to clear only formulae, i.e. data.

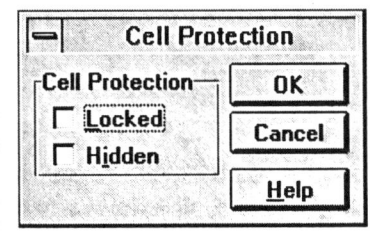

To make a template more robust against accidental changes when data is entered it is worth protecting all the cells that contain formulae or titles. After all, the user of the template shouldn't need to change these particular cells. To protect a cell or range of cells all you have to do is make a selection and use the command Format,Cell Protection - or use the pop-up right mouse button menu. In either case you will see the Cell Protection dialog box. You can select either Locked or Hidden or both of these options and then click on OK. The cells that you have set to Locked show with a small dot in the top right-hand corner. This is to indicate to the user which cells are locked. You can turn this indicator off using the command Options,Preferences and deselecting the Lock Indicator box.

A locked cell cannot be modified by the user in any way. A hidden cell doesn't hide its value as you might expect, only its contents. That is if you hide a cell containing a formula then you will not see the formula on the data entry bar when the cell is selected but you will see the result of evaluating the formula, i.e. its value, in the cell. The reasons for hiding the formulae stored in cells include trying not to confuse naive users and keeping the method of calculation to yourself!

If you select a range and apply protection you may be disappointed to find that you can still change the contents of the protected cells. The reason is that protection, including hiding, doesn't come into effect until you turn it on. The idea is that you can assign protection attributes to as many cells as you need to and then make them effective with a single command. Equally you can disable protection with a single command when you want to make changes.

To turn protection on use the command Options,Protect Document. This displays the Protect Document dialog box.

You can select three levels of protection. To enable the protection that you have just applied to individual cells select the Cells level of protection. You can supply a password if you want to and this will be required to disable document protection - so don't forget it. To make sure that you enter the password correctly SCW asks you to type it in a second time after you click the OK button. If you protect the document at the Cells level you will find that you cannot type any data into the cells that you have protected and you cannot modify the formatting of any cell. The Format options in the menus are greyed out indicating that they are not available.

If you select the Structure level of protection the Edit,Insert and Edit,Delete commands are also greyed out. This effectively means that the user cannot modify the spreadsheet in any way other than to enter data into the unprotected cells.

Finally, the Document level of protection demands the allocated password before the sheet can be opened. If you don't set a password then this level of protection is disabled.

» Practical - protection in action

As an example of how creating a template and protection go hand in hand, consider the task of creating a template from one of the monthly wine sales sheets. The first job is to remove all of the data by using the Edit,Clear command on B5:F8. Next use the Format,Cell Protection command to lock all of the titles and SUM formulae. It is also worth hiding all of the SUM formulae to stop users being distracted by the cell contents.

At this point we have a spreadsheet which looks as if it has a bad attack of the measles. The lock indicator is useful when you are working on a spreadsheet but the dot in the top right hand corner looks mystifying to a novice user. The solution to this problem is to use the Options,Display command to turn off the display of the lock indicator. It is much better to use a cell pattern or colour to indicate areas where data can be entered. To do this select the areas of the sheet that you have locked and use the Format,Patterns command to assign a solid fill with a grey foreground colour to all of the locked cells. Notice that this can be done in one operation if you use a multiple selection.

Sales of Red Wine April 1994						
	Bordeaux 78	Bordeaux 83	Burgundy 86	Rioja 86	Rioja 87	Total
High Street						0
Market Place						0
Long Lane						0
Back Avenue						0
Total	0	0	0	0	0	0

This leaves a white area in the middle of the sheet which from the user's point of view is obviously an area where typing is allowed. Finally change the colour of the font used to black to increase the contrast and add some rulings to make the table's structure stand out. It is also a good idea to use the Options,Display command to remove the gridlines and the row and column headings.

At this stage we have a template with protection in place but not turned on. To set protection on use the command Options,Protect Document and select at least Cell and Structure level protection. It is up to you to decide if Document protection, requiring the use of a password, is advisable.

» Debugging sheets

You may think that most spreadsheets are so easy to construct and so obvious in their use that errors never occur. Well you would be wrong because spreadsheet errors are easy to make and are commonplace. Many users rely on the results produced by a long-time and trusted spreadsheet only to discover one day that it has had a serious error all along! You have to take spreadsheet verification seriously if the results of a calculation are to be used for anything important.

» Notes

SCW provides a number of excellent tools and facilities to help get a spreadsheet right and to keep it right. Perhaps the simplest aid to keeping a spreadsheet correct is the cell note. You can enter a note, i.e. any text up to 255 characters long, into any cell without disturbing its contents. To enter a note you select the cell and use the command Formula,Note - or more simply press Ctrl-N. This changes the cell into note mode and you can enter the text of the note. To change back to normal mode, where you can see and edit the cells contents, you press Ctrl-N again. Cells with notes attached are indicated by a red dot in the top left-hand corner. If you don't want to see the note indicator you can turn it off using the Options,Display command. The edit line always shows a red dot to indicate that you are editing a note rather than the cell contents. The only danger in using a note is that you will edit the contents when you think you are editing the note and vice versa.

The question is what do you use notes for? The answer is whatever you want to use them for! Typically you should include a note when the calculation in a cell is less than obvious so that when you come back to it in a few days' time you have some hope of working out what it does. You can think of cell notes as documenting the spreadsheet so that you, or someone else, can understand what it is doing in times to come.

You can get rid of a note by selecting the cell and using the Edit,Clear command with the Notes option checked in the dialog box. This clears the note's text and the red marker dot from the cell.

Normally you can only see a note on the entry line - the cells value displays in the body of the sheet. However you can change what a cell displays in the body of the sheet using the Options,Display command.

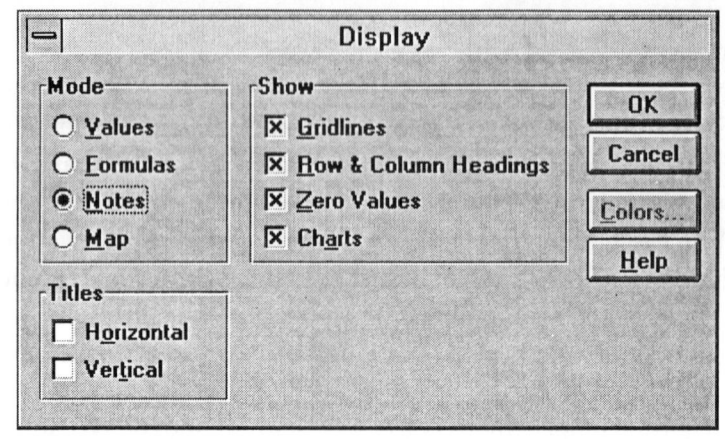

```
┌─────────────────── Display ───────────────────┐
│ ┌─Mode──────────┐ ┌─Show────────────────┐  ┌──OK──┐ │
│ │ ○ Values       │ │ ☒ Gridlines          │  └──────┘ │
│ │ ○ Formulas     │ │ ☒ Row & Column Headings │ ┌─Cancel─┐ │
│ │ ◉ Notes        │ │ ☒ Zero Values        │  └────────┘ │
│ │ ○ Map          │ │ ☒ Charts             │  ┌─Colors…─┐ │
│ └────────────────┘ └──────────────────────┘  └─────────┘ │
│ ┌─Titles────────┐                              ┌──Help──┐ │
│ │ ☐ Horizontal   │                             └────────┘ │
│ │ ☐ Vertical     │                                        │
│ └────────────────┘                                        │
└────────────────────────────────────────────────┘
```

If you select Notes in the Mode section of the Display dialog box then all of the notes entered into the cells can be seen at once.

» Formula and Map mode

If you select Formulas you will be able to see all of the formulae that you have entered and not the values that they work out to. This can be useful in finding a particular type of error - when a cell that should contain a formula in fact contains a value because the user overtyped the original contents by a value. The trouble with Formulas view is that the information presented can be overwhelming. If all you want to see is the pattern of values and formulae Map mode is a better choice.

In Map mode you can see more cells because each one is reduced to a single small character sized square. The content of each cell is categorised and shown as a pair of double quotes if it contains text, a # (hash) if it contains a number and f if it contains a formula. You can see that in Map mode it is very easy to see the overall pattern of the structure of a sheet and spot any irregularities or discrepancies.

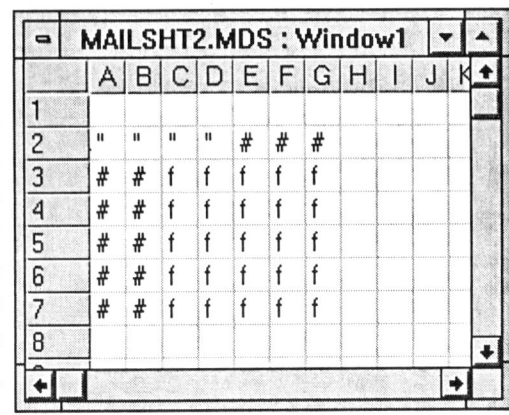

» Info window

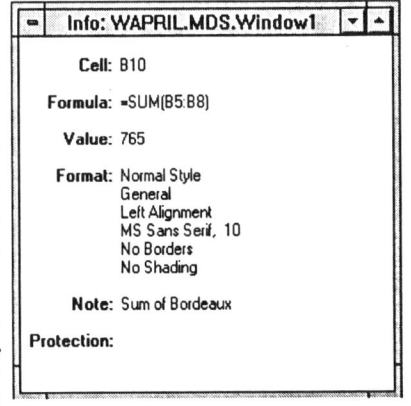

Another aid to discovering how a spreadsheet works is the Info window. To make this summary of cell status visible you use the command Window,Info Window. The Info window works in an obvious manner but you can alter what information it shows you by using the Info menu command which is only available when the Info window is selected. Of particular interest are the options to display Precedents and Dependents. A cell is a precedent of the current cell if it is referenced by the cell. This allows you to see which cells contribute to a particular cell's value. Similarly dependents are cells that make use of the current cell's value.

» Audit trail

The Info window is good for checking up on the details of individual cells but it is not an ideal tool to answer the question "how did this particular cell get to be this particular value". To answer this question we need the Audit Window. This can be used to display all of the cells, their contents and their values that are used by the current cell in working its value out. All you have to do to use this facility is to select the cell you want to analyse and use the command Tools, Audit Trail. The Audit window that appears will show the cell reference and content of the current cell.

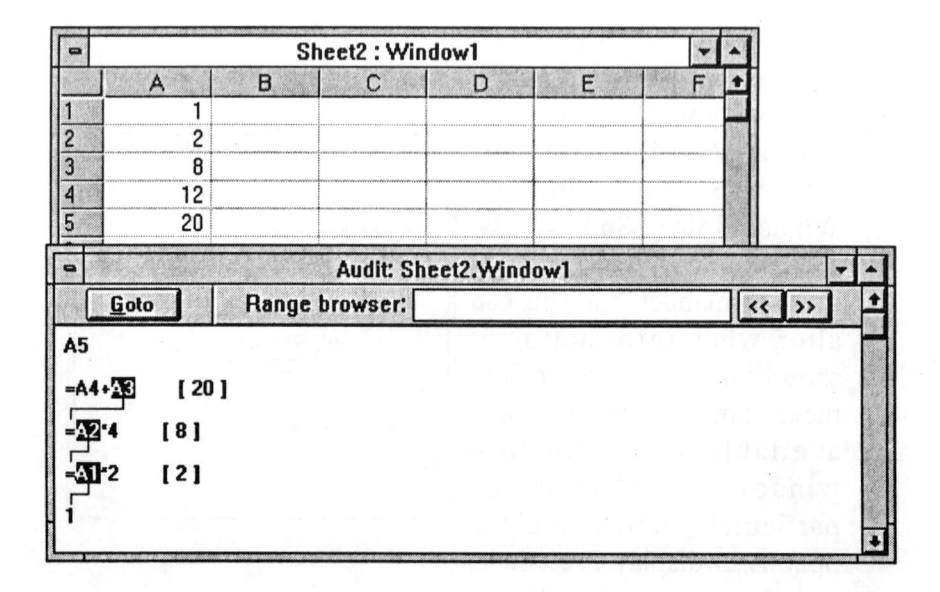

To see how this has been arrived at you have to click on any cell reference used in its formula. For example, if cell A5 is shown as containing the formula =A4+A3 then clicking on the reference to A3 in the Audit window will show what it contains and its value. You can repeat this process, following down the chain of dependency, until you reach a cell that contains a constant or is empty.

You can see that the Audit window is a powerful and easy way to find out why a cell works out to the value it does. Once you find a problem you can use the Goto button to transfer to the cell that you have selected in the Audit sheet.

The only problem in the use of the Audit window is what happens when a cell contains a formula that references a range? In this case you cannot show a single predecessor. The solution to the problem is to be found in the Range browser buttons. By clicking on the arrow buttons you can scroll through all of the cells in a referenced range and see what they contain.

» Select Special

Another useful command in debugging a spreadsheet is the Formula,Select Special menu command. This displays the Select Special dialog box which you can use to specify the type of cell you want to select. If you select a range before you use the command then the search for cells is restricted to this range. For some options you have to specify a range first. You can select all cells that store a given type of data or formula. These options are simple but useful. Slightly more complicated is the option to select all of the cells dependent on the currently selected cell, or all of its precedents. Clearly this can be used as another approach to the problem that the Audit window tries to help with.

```
┌─────────────────────────────────────────────┐
│ ═                   Select Special          │
│ ┌─Select──────────────────────┐  ┌────────┐ │
│ │ ○ Notes    ○ Column Differences│ │   OK   │ │
│ │ ◉ Values   ○ Row Differences │  ├────────┤ │
│ │ ○ Formulas ○ Precedents      │  │ Cancel │ │
│ │   ☒ Numbers  ☒ All levels    │  ├────────┤ │
│ │   ☒ Text   ○ Dependents      │  │  Help  │ │
│ │   ☒ Logicals ☐ All levels    │  └────────┘ │
│ │   ☒ Errors ○ Last Cell       │             │
│ │            ○ Visible Cells   │             │
│ └──────────────────────────────┘             │
└─────────────────────────────────────────────┘
```

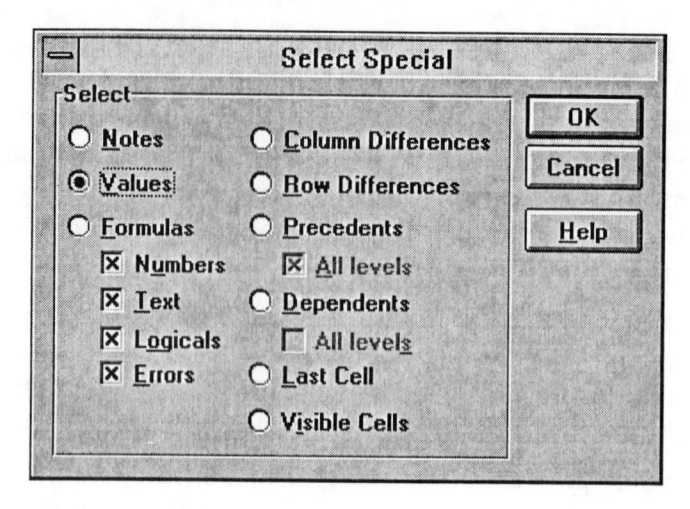

Finally there are options to select every row in a range that is different from the top tow and every column that is different to the left-hand column. You can also select all visible cells and the last used cell, i.e. the non-empty cell furthest from the left and from the top.

» Verification

SCW provides a great many tools to enable you to find problems in a spreadsheet but you cannot find problems if you don't know that they are there! It is important that any spreadsheet whose results you are going to make future use of is verified. Verification simply means making sure that the calculations performed by a spreadsheet give the correct results. You may think that this is unnecessary because spreadsheets automatically give the correct answer - every time. This is only true if the data is correct, the formulae are correct and the formulae all refer to the correct data. In practice it is all too easy to make a mistake that still produces a plausible answer.

The most common errors are -

» Incorrect range references - even if a formula starts out with the correct range reference it can be made incorrect by the insertion of rows and/or columns and by the expansion the area being used to store data. For example, the formula =SUM(A1:A10) stored in A11 will not be adjusted correctly if you insert additional rows at row 11.

» Failure to copy formulae into new rows and/or columns. Always remember that inserting rows and columns results in blank cells - remember to copy the necessary formulae.

» Formula transcription errors. When copying from paper it is very easy to enter a formula that looks right but calculates the wrong result.

» A value has overwritten a formula. As long as the value is the same as the result produced by the formula this error doesn't show. It is only when the data changes that the error comes to light.

Protection against such errors is usually a matter of anticipating how the sheet will be used. For example make sure that any new data areas are inserted within range references by using protection. Alternatively make sure that the user cannot alter the structure of the sheet and provide a macro to insert extra rows if this is necessary. Finally try to include checksums and check calculations (see Chapter 8) that prove that the spreadsheet is working.

Key points

» You can open multiple sheets and have multiple windows onto each sheet.

» Each window has its own display settings. When you open a sheet all of the windows that were open when you saved it are re-opened at the same position.

» A workspace is a collection of sheets (and models) complete with their windows. A workspace can be saved and opened in a single operation.

» You can insert and delete whole rows and columns. After an insert or delete operation, formulae are adjusted as necessary to ensure that they refer to the same data.

» As well as complete rows and columns, you can also insert and delete blocks of cells. In this case you have to decide whether to shift cells horizontally or vertically.

» Title locks are useful when you are working with large sheets because they enable you to keep the column or row titles visible at all times.

» It is difficult to use different areas of a sheet for different purposes without the risk of unwanted interactions. One solution is to use separate sheets and combine them together using merging or link them together using sheet links.

» Sheet links are just a special case of more general DDE links between SCW and any Windows applications.

» There are a wide range of tools to help you make sure a sheet is correct and stays correct - cell notes, formula and map mode, the info window, audit trail and select special.

» It is important that you verify that a sheet works before relying on it and make sure that it cannot be damaged in use.

Chapter 7

Printing and Reports

By formatting a sheet you can make it suitable for an on-screen presentation of results but in nearly all cases a printed report is required - if only to back up the on-screen display. Although report preparation is interactive and made easy because of the good match between what you see on the screen and what you see on the printer, there are also some important differences. Printers have different output characteristics and the size of the display area, i.e. the page size, is larger than a single screen. There is also the question of how to deal with the problems of multiple page output. Fortunately none of this is very difficult to master given a little planning.

» Windows printing

One of the advantages of using Windows is that it manages all of the output devices attached to a machine. If you are familiar with MS-DOS applications then you will know that getting a particular printer to work with a particular application was a matter of finding and installing the correct driver. Windows has simplified this problem down to installing a single driver for each device. Once the device is installed into the Windows system it can be used by all applications.

This means that the problems of installing and managing a printer are not unique to SCW but you still need to know a little about the general topic of printers and how Windows deals with them. The most important point is that you cannot use a printer with any Windows application without a suitable Windows driver specifically for the printer. It is also important to realise that the features and facilities that are actually available for use depends on the quality of the printer driver. Windows is supplied with many drivers for the most popular printers and these often work well. However some of the early drivers supplied with Windows have been improved and it is important to make sure that you are using the most up-to-date driver available. Usually the printer manufacturer can supply the most recent Windows driver but Microsoft also keeps the most common drivers. The on-line information services, such as CompuServe or manufacturers' bulletin boards, are also a quick and easy way to get hold of recent printer drivers.

Once you have the necessary driver you have to install it using the printers control in the Control Panel. This displays the Printers dialog box which you can use to install and configure a new printer. Clicking on the Add button displays a list of printers for which Windows has drivers. If your printer is in this list then select it and click on the Install button. If you have a driver on diskette then selected Install Unlisted or Updated Printer and click on Install. Before you can use the printer you have to click on the Connect button to let Windows know which port it is connected to.

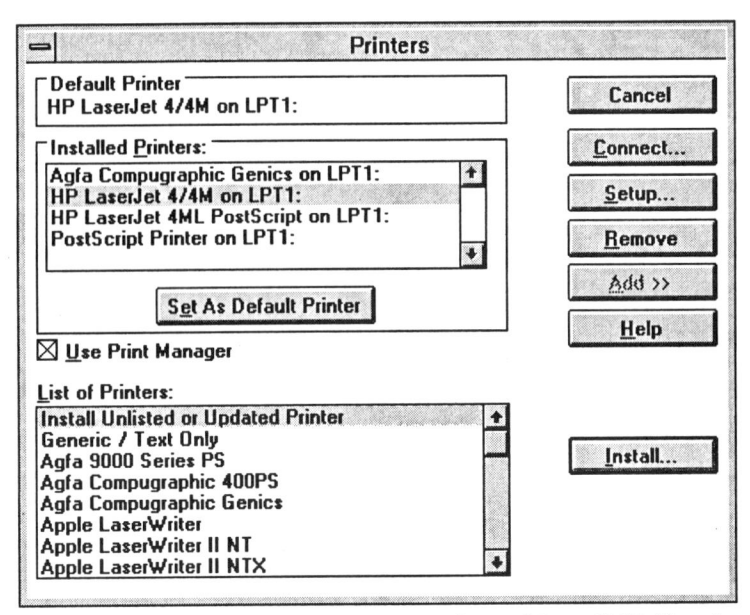

Also notice that you can select one of a set of installed printers to be the default. You can also opt to use or not to use the Print Manager. If you use the Print Manager printing occurs in the "background" - that is you don't have to wait until printing is complete before you can carry on using SCW. The disadvantage is that the entire print job takes longer. In practice it is a good idea to use the Print Manager as some printer drivers seem to work better with it - even though it should have no effect on what is actually printed. Another option that should speed up printing is the Fast Printing Direct to Port option in the Connect dialog box. When this works it does result in faster printing but again some printer drivers don't work correctly with this option selected.

» Printer setup

To set up the more advanced aspects of the way that your printer works you need to use the Setup button in the Printer dialog box. However, in most cases you can alter the details of the setup which most matter using the File,Print Setup menu command in SCW. The dialog box that is displayed varies according to the printer selected but it always gives you a way of changing the printer, the paper size and the paper orientation.

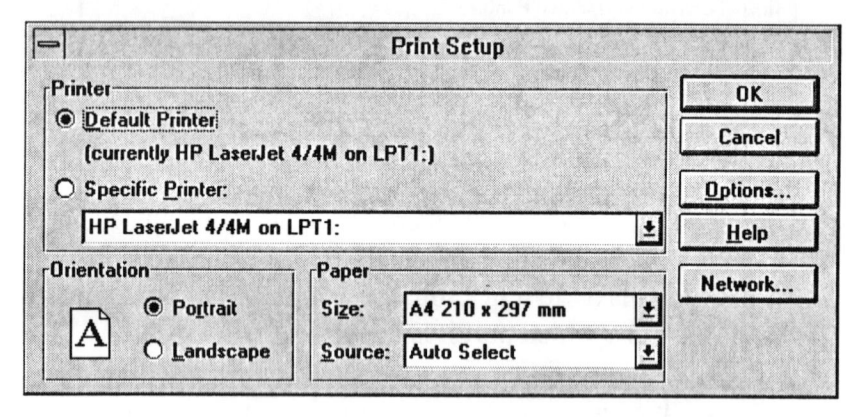

[Print Setup dialog box showing Printer options (Default Printer: HP LaserJet 4/4M on LPT1:, Specific Printer), Orientation (Portrait/Landscape), Paper (Size: A4 210 x 297 mm, Source: Auto Select), and buttons OK, Cancel, Options..., Help, Network...]

Sometimes it is exactly the same as the dialog box that you can display via the Control Panel - you should explore both dialog boxes to see what aspects of your printer's operation you can change.

» In most applications you can change the paper orientation using the Print Setup dialog box and using an application-specific Page Setup dialog box. This often causes problems when the two are set differently. The SCW Page Setup dialog box overrides the orientation settings in Print Setup, removing this source of confusion.

» Fonts

Fonts can be a complicated business but it all depends on the type of printer you are using. Until recently printers were expected to provide their own fonts and users had to buy font cartridges which plugged into the printer if they wanted to extend the range available. This is a slightly old fashioned approach as Windows 3.1 supports both TrueType and Adobe fonts. As long as the Windows printer driver is sufficiently up-to-date both TrueType and Adobe fonts can be down loaded to it so making built in fonts unnecessary. In other words, as long as the font you are using is a True Type or Adobe font you should be able to print it.

However, printers still come with some built-in fonts and this can cause difficulties. If you have a True Type or Adobe font that matches the built-in printer font then there is no real problem. If you haven't then you will only be able to use the printer font when the printer is selected as the current printer. In addition, without a matching screen font the look of the spreadsheet on screen and as printed will be different. If you are only using a single printer and never intend to print a document on another printer then this isn't a serious problem. However, you should try to find matching TrueType fonts for any fonts supplied as cartridges.

To manage the fonts installed on your system use the Fonts utility in the control panel. If you select the Show only TrueType fonts in the TrueType dialog box you can avoid the problem of selecting printer fonts but you will also be unable to use the SCW default font - MS-Sans Serif - which is not a TrueType font.

» Simple printing

Although you can achieve very presentable results by doing so, not every print job has to be set up carefully. You can obtain a rough print of any sheet simply by using the command File,Print or by clicking on the printer button in the toolbar. This displays the Print dialog box.

If you click on the OK button your spreadsheet will be printed to the current printer - as indicated at the top of the box. The area of your spreadsheet printed is automatically selected to include all of the cells that contain anything but notice that charts are not automatically included unless they happen to fall within the area of cells that are used.

In many cases this simple printing command is all that is needed but notice that even here it is still worth using the Preview button which will show you what your output looks like without wasting paper!

» Preview

In practice it is always worth looking at the output on the screen by using the Preview command before committing it to paper. Preview cannot guarantee to show you exactly how your output will look - the printer's resolution and colour handling is almost certain to be different to the screen's - but it does show you the most obvious errors. You can spot layout errors quite easily and correct the problem without having to wait for a printout.

As you can go directly from preview to printout you might as well acquire the habit of using the File,Print Preview command or the preview button in the toolbar as your standard method of printing.

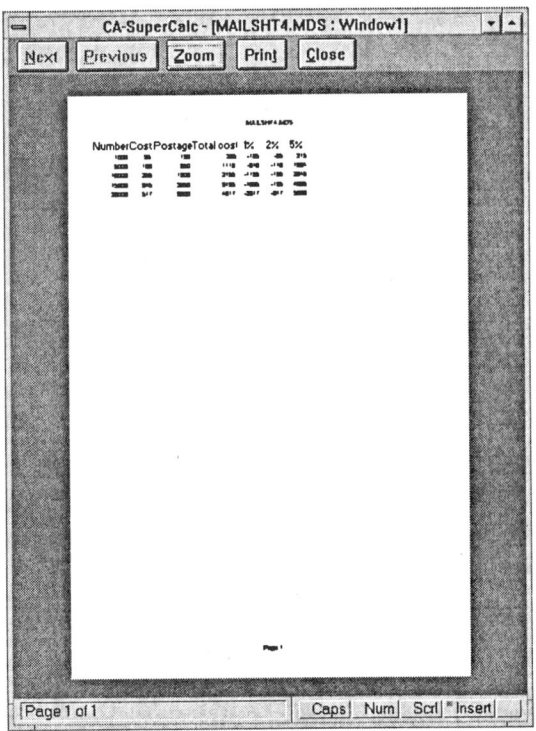

The preview window shows you the entire printout, page by page. You can move between pages using the Next and Previous buttons and you can zoom in by clicking on the Zoom button. The representation of the printout is faithful to the pagination, paper size, orientation and margins.

If you are satisfied with the preview you can click on the Print button which takes you to the Print dialog box. If you're not happy then click on the Close button and you will be returned to the sheet.

» The print range

Although you can rely on SCW selecting the range of cells to print, in many cases you either don't want to print the entire sheet or you will need to include charts. To set the range to be printed first select it and then use the command Options, Set Print Area. If this command isn't in the Options menu then a print range is already set and you first have to clear it using the command Options,Clear Print Area.

You can set multiple print areas by selecting them before using the command - but you also need to know that each rectangular range will be printed on a separate page in the order in which you selected them. So for example, if you select A1:A10, then F1:F10 and then D1:10 three pages of output would be produced with page one containing A1:A10, page two F1:F10 and page three D1:D10. Notice that this separation of ranges onto different pages even works if you select neighbouring blocks as a multiple range. So if you selected A1:A10 and then B1:B10 while holding down the Ctrl key two pages would be printed even though it may look as if only a single block A1:B10 was selected.

» Page setup

Most of the advanced control that you have over the output is contained within the Page Setup. You can reach the Page Setup dialog box by using the command File,Page Setup. You can use this to determine the initial settings of such things as page orientation and margins which will be used by subsequent Print and Print Preview commands. This raises the question, what do you do if the Print Preview reveals a need to change the page setup? The answer is that when you click on the Print button the Print dialog box that appears has a Page Setup button which you can use to alter the page setup. Once you have done this you can again return to the Preview.

[Page Setup dialog box image]

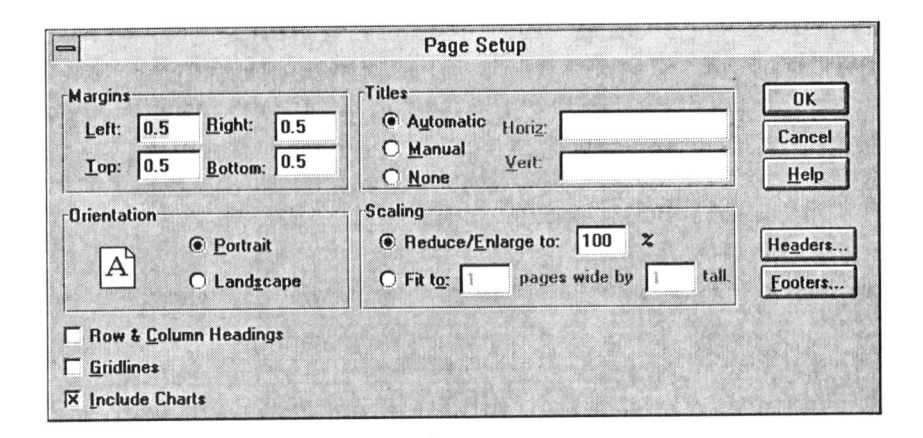

So you can modify the page setup from the preview - but only once. If you click on the Print button a second time the print job starts at once and you don't get another opportunity to use the Page Setup dialog box.

Most of the page setup controls are obvious and really the only problem is in remembering that they are available. You can set the page margins but remember that most printers cannot print right up to the edge of the paper. The page orientation can be set to suit the size of the print area and, as already mentioned, this overrides the setting in the Printer Setup dialog box.

You can also opt to show column headings and gridlines. In most cases you are better off adding your own headings as Titles and your own table rulings. If you don't want to spend the time printing charts make sure that the Include Charts option isn't checked.

» Titles

The Titles section of the dialog box is used to define a row and/or a column of text headings to be printed at the top and left-hand side of each page. The reason for using titles is simply that without them a multi-page printout of a single large table quickly becomes impossible to follow. However, if you are printing a report which has embedded tables and other text then repeating titles on each page will often be superfluous.

There are two ways to set titles. If you select Automatic then the titles that you defined using the Display dialog box accessed from the Options menu are used for the printout as well as the display. If you select Manual then you have to enter the rows and columns to be used as the titles as row or column ranges e.g. 1:2 or B:C. You don't have to enter both horizontal and vertical titles.

» Headers and footers

Headers and footers can be defined to print at the top and bottom of every page. Traditionally defining headers and footers that contain regular items such as a page number, the date etc. has been a difficult job involving cryptic codes. SCW still uses cryptic looking codes to define the layout of the header and footer but you don't have to worry what they mean because the process of creating a header and footer definition has been automated.

If you click on the Headers or Footers button in the Page Setup dialog box you will see the Header or Footers dialog box. You can define up to four lines of standard text to appear at the top and bottom of the page. Any lines that you don't use in the header or footer are used to print the sheet and are not left blank.

To enter text that will appear on a particular header or footer line you simply type it into the appropriate box. The array of buttons at the bottom of the box insert formatting and other special codes.

The first three buttons insert a code that determines the alignment of all of the text to the right of the code. The choices are left-aligned, centred or right-aligned.

The next button inserts a code that sets the font of the text to its right. You can select the font using the familiar Font Dialog box and allow SCW to insert the codes that are necessary.

The remaining buttons insert codes for the date, the time, the page number, the sheet name and the window name. You can, of course, combine these codes with alignment and font codes.

Although you don't really need to understand the codes to create a header or footer, it does help if you want to edit them. For example, if you click on the date button the codes &M, &D, &Y are inserted. It should be fairly obvious that these stand for month, day and year - but what is slightly less obvious is that you can edit these codes and enter them manually into other text. For example, if you want to change the standard &M &D, &Y format you can edit it to "Report for &Y" which would just print the year number. Similarly if you want to embellish the printing of page numbers you might change the default Page &p to -&p-.

The only other thing you need to know is that to print an ampersand you enter two i.e. &&.

» Making it all fit

One of the standard problems in getting output of any spreadsheet is making it fit on a convenient number of pages. SCW will automatically divide up the output but these divisions are sometimes not what you require. You can manually divide a printout up into pages using the command Options,Add Page Break. This divides up the output at the current position of the cursor. If the cursor is on the first cell of a row or column then the page break divides the sheet horizontally or vertically. If the cursor is anywhere else then a horizontal and vertical break is added. The page divisions are shown as dotted lines as you add them so it isn't at all difficult to see what parts of the sheet will print on the same page.

You can add multiple page breaks to divide up the sheet as you would like it paged but SCW will still automatically page any block of data that is too big to fit on a page.

You can remove a page break by placing the cursor so that the page break lines are at the top and/or right hand edge of the cell, i.e. in the location that you placed the cursor to create the page break, and then use the command Options,Set Page Break a second time.

If you want to clear all of the page breaks that you have set simply select the entire sheet and use the Options, Clear Page Break command. Notice that this command only appears when the entire sheet is selected.

» Scaling

As well as dividing output up into suitable pages you can also make use of the Page Setup dialog box to attempt to fit the output into a smaller number of pages.

If you enter a percentage scaling into the Page Setup dialog box the output will be that much smaller or bigger. For example, if you enter a scaling factor of 50% you will fit four times as much of the sheet on a single page by having twice as many lines down and twice as many columns across. Of course the disadvantage is that the font size will be that much smaller but often this is worth it to see more of the sheet. You can experiment with scaling factors to see what is workable on your particular printer.

An alternative to entering specific scale factors is to state the number of pages that you would like the sheet printed on. If you think of the individual sheets of paper as stuck together to form one huge page then what you are asking for is that the spreadsheet is scaled to exactly fit this huge page size. All you have to do is specify how many pages wide and by how many pages tall the output should be - entering 1 by 1 attempts to squash the output into a single sheet. You can also set the orientation of the paper to make the whole spreadsheet fit better. Of course there is no guarantee that after fitting the entire sheet to a given number of pages it will be acceptable.

» Layout

The tools that SCW provides for you to control the look of your spreadsheet, both on the screen and printed out, are very easy to use - but without some planning it can be difficult to produce a professional looking result. When you first create a spreadsheet your main concern is with the formulae and the results. This is exactly how it should be - always concentrate on constructing a working spreadsheet first and then move on to consider the presentation of the data and results. This second stage isn't just a matter of assigning styles and formats to the spreadsheet as it stands. You will probably have to move columns and rows of data to produce a better presentation and insert new rows and columns to add explanatory text or just white space.

There are a number of standard techniques that are used in producing a good looking report.

» Paragraphs

Inserting explanatory text as a number of paragraphs is something of a problem because of the limit of 255 characters on any single text string. That is, you cannot enter more than 255 characters into any single cell. As long as you can keep below this limit then the simplest way of creating paragraph text is to select the Wrap text option in the Alignment dialog box and set the column width and row height to format the text. Apart from the limit on the amount of text that can be displayed in this way, there is also the problem caused by having to set a single column very wide.

An alternative method of displaying paragraph text isn't as easy to edit but in general works better. Instead of trying to store a block of text in a single cell you store each line of the text in its own cell. As long as the cells to the right of the column are empty, the text will split over and display across the row. This avoids the 255 character limit because each line is certain to be shorter than this and it requires no adjustment to the column width. The only problem is that you have to decide where the line breaks go and any changes to the text usually involve altering the line breaks.

» Centred headings

You might think that all you need to create a centred heading is the Alignment dialog box but the Center alignment that it provides only centres text within a particular cell - not on the entire page. Sometimes you can find a column that is in the middle of a table and use it to centre the text but often you will find that there is no column that can be used to provide a centred heading. In this case the only approach is to insert a column where you would like the centred text, enter the text, set its alignment to Center and then reduce the column's width to .01. This allows the text to spill over to the right and left-hand side The narrow column width should make it small enough not to disturb the layout of the rest of the spreadsheet. Don't try to reduce the column width any more than this because this will hide the column and its data.

> Indents

	A	B	C	D
1				
2	Product A			
3		Metal finish		
4			1990	
5			1991	
6		Wood finish		
7			1990	
8	Product B			
9		Metal finish		
10			1990	
11			1991	
12		Wood finish		
13			1993	

When you are creating a table of categories and subcategories indenting can be used to help reveal the structure. To create a set of indented labels all you have to do is insert a number of columns and set the column widths to the size of the indent you require - 5 characters is usually enough. Then you can enter the label in the appropriate column to the right or left. The indenting effect looks particularly convincing when you turn off the gridlines and the row and column headings.

» Practical - the mailshot report

We have already added some formatting to the mailshot analysis spreadsheet. Now it is time to turn it into a printed report. The first thing to do is to add 9 or so new rows above the table to take the titles and headings. Inserting new columns A and B shifts the table over on the page. An alternative to entering the new columns would have been to alter the left margin using the Page Setup command. A new column F is used for the centred heading. Column F's width is set to .01 to effectively hide it. The heading is formatted using a new Style called Heading which has a centred alignment and a 28-point Arial font. The text of the report is entered into column C, one line per row. The only other change that is necessary is to change the money format so that a sign is used for negative values rather than red - which doesn't show well on a black and white printer.

Finally a chart is added showing the profit for each percentage response. The chart is created using a multiple range selection - C11:C15 and H11:J15. A scatter chart is the appropriate type and series C is used for the horizontal axis. To show the way the profit varies a simple curve, i.e. a straight line, can be added to the chart. The only other changes that are necessary is that the scale has to be adjusted to show £1,000 increments and the depth effect is removed. Finally the legend labels are changed to the appropriate percentages using the command Edit,Attributes while they are selected.

To ensure that the chart is printed the Print Area has to be set to A1:J42 - which results in a single page of output. Setting the first line of the header to a suitable title completes the print setup.

Number	Cost	Postage	Total cost	1%	2%	5%
1000	£95	£190	£285	£185	£85	£215
5000	£166	£950	£1,116	£616	£116	£1,384
10000	£255	£1,900	£2,155	£1,155	£155	£2,845
15000	£345	£2,850	£3,195	£1,695	£195	£4,305
20000	£517	£3,800	£4,317	£2,317	£317	£5,683

Practical - the mailshot report

Marketing Department Report Series 1

Direct Mail Campaign

The costings for the proposed direct mail campaign taking into account only direct postage costs and printing are not encouraging.

Clearly the response needs to be in the area of 5% before it is worth engaging in direct mail.

Number	Cost	Postage	Total cost	1%	2%	5%
1000	£95	£190	£285	-£185	-£85	£215
5000	£166	£950	£1,116	-£616	-£116	£1,384
10000	£255	£1,900	£2,155	-£1,155	-£155	£2,845
15000	£345	£2,850	£3,195	-£1,695	-£195	£4,305
20000	£517	£3,800	£4,317	-£2,317	-£317	£5,683

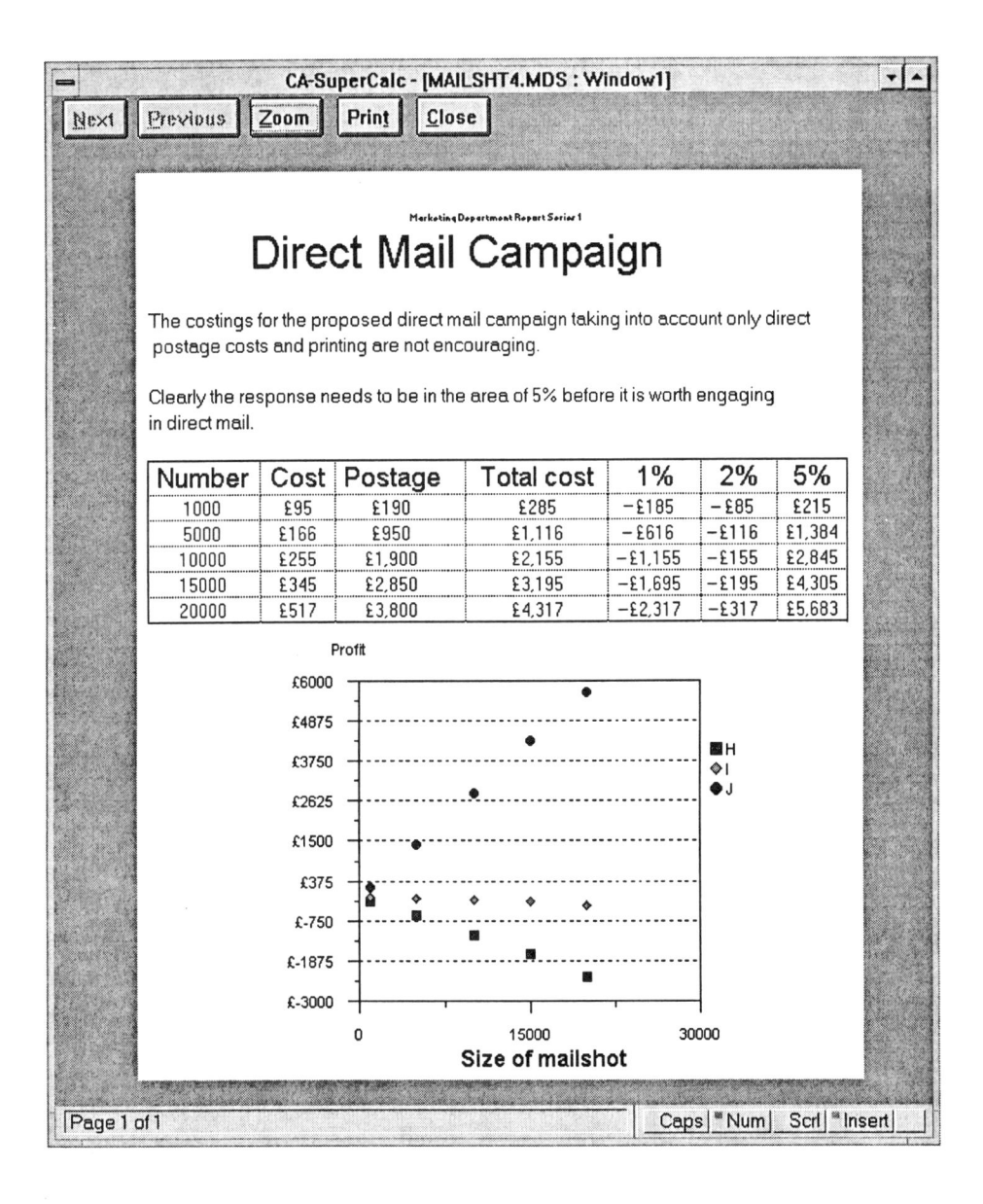

Key points

» SCW leaves all of the printer management and setup to the standard Windows utilities.

» To ensure that printed output matches the screen display make sure you have a TrueType font for any printer fonts you might use.

» Always use the Preview to check your output before printing.

» The File,Page Setup command controls the layout of the range that you are printing on the page. You can set margins, page orientation, scaling and set headers and footers.

» You can also opt for automatic scaling to fit the output into a given space.

» When you are ready to convert your spreadsheet into a printed report you may have to insert rows and columns and move the data to allow for explanatory text and white space.

Chapter 8

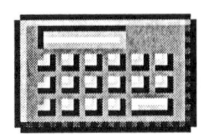

Using Functions

Achieving the results that you need from a spreadsheet is often a matter of knowing how to make use of the functions it provides. In this chapter we look at the commonly used functions that SCW provides with particular reference to how they differ from those in SC5.

The chapter concentrates on the use of the IF function and the various lookup and text handling functions. But before moving on to these more sophisticated topics it is worth looking briefly at the simpler arithmetic functions.

» The arithmetic functions

As well as the basic arithmetic operators +,-,*,/ and ^ you need to know about the arithmetic functions which SCW provides. These are:

ABS(*value*)	find the absolute value of *value*
EXP(*value*)	e raised to the power *value*
FACT(*value*)	factorial of value
INT(*value*)	integer (whole number) part of *value*
LN(*value*)	natural log of *value*
LOG(*value,base*)	log to *base* (default 10) of *value*
LOG10(*value*)	log to base 10 of *value*
MOD(*value1,value2*)	remainder of *value1/value2*
PI	the value of pi (3.14159)
RAND	a random number between 0 and 1
ROUND(*value,n*)	round *value* to *n* decimal places
ROUNDUP(*value,n*)	round up *value* to *n* decimal places
SQRT(*value*)	square root of *value*
TRUNC(*value*)	truncate *value*

We need to add to this list the three trigonometric functions SIN(x), COS(x) and TAN(x) which return the standard trig ratios for the angle x measured in radians and their inverses ASIN(r), ACOS(r) and ATAN(r) which return the angle in radians that has the corresponding trig ratio r. If you are not happy with working in radian measure then you can use the following rules:

radians=PI* degrees/180

and

degrees=180*radians/PI

You can also use the ATAN2(x,y) function to calculate the angle, in radians, that the line from the origin to the point at co-ordinates x,y makes with the x axis. This can be used to convert x,y co-ordinates into polar co-ordinates.

» Range functions

Perhaps the most useful of all spreadsheet functions are those that operate on lists, or vectors to use SCW's terminology, of data. The SUM function is the best known of these and on its own probably accounts for 90% of function use in any spreadsheet! The list functions that SCW supports are:

AVERAGE(*list*)   average of *list*
COUNT(*list*)   count number of cells in *list* that contain numbers
COUNTA(*list*)   counts the number of cells in *list* that are non-blank
MAX(*list*)   maximum value of the values in *list*
MEDIAN(*list*)   finds the median of the values in *list*
MIN(*list*)   minimum value of the values in *list*
STDEV(*list*)   sample standard deviation of *list*
STDEVP(*list*)   population standard deviation of *list*
SUM(*list*)   sum of all the values in *list*
VAR(*list*)   sample variance of values in *list*
VARP(*list*)   population variance of values in *list*

There are a large number of other functions that operate on ranges but these are mostly concerned with advanced statistical calculations such as curve fitting and evaluation. These are described in *Multidimensional Modelling with CA-SuperCalc for Windows*.

It is also worth mentioning again the fact that you can make use of range expressions to perform calculations on the values in a range taken one at a time. This makes it possible to use the simple arithmetic functions listed earlier with lists of data. For example, SUM(INT(A1:A10)) returns the sum of the integer part of each value in A1:A10 even though the formula INT(A1:A10) isn't valid on its own.

Function changes from SC5

SCW's function are broadly similar to those in SC5 with some major additions and simplifications. The major additions are easy to spot as are the major changes but there are also a few minor ones that might go unnoticed.

The only completely new arithmetic function is FACT(n) which will calculate the factorial of a number. For example FACT(4) is 4*3*2*1. Factorials are used in working out probabilities.

The ATAN2(x,y) function is also new but really it is just a modification of the ATAN(r) function. It will work out the angle of a right angle triangle with sides x and y. That is, it is identical to ATAN(y/x).

Although the COUNT function still works in the same way i.e. it counts cells with numeric values there is now an additional function COUNTA which will count non-blank cells.

The statistical functions have some welcome additions. The MEDIAN function will find the median of a series of data values - a difficult task without such a function. The VAR and STD (now renamed STDEV) functions have been changed so that they now calculate the variance and standard deviation for a population based on a sample of size N - that is they divide by N-1 and not N. The two new functions VARP and STDEVP calculate the population variance and standard deviation and are the equivalent of the original SC5 functions.

Finally you can no longer use the RND, RANDOM and AVG alternatives for RAND and AVERAGE.

» Using the IF function

After the SUM function, the IF function is probably the most useful but many users are intimidated by it. Understanding and using the IF function isn't difficult as long as you are very clear about the way that it works. The basic idea is quite straightforward. If you enter the formula

=IF(A1=0,A2+A3,A4+A5)

then SCW evaluates it by first determining if the condition A1=0 is true or false. If it is true, that is A1 is equal to 0, then the first formula to the right, that is A2+A3, is evaluated and used as the result. If it is false, that is A1 is any other value but 0, then the second formula to the right, that is A4+A5, is evaluated and used as the result. You should be able to see that the condition is used to select which of the two formulae to its right is evaluated and used as the value of the cell.

In general the IF function take the form:

=IF(condition,formula1,formula2)

and it is evaluated by first working out if the condition you have specified is true or false. If it is true formula1 is evaluated and used as the result otherwise formula2 is evaluated and used as the result. You can think of the condition as a switch that makes a choice between two possible formulae that determine the value that the cell shows as its result.

$$\text{Value} = \text{IF}(\underset{\downarrow}{\overset{\uparrow}{\text{condition}}}, \text{formula1}, \text{formula2})$$
$$\overbrace{}^{\text{True}} \quad \overbrace{}^{\text{False}}$$

This much isn't difficult to understand. The usefulness and the versatility of the IF function derives from the range of conditions and formulae that can be used within it. Many people find the type of condition that can be used particularly confusing so it is worth taking a closer look at this aspect of the IF function before going on to see how it can be used.

» Conditions

Most users know that they can write conditions using the following symbols:

    a=b   true if a and b are equal
    a<>b true if a and b are not equal
    a<b   true if a is smaller than b
    a>b   true if a is greater than b
    a<=b true if a is smaller than or equal to b
    a>=b true if a is greater than or equal to b

The only difficult parts are the use of the double symbols <> to mean not equal, <= to mean less than or equal to and >=to mean greater than or equal to. The conditions can be applied to text, date and time values as well as simple numeric values. Comparisons between date and time values are discussed in the next chapter.

Comparing text values is quite straightforward as long as you know that they are case insensitive. That is differences between text values due to the use of upper and lower case characters are ignored and, for example, as far as SCW is concerned "Hello"="HELLO" is true. You can also compare text using <, >, <= and >= but this isn't a common requirement. To understand how this works you need to know that the characters are considered to be in the standard order A to Z with A < B and so on. In other words, A is treated as the "smallest" letter and Z the "largest". Once again upper and lower case characters are treated equally.

An important point is that as well as comparing single values, as in A1=A2, you can also compare the results of formulae. For example, you can write conditions such as A1+A2<A3+A4 which is evaluated by first working out A1+A2, then A3+A4 and then comparing the two. You can even include functions within the condition. For example,

    SUM(A1:A10)>SUM(B1:B10)

is true if the sum of A1 to A10 is greater than the sum of B1 to B10. It is this sort of flexibility that can makes the IF function powerful and yet it can quickly result in an overall formula that looks intimidating.

» AND, OR and NOT

Once you understand the basics of the IF function you are bound to encounter a situation where the condition that you want to write is in fact a combination of two or more simpler conditions. In English we often use such compound conditions when we say things like "If it is sunny AND the temperature is above 25". You can also use the special logical functions AND, OR and NOT to form more complicated compound conditions in an SCW formula.

The AND, OR and NOT functions work more or less as you might expect from their English meaning. For example, AND(c_1,c_2) is only true if both conditions c_1 and c_2 are true, OR(c_1,c_2) is true if either (or both) c_1 or c_2 are true and NOT(c_1) is only true if c_1 is false. You can also use the operator versions of these functions c_1#AND#c_2, c_1#OR#c_2 and #NOT#c_1 if you want to. Many users find them easier.

Notice however that OR doesn't quite correspond to its English meaning because OR is still true if both c_1 and c_2 are true. In common use a choice between two things "A or B" would normally imply that you can have one of A or B but not both. This is called the Exclusive OR to make a distinction between it and the Inclusive OR that is used in logic.

> » Remember OR(c_1,c_2) is true if either or both c_1 or c_2 are true.

Compound conditions arise quite naturally when you need to select between two possible results based on more than one condition.

For example,
=IF(AND(A1=0,A2=0), *formula1*, *formula2*)
or
=IF(A1=0 #AND# A2=0, *formula1*, *formula2*)
will only work out *formula1* if both A1 and A2 are zero. Things can get a little more difficult when you need to use IF functions that involve three or more conditions. In this case you have to make use of more than one logical function. For example,
=IF(AND(A1=0,AND(A2=0,A3=0)), *formula1*, *formula2*)
will only work out *formula1* if all three of A1, A2 and A3 are zero! In this case the operator form of the AND function makes this easier to read.
=IF(A1=0 #AND# A2=0 #AND# A3=0,
formula1, *formula2*)
IF functions like the one above are usually easier to write than they are to read and this means that there is plenty of scope for making mistakes. For example, how do you write a condition that is true if A1 is within a given range 0 to 10 say? Is it
AND(A1>0,A1<10)
or is it
OR(A1>0,A1<10)
The answer is that it is the AND form but even this is incorrect in that to include 0 and 10 the formula should be
AND(A1>=0,A1<=10)
Compound conditions are difficult to write and even experts make mistakes. If you can't make a compound condition work, check it very carefully, especially the placing of the brackets.

» Multiple IFs

You can skip this section and return to it when you need to know more about IFs.

The most obvious use of the IF function is in choosing which of two formulae to apply to data. For example, suppose you give two rates of discount, a higher rate of 20% and a standard rate of 10%. If the rate to be applied is indicated by storing an H or an S in the cell named RATE, and the amount is stored in the cell named COST, then:

=IF(RATE="H",COST*.2,COST*.1)

will work out the appropriate discount. Notice that this IF function only checks to see if you have entered an H in RATE. You can enter any other letter, not just S, and the standard discount will be applied. In most cases this isn't too much of a problem because it allows a blank RATE to be treated as an indication that the standard rate should be applied. That is you only have to enter something into RATE if the higher rate is to be applied. But what if you try to type H but miss the key and type a J or something else? If you don't notice your mistake then the standard rate will still be applied. It is clear that if you don't want to make the standard rate the default in all cases other than an H you have to test for both H and S. It is clear that there is nothing wrong with the first part of the function:

IF(RATE="H",COST*.2,..

because if RATE is H you do want to calculate COST*.2. The part of the function that is causing the problem is the way COST*.1 is calculated whenever RATE="H" is false. What is needed is a positive condition, RATE="S", applied before the standard rate is calculated. This can be achieved if the final formula in the IF function is changed to :

..IF(RATE="S",COST*.1,"Enter H or S")..

This checks that the cell RATE really does contain S. If it doesn't then we already know that it doesn't contain H because of the first part of the IF function so the only reasonable thing to do is to give the user a message saying that the entry has to be one of H or S. Putting both halves of the IF function together gives:

=IF(RATE="H",COST*.2,
    IF(RATE="S",COST*.1,"Enter H or S"))

Notice how complicated this double IF function looks. There is plenty of scope for typing it incorrectly, by missing the brackets or commas! However even though the final form looks complicated it isn't difficult to understand if you think of the purpose of its two parts. Another way to understand this function is to work out the way the two conditions govern which formula is worked out:

```
                True
IF(RATE="H",   COST*.2,      True
                False    →  IF(RATE="S",  COST*.1,
                                          False   →   "Enter H or S"))
```

To make use of this double IF function notice that you have to initialise RATE to either S or H to avoid getting the error message before the user has had a chance to enter anything! You may decide that the advantage of the single IF function testing for H as the high rate and any other entry as standard rate is good enough for a particular application - but you should at least be aware that there is another way of doing it!

By "nesting" IF functions one inside another you can make positive selections between any number of options. For example, if you have formula *f1* that you want to work out when condition *c1* is true, formula *f2* that you want to work out when condition *c2* is true, and formula *f3* that applies in all other cases then this can be achieved by writing:

=IF(*c1*,*f1*,IF(*c2*,*f2*,*f3*))

In the same way:

=IF(*c1*,*f1*,IF(*c2*,*f2*,IF(*c3*,*f3*,*f4*)))

will work out *f1* if *c1* is true, *f2* if *c2* is true, *f3* if *c3* is true and *f4* otherwise. Notice the role of the final function as an "if all else fails" function. That is *f4* is only calculated if all of the conditions you specify are false. In most cases *f4* is either best regarded as the default calculation or an error message.

As an example of a three-way selection, consider the problem of applying a commission rate depending on which salesperson "HF", "JS" or "MJ" made the sale. This would be achieved using the IF function:

=IF(PERSON="HF",SALE*HFRATE,IF(PERSON="JS",
  SALE*JSRATE,IF(PERSON="MJ",
  SALE*MJRATE,"No such salesperson")))

where PERSON is the name of the cell holding the identity of the salesperson, SALE is the cell holding the amount of the sale and HFRATE, JSRATE and MJRATE hold the commission rates for the three salespersons respectively.

Notice that while it is reasonable to make selections between two, three or even four formulae, beyond this the multiple IF function quickly becomes complicated. If you need to make choices between more formulae than can easily be accommodated by a multiple IF function then the solution is to use a lookup table - see later.

» Checking validity

The IF function has an important role to play in checking that the data input to a spreadsheet is valid. For example, if a particular cell AGE is suppose to contain the age of a client then it is reasonable to suppose that its value will lie between certain limits. That is, AGE should be greater than 0 and less than 110. To check that this is indeed the case all you need is to enter:

=IF(AND(AGE>0,AGE<110),"","Verify age entry")

near the data entry cell. If the condition is false the user will see the message "Verify age entry" appear next to the data entry cell.

In general if you know that a cell's entry should be greater than L and less than H then you can test its validity using:

IF(AND(DATA>L,DATA<H),"","Error message")

If the entry should be greater than or equal to L and less than or equal to H then the function should be changed to:

IF(AND(DATA>=L,DATA<=H),"","Error message")

Simpler versions of the validity test often occur in practice but these are easy to make up for yourself. For example, checking that a value is less than some upper limit can be achieved using:

IF(DATA<H,"","Error message")

Whenever you construct a spreadsheet that contains cells that are used for data entry you should always write validation formulae that set sensible limits on the input if possible.

» Checksums

When you are doing arithmetic by hand or with a calculator a checksum is very often used to make sure that no error has been made. A checksum is a second calculation that has to work out to a particular value if the first calculation was correct. Spreadsheets don't make errors of calculation in the same way but it is still possible for them to arrive at the wrong answer. The reason is usually that the structure of the sheet has been changed either because the user has typed a value over a formula or has inserted a blank row or column that should contain formulae - see Chapter 6. To guard against this sort of mistake you can still make use of checksums but you have to work out what these should be in any particular case.

			SUM(row)
			SUM(row)
			SUM(row)
			SUM(row)
SUM(col)	SUM(col)	SUM(col)	

As long as every row and every column has a SUM formula the totals are equal and

SUM(column sums)=SUM(row sums)

			SUM(row)
			SUM(row)
			SUM(row)
			SUM(row)
SUM(col)	SUM(col)	SUM(col)	

If a row is inserted and the formulae are not copied to it then the row and column totals will no longer be the same and

SUM(column sums)<>SUM(row sums)

For example, if you have a table of data for which you compute column and row sums, then as a check to make sure that the row and column sums are set to the correct ranges, you should also compute the grand total in two ways. First by summing the row sums, and then summing the columns sums. If everything is alright then you will get the same answer in both cases. That is, you can add the formula:

=IF(SUM(ROW_SUM_RANGE)<>
    SUM(COL_SUM_RANGE),"Error","")

somewhere prominent in the spreadsheet where ROW_SUM_RANGE is a range name giving the location of the row sums and COL_SUM_RANGE is the range name giving the location of the column sums.

In practice you will discover that a check of the type described above sometimes doesn't work - it shows an error when there isn't one. The reason is that it is possible for small errors in the way that the sums are computed to result in the two quantities differing by tiny amounts. A more robust check results from taking the difference between the two quantities and comparing this to the smallest difference that you consider worth reporting. For example:

=IF((SUM(ROW_SUM_RANGE)-
    SUM(COL_SUM_RANGE))<.01,"Error","")

would only show the error message if the difference was greater than .01. Unfortunately this IF function doesn't work because the difference can be either positive or negative depending on which of the two sums is larger. The solution to this is to use the ABS function which converts all values to positive values. For example, ABS(43)=43 and ABS(-43)=43. Using the ABS function in the IF function given above produces:

=IF(ABS(SUM(ROW_SUM_RANGE)-
    SUM(COL_SUM_RANGE))<.01,"Error","")

which will show the message "Error" if the two sums differ by more than .01.

» Logical functions

You can skip this section until you need to know about the inner workings of conditions.

When you write a condition, like B10>10, SCW actually uses the numeric value 0 to stand for false and 1 for true. This means that logical operations evaluate to numeric results and numeric results can be used in logical operations. For example, you can write IF(A1,"NON-ZERO","ZERO") which will evaluate to ZERO if the A1 is zero i.e. the value that corresponds to false.

The idea of using 0 and 1 to represent true and false takes a little getting used to. SCW provides two simple functions, FALSE and TRUE, that return the numeric values 0 and 1 so that you can write logical expressions that read a little more naturally. For example
    =IF(A1=TRUE,"NON-ZERO","ZERO")
is another way to write the earlier IF function.

SCW also provides a range of logical functions which return true or false (1 or 0) depending on the type of contents of any given cell. These are:

ISBLANK(*cell*)	true if *cell* is blank
ISDATE(*cell*)	true if *cell* contains a date
ISERR(*cell*)	true if *cell* contains any error except N/A
ISERROR(*cell*)	true if *cell* contains any error
ISLOGICAL(*cell*)	true if *cell* contains a logical value
ISNA(*cell*)	true if *cell* is N/A (not available)
ISNONTEXT(*cell*)	true if *cell* contains any nontext value
ISNUMBER(*cell*)	true if *cell* contains a number
ISPROT(*cell*)	true if *cell* is protected
ISRANGE(*cell*)	true if *cell* contains a range reference
ISREF(*cell*)	true if *cell* contains a cell reference
ISTEXT(*cell*	true if *cell* contains a text value
ISTIME(*cell*)	true if *cell* contains a time

As well as these sheet logical functions there is also ISCONSISTENT(*cell,tol*) which is used in models to check that functions that apply to the same cell give the same answer to a specified tolerance.

These logical functions are most often useful within macros, but they are sometimes useful in avoiding working out a formula when the cell that it uses is blank or some other inappropriate value. For example,
    =IF(ISNUMBER(A1),A1*.15,"Cannot calculate")
will work out A1*.15 only if A1 contains a numeric value.

> **Changes from SC5**
>
> The logical functions have changed little from SC5. The biggest change is that ISVAL has been replaced by a combination of logical functions which can test for any particular type of value - ISLOGICAL, ISTEXT, etc. Notice that ISSTR has been change to ISTEXT and there are now two forms of ISERR.

» Text functions

There are a whole range of text, (which used to be called "string") functions which are provided to allow you to manipulate text or text values stored in cells. Most of these are fairly specialised and really only come into their own when you start to write macros but they are sometimes useful in general spreadsheet work.

The text functions are:

CHAR(*n*)	ASCII character *n*
CODE(*text*)	ASCII code of first character in *text*
CLEAN(*text*)	Removes nonprintable characters from *text*
CONTENTS(*cell*)	the contents of *cell* as text
DISPLAY(*val,for,wid*)	the value *val* formatted according to *for* and *wid*
DOLLAR(*val,n*)	converts *val* to currency format text
EXACT(*txt1,txt2*)	true if *txt1*=*txt2* exactly
FIND(*txt1,txt2,n*)	the position of *txt1* if it is contained in *txt2*, the search starts at character *n*
FIX(*val,n*)	rounds *val* to *n* decimal places as text
FORMAT(*cell*)	gives the format of *cell*
LEFT(*txt,n*)	the first *n* characters of *txt*
LEN(*txt*)	the length of *txt*
LOWER(*txt*)	converts *txt* to lower case
MID(*txt,n,m*)	part of *txt* starting at character *n* and going on for *m* characters

PROPER(*txt*)	changes the first letter of each word in *txt* to a capital letter
REPT(*txt,n*)	repeats the *txt* *n* times
REPLACE(*txt1,s,n,txt2*)	removes the *n* characters in *txt1* starting at character *s* and inserts *txt2*
RIGHT(*txt,n*)	the last *n* characters of *txt*
STRING(*x,n*)	converts the numeric value *x* into text with *n* digits after the decimal point
SEARCH(*txt1,txt2,n*)	as FIND but not case sensitive and accepts wildcards
SUBSTITUTE(*txt1,txt2,txt3,n*)	Substitutes *txt3* for occurrences of *txt2* in *txt1*; if *n* is specified then only *n*th occurrence is substituted
TEXT(*val*)	converts *val* to text
TRIM(*txt*)	removes redundant spaces from *txt*
UPPER(*txt*)	changes *txt* to upper case
VALUE(*txt*)	converts a number in *txt* into a numeric value

In general when you are working on a spreadsheet that needs the use of any of the text functions then their meaning will become quite obvious. However, it is worth saying a little about some of the more difficult or obscure functions at this point.

It is probably a good idea to just skim read the following paragraphs and return to them when you really need to know more.

The basic operations concerned with manipulating text are adding text together, breaking text down into smaller parts, and altering sections of specified text.

Joining text together is generally called "concatenation" and it is signified using the ampersand character &. For example, A1&A2 gives the text that is the result of joining the text in A1 to the text in A2. So if A1 contained HELLO and A2

Changes from SC5

The changes to the text functions from SC5 are mostly additions. The new CLEAN function will remove non-printable characters; DOLLAR will convert a value to currency formatted text - using the Windows system currency symbol and FIX will round a value to n decimal places before converting it to text. Finally there are two improved search and replace functions. SEARCH will search for target text ignoring upper and lower case differences. You can also use the wildcard characters * and ? in the target text. SUBSTITUTE is a complicated looking function but it is the quickest way of changing one portion of text to another.

The name of the STR function which converts numbers to text has been changed to TEXT. In fact this conceals a larger change because SCW will actually convert between text and numbers and vice versa entirely automatically. If you use a text value where a number is required it will be converted provided it is in a recognisable format. This applies to currency format and dates and times. The reverse is also true. That is, numbers will be converted to text if the situation demands it.

The single change that is most likely to cause you problems is that to the numbering of characters in a text value. SC5 numbers the first character as character 0 whereas SCW refers to it as character 1.

Also notice that the format specifiers used in DISPLAY and FORMAT have changed to be the same as those used in a numeric format. This is more logical but it also means that you can no longer set alignment using these functions.

contained THERE the result of the formula would be HELLOTHERE. If you wanted a space between the two words then you actually have to write it into the formula. That is, A1&" "&A2 would give HELLO THERE.

There are a number of functions concerned with extracting sections of text. The easiest to use is the LEFT function which can be used to extract the left-hand part of a text value. The form of the function is very simple in that all you have to specify is the text and how many characters you want to extract. For example,

=LEFT("HELLO",3)

returns HEL, that is, the first 3 characters from the left-hand end of the text HELLO. You can use LEFT to extract the first letter from the text stored in a cell. For example, if A1 contained YES then LEFT(A1,1) is just the first letter, Y.

The RIGHT function performs the corresonding action but it takes the *n* characters from the right of the text. For example,

=RIGHT("HELLO",3)

returns the string LLO.

A more complicated but more versatile function that can be used to extract any part of a text value is the MID function. This function is a little more difficult to follow at first as it involves specifying the starting position, S, of the text that you are interested in and its length, L. The first character in the text is character 1 so

=MID("HELLO",2,3)

starts from character 2 and returns 3 characters and therefore returns the string ELL.

You can use the REPLACE function to change any part of a text value. For example, if you want to replace the EFG by XX in the string ABCDEFGHI stored in cell A1 you would use

=REPLACE(A1,5,3,"XX")

which works by deleting the 3 characters starting at letter 5 and then inserting 2 characters, XX, into the place they used to occupy. This gives ABCDXXHI.

An alternative to using REPLACE and the position and length of the text to be replaced is to use SUBSTITUTE. This is a complicated looking function because it has so many arguments. If you want to replace every occurrence of a given text value by another then the function

=SUBSTITUTE(*text,old,new*)

will do the job. You can think of it as a search and replace function because it will change every occurrence of *old* in *text* to *new*. If you don't want to change every occurrence then you can use

=SUBSTITUTE(*text,old,new,n*)

where *n* is the number of the occurrence that you want to change.

If you don't know the length of a string then you can always use the LEN function which returns the number of characters in a string.

The FIND and SEARCH functions are used to discover if a given string contains another. They return the position of the first letter of the string that you are looking for if it is present, and VALUE otherwise. For example, if you want to know if a string in cell A1 contains the word Yes you would use

=FIND("Yes",A1,1)

This searches for Yes in A1 starting from the first character.

Notice that the matching is done in a case sensitive way. That is, if A1 contains yes the previous find will fail because Yes and yes are different in that their first letters are upper and lower case respectively. If you want to search ignoring case then use the SEARCH functions. The SEARCH function also allows you to use wildcard characters - see Chapter 10.

The EXACT function can be used to test to see if two text values are identical taking captialisation into account. So

=EXACT("Yes","yes")

returns a value of false. You can, of course, use EXACT within an IF function.

» Converting to a format

One of the jobs often tackled using text functions is formatting data. The DISPLAY function, for example, will format a value to any format and any column width. The result of the format is returned as text which can be further processed if necessary. For example,

=DISPLAY(A1,"£##0.0",9)

will convert the value in A1 to the specified format with a maximum of 9 characters.

If you want to discover what format is in effect at any cell then you can use the FORMAT function which uses the same format symbols. The text returned by the FORMAT function can be used by the DISPLAY function.

The function PROPER can be used to ensure that the first letter of each word is a capital letter. In other words, it can be used to capitalise proper nouns. For example,

=PROPER("john smith")

returns the string John Smith.

Another function which can be useful for tidying up text is TRIM which removes redundant spaces to make sure that the string has no leading or trailing spaces and no more than one space between each word. For example,

=TRIM("   john   smith   ")

returns the string john smith. You can use functions in combination to alter strings.

For example
    =PROPER(TRIM(" john smith "))
returns the string John Smith. Much of string manipulation is a matter of thinking up the correct combination of functions to achieve your desired result.

» Other characters

The CHAR and CODE functions are useful for working with characters that are not easy to obtain by pressing keys. The CODE function will return a number that is the ASCII code of any character and the CHAR function returns the character that corresponds to the ASCII code. For example, CODE("A") is 65 and conversely CHAR(65) is A. Exactly what character you see corresponding to a particular ASCII code also depends on the font you have selected.

» Numbers to text

There is a fundamental difference between text and numeric values but SCW often automatically converts between them when appropriate. For example, if you enter
    ="1"+"2"
then you will see the result 3 - although strictly speaking two text values shouldn't add up to give a numeric value. SCW will perform this automatic conversion for you whenever it can make sense of the operation.

If you want to convert between numbers and text explicitly then you need to use the function TEXT(*value,format*) where *format* is a standard format specifier e.g. TEXT(1.1,"#0.00") returns the text 1.10. The VALUE(*text*) function will convert any text to a numeric value as long as it is recognisable as such. In practice you don't need VALUE because the conversion will be performed automatically.

» Lookup functions

Lookup functions are very important and are the key to constructing many advanced spreadsheets. A lookup function can be thought of as simply finding a given value in a table. For example, if you have a table of percentages to be applied in different situations then a lookup function can find the percentage that applies. In the broader view a lookup function is concerned with retrieving some piece of information from a variable location.

The lookup functions are:

CHOOSE(n,*list*)   the nth value in *list*
HLOOKUP(x,*range*,*r*)   a horizontal lookup table
INDEX(*range*,*c*,*r*)   the contents of the cell at column *c* and row *r* of *range*
LOOKUP(*res*,*look*,*x*)   lookup *x* in *look* and return *res*
MATCH(*x*,*look*,*type*)   looks up *x* in *look* matching according to *type* and returns the position
VLOOKUP(x,*range*,*c*)   a vertical lookup table

The most important and flexible lookup function is LOOKUP. This accepts two lists of values - the lookup list and the result list - plus a single value. The exact workings of the LOOKUP function are not difficult to describe. What happens is that the value specified is compared in turn with each item in the lookup list. If an exact match is found then the corresponding item in the results list is returned. So for example, if the value matches with the fourth item in the lookup list then the fourth item in the results list is returned.

If there is no exact match then what happens is a little more tricky. The value is compared with the items in the lookup list in turn until one is found that is bigger. This is not the item that is considered to match the value but the item one before. You can think of the bigger item as being a sort of "end stop" which halts the search and forces LOOKUP to return a value based on the item before the end stop.

A few moments' thought will reveal that it is important that the lookup list is sorted into ascending order for the lookup to work properly. As long as the list is in ascending order then the LOOKUP function will find the largest item in the lookup list that

The LOOKUP function searches down the list of values specified by *look* until it finds a match for *value*. It then returns the corresponding item in the list specified by *res*.

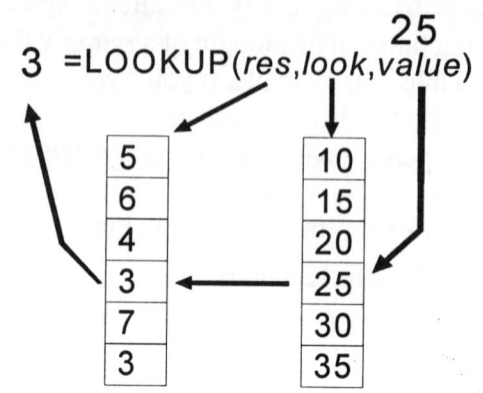

$$3 = \text{LOOKUP}(res, look, \overset{25}{value})$$

look	res
5	10
6	15
4	20
3	25
7	30
3	35

is less than the search value. Another way of saying this is that the lookup criterion is to match value to the largest value in the table that is smaller than or equal to the value.

When there is no exact match the search stops at the first item larger than *value* and backtracks to the item one earlier.

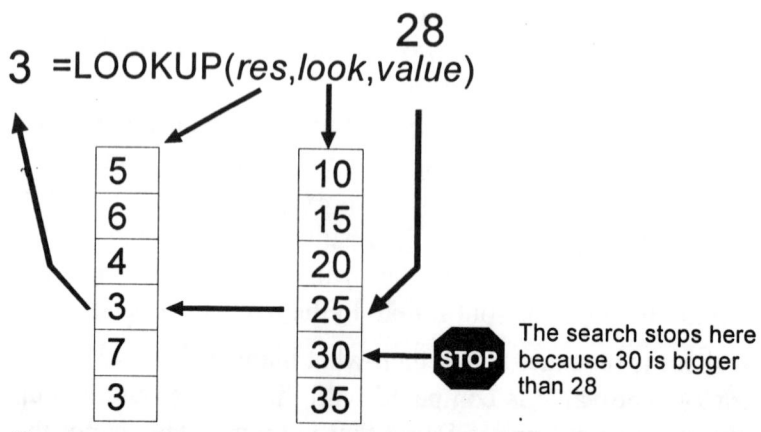

$$3 = \text{LOOKUP}(res, look, \overset{28}{value})$$

look	res
5	10
6	15
4	20
3	25
7	30
3	35

The search stops here because 30 is bigger than 28

For example, suppose you have a table that gives the equivalent temperature in Fahrenheit for a temperature in centigrade. The first column of the table, A1:A4 say, could be used as the lookup and the second column B1:B4 the result. If the centigrade values are sorted into ascending order then the function LOOKUP(B1:B4,A1:A4,*value*) could be used to look up the value in centigrade and return the corresponding value in Fahrenheit.

Notice that the lists used for the lookup and the result do not have to be columns. They can equally well be rows or any one-dimensional series that can be treated as a list. In particular, although it is usual for the two lists of items to be next to each other in the spreadsheet, this isn't necessary. You could for example, look up a value in D5:D10 and return the corresponding value in F25:F30. All you need is a list to look the value up in and a list to return a result from. You can use lookup tables to look up text values and you can return values that are calculated by formulae. In the case of a text lookup differences between upper and lower case are ignored.

» If you try to lookup a value that is smaller than any in the table the result is an error condition.

» If you try to lookup a value larger than any in the table the last, i.e. largest entry will be used.

Although the LOOKUP function is very flexible the traditional pair of lookup functions HLOOKUP and VLOOKUP are also supported in SCW. These implement horizontal and vertical lookup tables respectively.

A horizontal lookup table consists of rows of values. The top row acts as the lookup portion of the table and one of the rows below is the result portion of the table. What happens is that the HLOOKUP(*x,range,r*) function scans the top row of *range* until it finds a cell containing the value *x* or the first value that is just less than *x* and then returns the value in row *r* below. The top row is numbered as row 1 and so on. For example, HLOOKUP(A1,B1:E5,3) would lookup the value in A1 in the row B1:E1. When a match for the value was found it would return the corresponding value in the third row of the range i.e. B3:E3. The way that the value is matched is exactly the same as in the case of the LOOKUP function - that is if the value isn't in the lookup table then the largest value not bigger than it is used.

» The function VLOOKUP works in exactly the same way but the table is arranged as columns of values rather than rows.

The standard way of matching the value against the lookup table works in most cases but sometimes you don't want to return a value that is just smaller than the target. Sometimes only an exact match or a value just larger will do. The solution to this problem is to use the MATCH(*value,look,type*) function. This will lookup a value in a lookup list but you can specify the match criterion. If *type* is 1 then the usual lookup criterion is used - that is, the largest item that is less than or equal to the value. If *type* is -1 then the smallest value that is greater than or equal to the lookup value is used. If *type* is 0 then only an exact match will do. If you use *type* -1 then the lookup list has to be sorted into descending order. Notice that in this context exact means ignoring upper and lower case differences. Unlike the other lookup functions MATCH doesn't return a value from another row or column, it simply returns the position of the match in the lookup list. It isn't difficult to use this information to pick a value from a results list - see the post room calculator practical.

A simpler form of lookup table is provided by the CHOOSE function. This will return a single value from a list. For example, you can convert a numeric value to the days of the week using:

=CHOOSE(A1,"MON","TUE","WED",
    "THR","FRI","SAT","SUN")

which would return "WED" if A1 is 3, "FRI" if A1 is 5 and so on. You can use the same technique to select say the percentage commission paid to a given salesperson etc..

Changes from SC5

The biggest change to affect the existing lookup functions is that the row and column offset within ranges is counted starting from 1 not 0. Thus the first row of any range is row 1 not row 0. This change affects all of the lookup functions including INDEX.

Although the original lookup functions HLOOKUP and VLOOKUP are still supported you would be well advised to switch to using the new LOOKUP function. This allows you to specify the lookup part of the table and the results part of the table independently i.e. as two separate ranges. The two ranges don't have to be near each other and they can be anywhere in the spreadsheet. The values are matched up by the order that they come in and not by row or column number. Also notice that the new LOOKUP isn't the same as the rather weaker function of the same name in SC5.

SCW has added a function which solves a longstanding problem common to most spreadsheets. The MATCH function will perform a lookup either using the usual "largest value that is smaller than or equal to", or an exact match, or "smallest value that is larger than or equal to". This allows you to tailor the lookup to your needs without having to use tricks such as including IF statements to check for an exact match or looking up the negative of the value to find the item "just less than" in the table. The only problem is that MATCH only returns the position in the lookup list but this is easily converted into an appropriate value - see the post room calculator practical later in this chapter.

And finally, an even simpler lookup table is provided by the INDEX function which will return the contents of the cell at a given row and column. For example,

=INDEX(A1:B4,1,3)

will return the value in cell A3, i.e. first column third row.

There are also a great many new lookup functions that work only with models.

» Practical - Sales commission spreadsheet

Suppose commission on sales varies according to total sales as follows:

less than £100	0%
£100 to less than £500	1%
£500 to less than £1000	3%
over £1000	5%

This can be converted into a lookup table by typing the sales values into column A and the percentages into column B. To find the commission rate using this table all you have to do is look down column A until you find the largest value that is less than or equal to your sales and your commission rate is in the same row in column B. For example, if your sales on a particular day are £250 then the largest value that is less than or equal to £250 is in A3, so your commission rate is in B3.

	A	B	C	D
1	Sales	Commission		
2	£0.00	0%		
3	£100.00	1%		
4	£500.00	3%		
5	£1,000.00	5%		
6				
7				
8	Takings	£500.00	3%	£15.00
9				
10				

You can achieve the same result automatically using the LOOKUP function. Enter the day's takings in B8 and in C8 the formula:

$$=\text{LOOKUP}(B2:B5,A2:A5,B8)$$

This will search the column A2:A5 to find the largest value that is just less than or equal to the value in B8, it then returns the value in the next column as the result. This gives the commission rate to use. You can then use this to work out your profits by entering the formula

$$=B8*C8$$

into D8.

» Practical - Post Room Calculator

An obvious application of a lookup table is to calculate the postal charge for a letter of a given weight. The lookup table itself isn't difficult to create. A column of weights and the corresponding first and second class postage charges does the job very nicely. The difficulty is that if you use the obvious lookup formula you will discover that in some cases it doesn't work. The reason is that

$$=\text{LOOKUP}(B11:B26,A11:A26,C2)$$

looks for the weight in A11:A26 that is just just less than the value in C2. However a postal table gives weights that a packet cannot exceed in order to qualify for the price. For example, a packet just less than 200 grams will qualify for the 200 gram price but a weight of 210 grams moves it into the next category of 250 grams or less. The trouble is that the lookup function still matches 210 grams to the 200 gram entry in the table, i.e. the largest value less than or equal to 210.

	A	B	C
10	Weight	First	Second
11	60	25	19
12	100	38	29
13	150	47	36
14	200	57	43
15	250	67	52
16	300	77	61
17	350	88	70
18	400	100	79
19	450	113	89
20	500	125	98
21	600	155	120
22	700	190	140
23	750	205	145
24	800	215	
25	950	235	
26	1000	250	

The solution to the problem is to use the MATCH function with a search type of -1 i.e. the smallest value greater than or equal to 210. Using this function introduces some problems of its own. The first is that the table has to be sorted so that the weights decrease. You can do this manually but it is much easier to use the Data,Sort command - see Chapter 10.

Once the table is in decreasing weight order the formula to look up the weight is

=MATCH(C2,A11:A26,-1)

This works correctly but it returns the position in the list of the weight that matches rather than the cost.

To convert this into a cost we need to use the INDEX function. This will pick out the value in a given row and column of a specified range. For example, if MATCH has identified the row with the matching weight as row r then the 1st class postage is simply

=INDEX(B11:B26,r,1)

or putting the MATCH together with INDEX

=INDEX(B11:B26,MATCH(C2,A11:A26,-1),1)

In fact we can be a little cleverer than this by making the range used in INDEX contain both the first and second class costs and using a 1 or 2 to pick out which one the user wants. That is, the cost of postage is given by

=INDEX(B11:C26,MATCH(C2,A11:A26,-1),C3)

where C3 is 1 or 2 for first or second class mail.

» User defined functions

If you are creating a spreadsheet which uses very complex looking formulae then the best way of making these look simpler is to write a user defined function. A user defined function is in fact a special case of a macro but you should be able to create one even if you find macros difficult.

To create a user defined function open a macro sheet called GLOBAL.MDM in the same directory as SCW.EXE is stored in. This is usually the SCW directory. If the macro sheet doesn't exist use File,New to create a new macro sheet and save it as GLOBAL.MDM. When you open a macro sheet you will see a new type of window and menu. You can type into the window as if it was a text editor. To create a user defined function you first enter the line

Function *name(arguments)*

where *name* is the name that you want to give your new function and *arguments* are the values that you want it to work with. You then write formulae that work out whatever it is you want to work out. You can use the full range of macro functions (see Help under CA-ble functions) and simple arithmetic. When you have finished you can return a value as the result of the function using the line

Return *value*

The final line of every function is

End Func

You can begin the definition of any other function you want to specify after the line End Func so GLOBAL.MDM can store as many user defined functions as you like - each with its own End Func statement.

For example, try the simple and quite useless function

>   Function test(a,b)
>   ans=a+b
>   return ans
>   end func

Once you have typed this into the macro sheet and saved it as GLOBAL.MDM you can use this new function in any sheet. For example, if you enter

>   =test(A1,A2)

then the contents of A1 and A2 will be added together. Of course in a real user defined function the calculation would be more useful and, very probably, much more complicated.

Notice that the parameters that you pass to a user defined function have to be values. If you try to pass a range to a user defined function it will return an error. So for example, it isn't possible to write a user defined function which simplifies the lookup function in the Post Room Calculator using the simple techniques discussed here. It is possible to extend user defined functions to work correctly with ranges but you have to know more about programming in SCW's macro language CA-BLE, see Chapter 12.

» What's missing

If you look at the full list of functions offered by SCW you will discover that it is a very long list. The reason for this is that, as well as the sheet functions that we have examined in this chapter, there are a long list of CA-BLE macro functions which are common to all CA applications and a list of CMD functions which enable CA-BLE to work with SCW in particular. There are also a number of functions concerned specifically with models that are described in *Multidimensional Modelling with CA-SuperCalc for Windows*. There is also a whole class of information functions which are concerned with returning details concerning cells, cell references or range references. Although these occasionally find use in formulae their original purpose was to be used in SC5 macros. As these functions are no longer used in SCW macros, having been replaced by CMD functions, they are no longer as important.

As well as these there are a large number of functions concerned with specialised areas. There are advanced statistical functions, concerned with modelling and curve fitting, financial functions concerned with working out payments on loan and returns from investments. If you are interested in this latter group, and in financial applications of a spreadsheet in general, see *Financial Functions Using a Spreadsheet* by Mike James and Janet Swift, (I/O Press, ISBN 1-871962-01-3).

SCW's date and time functions are dealt with in the next chapter and database functions are described in Chapter 10.

Key points

» The ability to do range arithmetic has enhanced the usability of the simple arithmetic functions in SCW.

» The IF function is the key to creating more sophisticated spreadsheets. It can be used to select which of two formulae have to be used.

» Making up more sophisticated IF functions is a matter of using AND, OR and NOT.

» The logical functions can be used to test the type of value in a cell and, in combination with the IF function, apply an appropriate calculation.

» The text handling functions can be used to manipulate text.

» SCW will always attempt to convert between text and a value where possible.

» The lookup functions can be used to look up a result based upon a given value.

» You can create your own user defined functions but you also need to program in CA-ble to make best use of these.

» A number of esoteric functions have been included to ensure compatibility with SC5, although the primary need for many of these functions (i.e. to be used within macros) has been removed.

Chapter 9

Dates, Times, % and Precision

Although most of the time the difficulty in constructing a spreadsheet is in knowing what functions to use and how - sometimes the problem is the data. Some types of data are just more complicated than others. In particular, performing calculations with dates and times can be puzzling.

In this chapter the topic is difficult data. We start off by looking at dates and times, then we look at how to handle percentages, and finally tackle the difficult question of precision. Spreadsheet users get used to the idea that what a cell displays is not necessarily the same as what it contains but even experienced users can sometimes forget this simple fact.

» Date serial numbers

Dates and times are very messy quantities from a spreadsheet's point of view because they are generally not expressed as a single value. For example, the date 31/3/1900 may look like a single date value at first glance but a more careful examination reveals that a date is composed of a day, month, and year value. This makes apparently simple tasks such as finding the difference between two date values very difficult. For example how many days are there between 31/3/1900 and 2/4/1964? The same sort of problems arise with times expressed in hours, minutes, and seconds.

To solve all of these problems in one stroke SCW converts dates into a single value called the "date serial number". This is simply the number of days from a given fixed date called the "date base". SCW uses the date base of 1/1/1900 so a date serial number is the number of days since the start of the century. You can see this for yourself by entering 1 into any cell and then applying a date format to it. The largest date serial number that SCW can work with is 73109 which corresponds to 28th February 2100.

» Entering dates

Any numeric value that you type in, within the allowable range can be treated as a date. All you have to do is select a data format and it will display as a date as you requested. This means that there is a small potential for making errors, for example, you could show your total profit as a date, but in general it is a simple and effective method, as long as you understand it.

If you want to enter the date serial number for a known date the simplest way is to enter the date using one of the recognised date formats. SCW will automatically recognise this as a date and converts it to a date formula. A date formula is best thought of as an expression like 31/12/1991 which evaluates to the corresponding date serial number. The format of a data formula is controlled by the international settings in Windows as a whole.

To set the date format you have to use the International utility in the Control Panel. This displays the International dialog box and if you click on the Change button in the Date section you will finally see the Date Format dialog box.

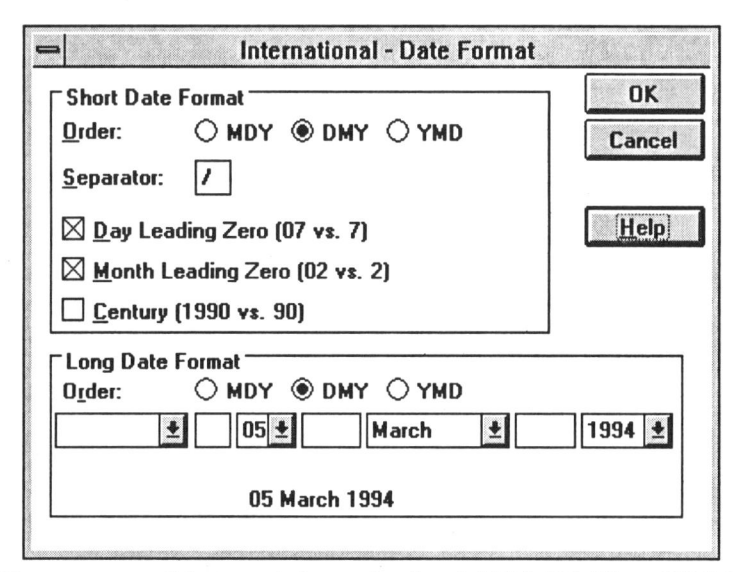

```
┌─────────────────────────────────────────────────────┐
│ ═          International - Date Format              │
│ ┌─Short Date Format────────────────┐   ┌────────┐   │
│   Order:    ○ MDY  ● DMY  ○ YMD        │   OK   │   │
│                                        └────────┘   │
│   Separator:  / 
│                                        ┌────────┐   │
│   ☒ Day Leading Zero (07 vs. 7)        │ Cancel │   │
│   ☒ Month Leading Zero (02 vs. 2)      └────────┘   │
│   ☐ Century (1990 vs. 90)              ┌────────┐   │
│ └──────────────────────────────────┘   │  Help  │   │
│                                        └────────┘   │
│ ┌─Long Date Format────────────────────────────────┐ │
│   Order:    ○ MDY  ● DMY  ○ YMD                     │
│        [  ▼] [05▼] [March  ▼] [1994▼]               │
│                 05 March 1994                       │
│ └─────────────────────────────────────────────────┘ │
└─────────────────────────────────────────────────────┘
```

You can use this to set the order i.e. MDY, DMY or YMD that you would like dates to be represented in. Notice that this setting doesn't restrict the way that you can format dates in SCW it just determines the default format for date formula. Once you have entered a date you can apply any date format that you want to using Format,Number.

This idea of a date formula is important to the complete understanding of how SCW handles dates so it is worth looking at some examples. If you enter a date like 1-Feb-94 this is converted into the date formula 01/02/1994 when it is stored in the cell. If you now use the Info window to see exactly what is stored in the cell, this will show that the cell contains a formula - 01/02/1994 - and its value is 34366 which is, of course, the corresponding date serial number. The Info Window will also show that the cell's value has been formatted using the dd/mm/yyyy number format. This is the reason why the displayed value looks like the formula stored in the cell.

```
Info: Sheet1.Wind
Cell: A1
Formula: 01/02/1994
Value: 34366
Format: Normal Style
        dd/mm/yyyy
        General Alignment
        MS Sans Serif, 10
        No Borders
        No Shading
Note:
Protection:
```

Now compare this with what happens when you enter the date serial number directly. If you type 34366 into a cell then that's exactly what you will see - its formula and value are the same. However if you apply the dd/mm/yyyy number format the date serial number will be displayed as a date that is indistinguishable from 01/02/1994. If you use the Info Window to look at the contents of the cell you will see that there is indeed a difference.

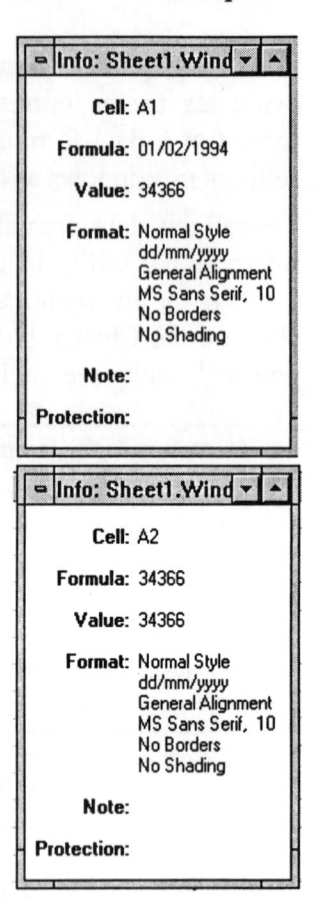

```
Info: Sheet1.Wind
Cell: A2
Formula: 34366
Value: 34366
Format: Normal Style
        dd/mm/yyyy
        General Alignment
        MS Sans Serif, 10
        No Borders
        No Shading
Note:
Protection:
```

The important facts about date entry are:

» any cell with a numeric value in the correct range can be treated as a date serial number and formatted as a date.

» If you enter a date using one of SCW's primary date formats then it will be recognised as a date, converted to a date formula - the value of which is a date serial number, and a date format will automatically be applied.

Notice that if you don't enter a value for the year the current year, as indicated by your machine's built-in clock and calendar, will be used.

> ### How do I enter a fraction?
>
> SCW's date entry methods are very easy to use but they do pose one problem.. If 1/2 is recognised as a date - the 1/2 in the year indicated by the machine's clock - how do you enter a 1/2 as a fraction? In this particular case you could enter .5 but in general you would want SCW to work out the division for you. The solution is to enter it as arithmetic i.e. =1/2. This is of course no different to having to enter =1+2 if you want the addition worked out for you.

The fact that all dates, whether entered as dates or not, are represented as numeric values means that you can use dates within arithmetic that mixes dates and numbers and you can compare dates as if they were numeric values. That is date1<date2 is true if the date serial number corresponding to date1 is smaller than date2, i.e. if date1 is earlier than date2. In the same way sorting a column of dates into ascending order, that is increasing date serial number, results in earlier dates first.

» Times

After discovering how SCW handles dates, time values should come as no surprise. A time expressed as hours, minutes, and seconds is a multi-value quantity just like a date and so to deal with it SCW converts it into a single time serial number which is simply the fraction of a day that the time represents. For example, .5 is 12 noon, i.e. half way through the day, .75 is 6 o' clock in the evening and so on.

As in the case of date serial numbers, any fraction can be treated as a time fraction. All you have to do is apply one of the time formats to the value and it will display as a time. If you apply a time format to a value greater than 1 then the fractional part is used as the time value. For example, 1.5 displays as 12:00, as does any value ending in .5.

If you enter a time using one of the standard formats then it is recognised as a time and converted into a time formula which has the format hh:mm:ss. A time formula evaluates to an appropriate fraction and this is displayed using the default time format.

》 As in the case of dates, time values can be added and subtracted and generally treated as ordinary numbers.

» Mixed dates and times

As times are recorded as fractional parts of a day it doesn't seem unreasonable to allow a mixed time and date serial number. In this case the whole number part of the date/time serial number is taken to be the days since the date base and the fractional part is the time of day. For example, a date/time serial number of 1.5 is just 12 noon on 1/1/1900.

You can format any numeric value to show as a date and time. When you enter a mixed date and time it will sometimes only show as a date even though it is stored in the cell as a combined date and time formula which evaluates to a date and time serial number. For example, if you type in 1-May-1994 12:00 it will be displayed as 1/5/1994 although the date/time formula 1/5/1994 12:00:00 will be stored in the cell and evaluated to 34455.5. The reason for this is that a pure date format has been applied to the cell and the time fraction is ignored. In most cases if you want to work with mixed times and dates you will need to assign your own format.

Differences from SC5

SCW has changed the handling of dates from SC5, considerably simplifying everything. There is no longer any need to use the date entry functions EDAT and JDATE. You can now type in a date using any reasonable format and it will be automatically evaluated to a date serial number and a date format will be applied. This makes date entry easier but you have to be slightly more careful because any numeric value can now be treated as a date. The only other significant change is that that date base has been changed from 1 March 1900 to 1 January 1990 but this shouldn't cause any problems.

Even though you don't need to use the date entry functions like EDAT and DATEVALUE to enter dates they are still occasionally useful in converting dates in one format into another. Notice that the WDAY has changed its name to WEEKDAY.

The same is true of time values. A time is automatically recognised and converted into a time formula - hh:mm:ss. Time formulae evaluate to time fractions which can be used just like ordinary numbers.

A combined date/time serial number behaves like a date for date functions and like a time for time functions. In other words, a date function will ignore the fractional part of a combined date and time value and a time function will ignore all but the fractional part. You can, of course use a date/time serial number in ordinary arithmetic.

» Formatting dates and times

Although there are a number of date and time formats included as standard in the Format,Number dialog box you can easily define your own.

Essentially you can describe exactly how you would like a date or time to appear using a set of standard symbols to create a "picture" of the format. For example, dd/mm/yy is a picture of a date specified by a two digit day number, a two digit month number and a two digit year number separated by / (slash) characters. The picture that you specify is followed more or less exactly. For example, if you specify dd / mm / yy then the spaces included in this picture between each date value and the separating slashes will be included in the resulting format.

You can also include text in the picture, for example:

"Today's date is" dd/mm/yy

Notice that you have to enclose the text in double quotes to avoid the ds and ys being confused with date formatting symbols.

The date and time formatting symbols that you can use are -

d, m, y   A single digit day, month, or year value. If the value needs more than one digit then two are used. If m occurs after an h then it is taken to mean a single digit minutes value.

dd,mm,yy,hh,ss   A double digit day, month, year, hour,or second value. A leading zero is used if necessary. If mm follows hh it is taken to mean a double digit minutes value.

yyyy   A four digit year value.

ddd, mmm   A three character abbreviation for the day or the month name.

dddd, mmmm   A full day or month name.

Finally there is the question of using a 24hr or 12hr clock for time display. If you include AM/PM am/pm, A/P or a/p in the format then a 12-hour clock is used and the corresponding am/pm indicator is used.

» Working with dates and times

After you have entered a date or time there are occasions when you need to break it back down into one or more of its constituent parts. There are a range of functions that allow you to do this. If you have a date/time value then:

DAY(*date-time*)	gives the day of the month
MONTH(*date-time*)	gives the month number
YEAR(*date-time*)	gives the year
HOUR(*date-time*)	gives the hour of the day
MINUTE(*date-time*)	gives the minute value of the time
SECOND(*date-time*)	gives the seconds

As well as the functions that split a date or time into its component parts, there is also the WEEKDAY(*date-time*) function which returns the number of the day of the week corresponding to the day value of the date, using 1 for Sunday to 7 for Saturday. You can use this function in conjunction with a lookup table or with the CHOOSE function to produce the day of the week as a text value. For example, if A1 contains a date, the formula:

=CHOOSE(WEEKDAY(A1),"Sunday","Monday", "Tuesday","Wednesday","Thursday","Friday","Saturday")

will select the correct name for the day of the week. If you only want to convert a small number of dates to day names then the CHOOSE function is effective but if you want to convert a lot of dates in this way a single lookup table will save having to repeat the list of day names each time. You can of course use the same technique to convert month numbers to names but with a choice of 12 names in this case! For many purposes it is simpler to set a special user-defined date format than it is to actually convert to day names. For example, the user-defined format WWW will produce a three letter weekday name and the format WWWW will display a full weekday name.

Also notice that all of the date and time functions will accept dates as text in any of the usual acceptable formats. For example,

=MONTH("1-FEB-1994")

returns 2.

Just as it is sometimes necessary to "pull a date apart" it is also necessary to build one up from its constituents. To do this, and similar tasks, you need to use the following date and time functions:

DATE(yy,mm,dd)   converts separate numeric values into a single date serial number.

EDAT(dd,mm,yy)   a European form of DATE.

DATEVALUE("date")   convert text in date format into a date serial number.

TIME(hh,mm,ss)   converts separate numeric values into a single time fraction.

TIMEVALUE("time")   converts text in time format into a time serial number.

As an example of using these functions, consider the problem of converting a column of day numbers for a given month, January say, into full dates. If the day numbers are stored in A3:A7 then you can generate a column of dates by entering:

=DATE(1994,1,A3)

	A	B
1	January	
2	Day	Dates
3	1	DATE(1994,1,A3)
4	2	2-Jan-94
5	5	5-Jan-94
6	10	10-Jan-94
7	11	11-Jan-94

in B3 and copying this into B4:B7. To see the results as dates you also have to remember to apply a date format to B3:B7.

» Entering today's date and time

The easiest way to enter the current date is to use the TODAY function. The only problem being that TODAY returns the current date each time the spreadsheet is recalculated. That is, it isn't a fixed date serial number but behaves more like a ticking clock. If you want to see a demonstration of the way TODAY is re-evaluated each time the spreadsheet is recalculated then you will have to wait up to a full 24 hours! A quicker demonstration is provided by the NOW function which returns the date and the time. To see NOW 'ticking' simply start with a fresh spreadsheet and enter =NOW() into A1 and format it to hh:mm:ss. You will then see the time value in A1 change each time you press the F9 key. You would see the same behaviour from the TODAY function but it only changes once every 24 hours.

To fix the value returned by TODAY or NOW before entering it into the spreadsheet all you have to do is remember to press the F9 key, or the recalculate icon on the toolbar, before pressing Return. This will evaluate any function on the date entry line allowing you to enter a simple value rather than the function. If you have entered date values using TODAY or NOW without recalculating then simply edit the value and press F9 or the recalculate icon before pressing Enter to return the value to the sheet.

» Date arithmetic

Although the basic idea of a date/time serial number simplifies calculations and comparisons between dates and times, it is still easy to find yourself unable to do something that seems straightforward. For example, it is obvious that the number of days between two dates, d1 and d2 say, is simply d2-d1, assuming d2 is the later date. Now try the same problem but work out how many calendar months there are between the two dates.

You can easily work out the approximate answer by dividing the number of days between them by 30 but a more exact answer needs some date functions. You can extract the month number from two dates using MONTH so

=MONTH(d2)-MONTH(d1)

gives you number of months between the two dates. If you try this out on some real dates you will find it works as long as the two dates are in the same year. If not then the year differences cause the method to fail.

For example,

=MONTH("1/1/1994")-MONTH("1/12/1993")

gives the answer -11 because of the year change. The solution is to calculate the difference in the year numbers and add 12 months for each year difference. That is, if the two dates are in A1 and A2 respectively the formula to calculate the number of calendar months between two dates is:

=(YEAR(A2)-YEAR(A1))*12+
        (MONTH(A2)-MONTH(A1))

Converting everything to calendar months is also useful in solving another problem of date arithmetic - ages. If you need to work out an age in years and months the simplest way of doing it is to work out the age in calendar months and then translate this to years and months by dividing by 12. Specifically, if M is the age in months then the age in years is:

=TRUNC(M/12)

The TRUNC function is needed to get rid of any fractional part of the division. To find the months part of the age we need the remainder after dividing by 12. This can be calculated using the MOD function. Whenever you need the remainder after dividing by a value, D say, simply use MOD(value,D). In this case we need the remainder after dividing M by 12, i.e.

=MOD(M,12)

As the difference in calendar months between two dates is given by the formula explained earlier we can now easily put the two parts together to calculate the age in years and months. If the birth date is stored in B1 the formula

=(YEAR(TODAY())-YEAR(B1))*12+
    MONTH(TODAY())-MONTH(B1)

stored in B2 will calculate the number of months difference between the birth date and the current date. Next the age in years can be worked out in B3 using

    =TRUNC(B2/12)

and the months in C3 as

    =MOD(B2,12)

If you try this formula out for different dates you will find that it works - except when the anniversary falls in the current month. That is, it counts you as one month older as soon as the current date reaches the month of birth. This isn't unreasonable as the formulae doesn't compare the current day part of the dates. If you want to only count the extra year once the birthday has passed you need to add a correction to the number of months. Before the birthday you need to subtract one and this can be worked out using the following IF function:

=IF((MONTH(TODAY())=MONTH(B1))#AND#
    (DAY(TODAY())<DAY(B1)),1,0)

in C2.

	BIRTH2.MDS : Window1			
	A	B	C	D
1	When were you born	12/03/1984		
2		119	1	
3	Your age is now	9	11	
4				
5				

This correction then has to be subtracted from the number of months in B2 giving

=(YEAR(TODAY())-YEAR(B1))*12+
    MONTH(TODAY())-MONTH(B1)-C2

as the final formula. This at least now shows the correct age just before a birthday.

You may be horrified at how complicated this example has become. This isn't untypical of date arithmetic, mainly because of the way calculations have to be done in different units - days, months and years. However once you have seen how to work in calendar months nothing is quite as complicated!

» Time arithmetic

Time arithmetic also has its complications but these are more to do with what happens when two times are separated by a day or more. For example, t2-t1 gives you the difference between the two times as a time fraction. This you can format as hh:mm:ss or use one of the time functions to convert it into hours and minutes as appropriate. However, if the two times are a day or more apart then there are differences in the date part of serial number to take into account.

For example, if you record the on and off times for something in two columns then you can work out the time period for which it has been on by subtracting. However, if the on and off times cross the midnight divide into another day then the result of the subtraction will be negative and this cannot be formatted as a time period and will show as a set of # characters if you try to do so.

The solution to the problem depends on exactly how you want to record times and what assumptions you can make. For example, if you can always assume that an "off" time that is less than an "on" time is due to crossing the midnight barrier just once then you can use the formula

=IF(B2-A2<0,B2-A2+24,B2-A2)

which adds 24 hours to adjust for the change of day. If you cannot assume that the time differences will be this regular you have no choice but to enter the full date and time of the on and off events. Now if you subtract the off time from the on time you should always get a positive quantity but it is possible that it will be bigger than one. This cannot be displayed as a time using a time format because the whole number part of the result will simply be ignored. For example, if you subtract two date/time serial numbers and get 1.5 then displaying this as a time will show 12:00. As the value actually indicates the period as days and fractional days multiplying by 24 converts this to hours. That is the formula that has to be entered is simply

=(B2-A2)*24

The only problem remaining is that there isn't a suitable format to display the result in as hours and minutes because a time serial number has to be less than one and a time format cannot show more than 24 hours. You can display the result as hours and fraction of an hour using the format

#0.00 "hours"

but this carries with it the danger that 10.50 hours will be interpreted as 10 hours 50 minutes when it really is 10 hours 30 minutes, i.e. 0.5 of an hour. However, the hours and fractional hours format is exactly what you need to do time calculations. For example, if you multiply by an hourly rate you get the correct result for parts of a full hour worked.

If you do want to show the time as hours and minutes the only way you can do it is to separate the two. The hours are simply the whole number part of the result and the minutes are simply the fractional part times 60. That is, to calculate hours in D2 from the hours and fractional hours in C2 you would use the formula

=TRUNC(C2)

and to calculate the minutes in E2 you would use the formula

=(C2-D2)*60

As long as you are not going to need to perform calculations with the result you can even combine the two results as a single text item using the complicated looking formula

=TRUNC(C2)&"h "&(C2-TRUNC(C2))*60&"m"

If you look at this formula carefully you will see that it just works out the hours and minutes as described earlier and adds some text to make the hours and minutes parts clear. Notice that the result of this formula is text and you cannot use it to perform arithmetic.

	A	B	C	D	E	F
1	On	Off	hours.00	hours	mins	hours mins
2	5/1/94 12:00	5/1/94 15:00	3	3	0	3h 0m
3	5/2/94 20:00	5/4/94 03:30	31.5	31	30	31h 30m
4						

You can use the TIME function to provide the appropriate fractions of a day for any time period. For example, TIME(0,1,0) is the time serial number for one minute and TIME(1,30,23) is the time serial number for one hour, thirty minutes and twenty three seconds. Typically this would be used to add an increment to another time value. For example, if A1 contains a time then the formula A1+TIME(0,1,0) evaluates to one minute later.

» Practical - Days360

As you can see from the preceding discussion of time and date arithmetic, working out the period between any two dates isn't always easy. In the days before computers were available it was considered much easier to assume that each month had exactly 30 days. SCW provides a built-in function DAYS360 that will calculate the number of days between two dates assuming a 360 day year. That is,

difference=DAYS360(D1,D2)

However, there are a number of ways of calculating a 360 day calendar and SCW uses the simplest interpretation. If the two dates are D1 and D2 then the number of years between them is YEAR(D2)-YEAR(D1) and 360 times this gives the number of days difference. The difference between the months is MONTH(D2)-MONTH(D1) and 30 times this gives the number of days difference. Finally the number of days between the two dates is DAY(D2)-DAY(D1) and adding all of these terms together gives the total number of days between the two dates, i.e.

(YEAR(D2)-YEAR(D1))*360+ (MONTH(D2)-MONTH(D1))*30+DAY(D2)-DAY(D1)

This formula agrees with the result produced by DAYS360.

The only problem is that some definitions of the 360 day calendar correct for the start or finish date being the 31st of a month. If the later date, D2, ends on the 31st of a month then we have counted a day too many for a 30-day month. This can be dealt with by adding in the result of the formula IF(DAY(D2)=31,-1,0).

Similarly if the earlier date, D1, starts on the 31st of a month then we have counted a day too few for a 30-day month. This can be dealt with by adding in the result of the formula IF(DAY(D1)=31,1,0).

228 *Dates, times, % and precision* Chapter 9

Putting all of this together gives:

(YEAR(D2)-YEAR(D1))*360+
    (MONTH(D2)-MONTH(D1))*30+
        DAY(D2)-DAY(D1)+
            IF(DAY(D2)=31,-1,0)+IF(DAY(D1)=31,1,0)

as the number of days between two dates D1 and D2 on a 360 day calendar.

	A	B	C	D
1		First date =		01/05/1991
2		Second date=		31/07/1991
3				
4				
5	Days difference=	90	using Days360 function	
6		90	using equivalent date formulae	
7		89	adjusting for 31st of months	
8				
9				

Notice that even this calculation may not conform to custom and practice in all financial areas and countries. In particular, it doesn't conform to the method used by the USA securities industry where if the ending date is a 31st and the starting date is the 30th or the 31st then the ending date has to be changed to the 30th. Before using any financial formula or calculation you should always check that it gives the same results as the traditional method. You should find it relatively easy to create a 360 day formula to meet your needs given the example above.

» Practical - Named day of the month

A common requirement when working with dates is to find the first Monday, or some other named day, of the month. Once you have the date of the first named day of the month it is easy to find the second by adding 7 days or the third by adding 14 days etc..

It is possible to write a formula that will automatically give you the date of the first occurrence of any named day in a month. This works by using the WEEKDAY function to discover the weekday number of the first day of the specified month. That is

$$WEEKDAY(EDAT(1,mm,yy))$$

is the day number of the first day of the month - where *mm* and *yy* are the month and year numbers that you are interested in. If you know the weekday number of the first day of the month then you can work out by how many days it differs from the day that you want, that is

$$wd\text{-}WEEKDAY(EDAT(1,mm,yy))$$

where *wd* is the weekday number that you are looking for. Adding this to the first of the month gives you the day of the week that you are looking for in the same week as the first day of the month.

As long as this quantity is positive it can simply be added to the date of the first day of the month to give the date of the first occurrence of the weekday that you are looking for. If it is negative then you have to add 7 to the difference to move the day into the following week and so keep the date in the same month.

For example, if you are looking for the first Friday, i.e. weekday number 6, in May 1990 then as the 1st of May was a Tuesday, i.e. weekday number 3, the difference, 6-3, is 3 and so three more days have to be added to the start of the month to reach the first Friday. However, if you want the first Monday, i.e. weekday number 2, then as 2-3 equals -1 the

Monday in the same week as the start of the month is in the previous month. To find the first Monday in May you have to add 7 to -1, giving 6 and add this to the date of the first of the month.

Putting all of this together gives the formula:

=EDAT(1+A1-WEEKDAY(EDAT(1,A2,A3))+
    IF(A1<WEEKDAY(EDAT(1,A2,A3)),7,0),A2,A3)

where it is assumed that A1 contains the number of the day of the week which you are interested in, A2 contains the month number, and A3 the year number. This formula may look intimidating but if you break it down into its constituent parts you should see that it is working exactly as described above.

Using this formula it is not difficult to create a spreadsheet that lists the first week day of every month. The basic idea is that the user enters the year and the day required and then the spreadsheet constructs a table of the date of the first such weekday of each month.

	A	B
1	First Day Scheduler	
2	YEAR	1994
3	DAY	Monday
4		
5	Month	Date of first
6		Monday
7	January	03-Jan
8	February	07-Feb
9	March	07-Mar
10	April	04-Apr
11	May	02-May
12	June	06-Jun
13	July	04-Jul
14	August	01-Aug
15	September	05-Sep
16	October	03-Oct
17	November	07-Nov
18	December	05-Dec
19		
20	Fri	6
21	Mon	2
22	Sat	7
23	Sun	1
24	Thu	5
25	Tue	3
26	Wed	4
27		
28	2	

To create the spreadsheet we first need a column of dates corresponding to the first of each month. This can be done automatically by entering

=EDAT(1,ROW()-6,$B$2)

into A7 and copying it into A8:A18. The ROW function gives the row number in which the formula is stored and so changes the month number automatically.

We could insist that the user enters the day number but is is better to use a lookup table to convert the usual day name into a number. This requires the day names to be entered into one column A20:A26 in alphabetical order and their corresponding day numbers into another B20:B26. If the day name is entered into B3 the number can be looked up using the formula

=LOOKUP(B20:B26,A20:A26,LEFT(B3,3))

in A28.

Notice the way that the LEFT function is used to look up only the first three letters of the weekday name. This allows the user to enter Monday or Mon or any word starting Mon and have it recognised as Monday.

Finally, entering the formula
=EDAT(1+$A$28-WEEKDAY(A7)+
  IF($A$28<WEEKDAY(A7),7,0),MONTH(A7),YEAR(A7))
into B7 will work out the date of the first named day in January. When this is copied into B8:B18 the table is complete. All that is left is to apply the mmmm format to the months and the dd-mmm format to the days.

» Practical - A calendar

A surprisingly difficult application is to use the date functions to create a reasonably standard calendar display. However, if you follow the reasoning step-by-step you will be able to make sense of the rather long formula that results.

The first step is to create a formula that will number the squares of the calendar layout. That is it must evaluate to 1 in the first square 2 in the second and so on. The function COLUMN() returns a number according to the column it is stored in 1 for A, 2 for B and so on. So if we store the formula

=COLUMN()

in the first row of the layout which is in columns A to G it will number them 1 to 7. If the columns used were any other range you could correct the numbering by subtracting an appropriate value. This simple formula will not do in the second row but the function ROW() will return the row number in which it is stored, so the formula

=COLUMN()+(ROW()-7)*7

copied into A7:G12 produces the correct numbering of the squares.

This numbering would be correct for a display of the days of the month but it always starts with day 1 on a Sunday. We can easily work out what day number the first day of the month is. If the year is in B1 and the month number in B2, the first day of the month can be calculated in B3 using:

=WEEKDAY(EDAT(1,B2,B1))

This value can be used to correct the numbering of the calendar. Let us assume that the first day of the month works out to be 3, i.e. a Wednesday. At the moment the first Wednesday is numbered as day 3 of the month so subtracting 2 makes it day 1. In fact subtracting 2 from the value in each square produces the correct numbering for the days of the month. That is the formula that should be entered into A7:G12 is

=COLUMN()+(ROW()-7)*7-$B$3+1

The only problem that now remains is that the calendar shows negative values before the 1st day and shows values beyond the end of the month. Clearly what is needed next is an IF function to remove the silly values. This is easy enough but what should the condition be? The key to this is to notice that if the date functions are given "silly" dates that are before a month start or after a month end then they simply convert them to sensible dates in the previous or next month. For example, the function EDAT(32,5,1994), i.e. one day beyond the end of May, is converted into 1/6/1994, i.e. the first of

June. What this means is that if you give EDAT a sensible date it returns a date in the same month but if the date is before the month start or after the month end it gives you a date in a different month. In other words, the IF function should be

IF(MONTH(EDAT(*date in square*))<>$B2,
".", *date in square*)

This formula enters a dot if the date implied by the calendar numbering isn't a sensible date for the month in question.

The only problem is that working out the date from the calendar numbering looks complicated

MONTH(EDAT(COLUMN()+
7*(ROW()-7)-$B$3+1,$B$2,$B$1)

but if you look at it carefully you will see that it is just the formula for numbering the squares plus the month and year number entered by the user.

	A	B	C	D	E	F	G
1	Year	1994					
2	Month	3					
3	First day	3					
4							
5							
6	Sun	Mon	Tue	Wed	Thu	Fri	Sat
7	.	.	1	2	3	4	5
8	6	7	8	9	10	11	12
9	13	14	15	16	17	18	19
10	20	21	22	23	24	25	26
11	27	28	29	30	31	.	.
12	.	.	.	.	.	.	.
13							

CALENDAR.MDS : Window1

Putting this all together gives the very long formula:
=IF(MONTH(EDAT(COLUMN()+7*(ROW()-7)-$B$3+1,
    $B$2,$B$1))<>$B$2,".",
            COLUMN()+7*(ROW()-7)-$B$3+1)

This should be copied into A7:G12. Notice that it doesn't work correctly in any other position within the spreadsheet unless you adjust the results produced by COLUMN and ROW.

The final touch is to alter the column and row spacing and add some gridlines. You can even use the cell note facility to mark appointments on the dates.

» Practical - Graphing Biorhythms

There is a particular problem with creating charts in that you cannot format values shown on the axes as dates. A spreadsheet that calculates your biorhythm is a good example of this problem and how to solve it - even if you don't believe in biorhythms.

The theory of biorhythms is that there are three independent cycles - Physical with a period of 23 days, Emotional with a period of 28 days and Intellectual with a period of 33 days - which start on the day a person is born and affect their life from then on. If you want to know more about this theory a text file is included on the companion disk that relates to this book.

To calculate the biorhythm for any given date all we have to do is work out how many days since the person was born and where it is located in each of the three cycles.

If the birth date is stored in B1 and today's date, which can be entered using =TODAY(), in B2 you can work out the number of days that the user has been alive in B4 using the formula
              =B2-B1

	A	B	C	D	E	F
1	Enter your birthday	6/5/53				
2	Today	4/3/94				
3						
4	Number of days alive	14912				
5	Physical	0.82		HIGH		
6	Emotional	-0.43		MEDIUM		
7	Intellectual	-0.69		LOW		
8						
9						
10			Date	Physical	Emotional	Intellectual
11			18-Feb 18-Feb	-1.00	0.43	0.28
12			19-Feb 19-Feb	-0.98	0.62	0.10
13			20-Feb 20-Feb	-0.89	0.78	-0.10
14			21-Feb 21-Feb	-0.73	0.90	-0.28
15			22-Feb 22-Feb	-0.52	0.97	-0.46
16			23-Feb 23-Feb	-0.27	1.00	-0.62
17			24-Feb 24-Feb	0.00	0.97	0.76

The current state of the physical biorhythm with period 23 days can be worked out in B5 using

=SIN(B4/23*2*PI())

Dividing B4/23 gives the number of periods and the factor of 2*PI converts this into radians so that the SIN function can work out the current level of the cycle. Similarly you can work out the emotional state in B6 using

=SIN(B4/28*2*PI())

and the intellectual state in B7 using

=SIN(B4/33*2*PI())

As well as just quoting bare figures it would also be nice to comment on the levels - low, medium and high. This isn't difficult to do by entering the formula

=IF(B5<-0.5,"LOW",IF(B5>0.5,"HIGH","MEDIUM"))

in D5 and copying it into D6:D7.

The next step is to work out a table of values that surround the current date by two weeks on either side so that a chart can be constructed. Given that the current date is in B2, a date two weeks earlier is just

=B2-14

This should be entered into B11 to start the table. Then entering

=B11+1

into B12 and copying it into B13:B39 to generate the rest of the values. Now that the dates are entered into the column B2:B39 calculating a table of biorhythms is easy. The formula for the physical curve

=SIN((B11-$B$1)/23*2*PI())

has to be entered into D11; the similar one for the emotional curve

=SIN((B11-$B$1)/28*2*PI())

goes into E11 and the one for the intellectual curve

=SIN((B11-$B$1)/33*2*PI())

into F11. Then these three formulae can be copied down into D12:F39.

Now we have a table of biorhythm values it is easy to construct a chart using B11:B39 as the X axis series and D11:F39 as the Y axis series. If you do this you will discover that the X axis shows as a date serial number which isn't very informative to the casual onlooker! To force the X axis values to be shown as dates we need to convert the dates to text in column C. Enter the formula

=DISPLAY(B11,FORMAT(B11),7)

into C11 and copy it down the column C12:C39. This formula converts the contents of B11 into text with the same format that has been applied to B11. In other words, C11 and B11 appear to have exactly the same contents but B11 is a date value and C11 is text.

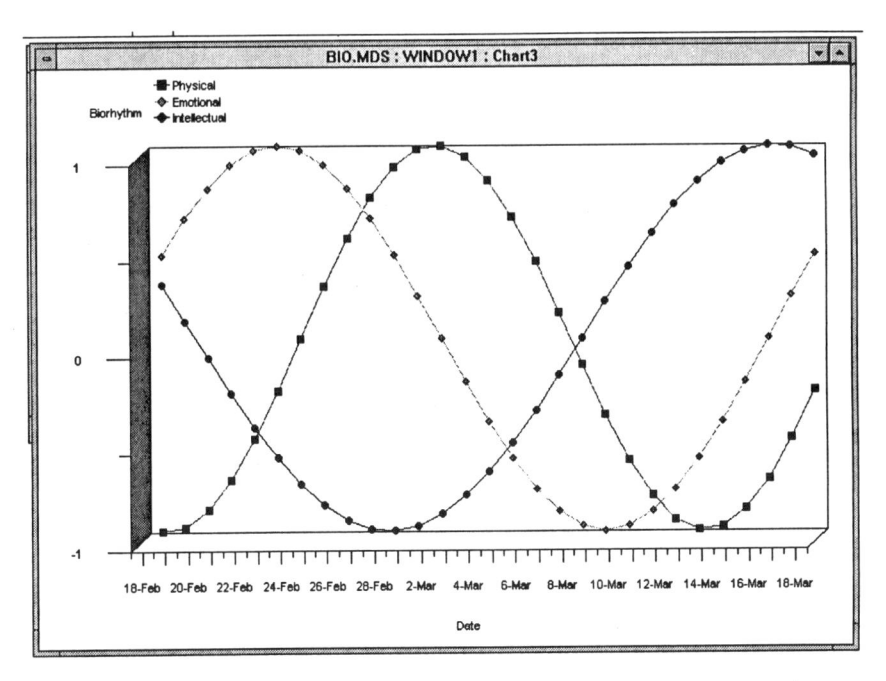

Now when a line chart is constructed using C11:C39 as the X axis series, the dates show as dates. The only other changes that are necessary are to set the maximum Y value to 1 and the minimum to -1.

» Percentages

Dates and times are an example of complicated data values and how to handle them. In both cases the solution to the problem is to store the value in one form, i.e. the date serial number, and display it in another, i.e. a conventional date. Percentages are another, but far less complicated example of this idea.

A percentage is a fraction expressed in hundredths. It is usual to write a percentage ignoring the 1/100. So for example, 50% actually means 50/100. When you work with percentages it is easier to convert the fraction to a decimal, i.e. 50% is

50/100 or 0.5. The reason why a decimal fraction is easier to work with is that taking a percentage is just a matter of multiplication. For example, 50% of the contents of A1 is either -

=A1*50/100

or

=A1*0.5

To make it easier to work with percentages SCW will automatically recognise a percentage, convert it into a decimal fraction and apply a percentage format. For example, if you enter the value 50% into a cell SCW converts this to 0.5 and applies the percentage format 0% to make it display as 50%. In other words, the cell may appear to contain 50% but it in fact contains 0.5.

What this means is that when you work with percentages in SCW you don't need to divide by 100 even though the values used look as if they need you to. In addition to entering a percentage value SCW allows you to use a percentage operator. This divides the value to its left by 100 to give a decimal fraction. For example,

=100*3%

is   100*(3/100) or 3

» Notice that when you enter a formula that uses the percentage operator the cell is not automatically formatted to show as a percent. This give you a way of entering percentages and having them show as decimal fractions. For example, if you enter =3% the cell contains and displays 0.03.

» Fixed decimal entry

A similar idea to the entry of percentage values is the Fixed Decimal option. Using this you can specify as decimal multiplier to be use with all entries. For example, if you set the Fixed Decimal option to 3 then the multiplier is 1/1000 and all values that you enter are divided by 1000. If you set the Fixed Decimal option to -3 then the multiplier is 1000 and every value that you enter is multiplied by 1000. To set the Fixed Decimal to any given value use the Option,Preferences command. Value is the number of zeros after the 1 in the multiplier. Positive values divide and negative values multiply. Obviously if you are working in units of 1,000s, or even 1,000,000s, then setting the fixed decimal to -3 or -6 saves typing zeros.

If you enter a value as a formula, i.e. by preceding it by an equals sign, then the multiplier isn't applied. You can use this as an override when you want to enter a value that shouldn't be adjusted.

» Accurate arithmetic?

Spreadsheet users quickly get used to the idea that a cell's contents and what it displays aren't one and the same thing. However, there are still times when this fact leads to unexpected results. For example, if you store 1.4 in a cell and set its format to 0 then it will show as 1. Rounding the display of a value to a given number of decimal places doesn't cause any great difficulty until you come to use the values in formulae. For example, suppose you store 1.4 in A1 and 1.4 in A2 and the formula =A1+A2 in A3. In this case you will see the correct answer 2.8 in A3. Now if you set the format of A1,A2 and A3 to 0 you will see the surprising result that 1+1 = 3, because 1.4 rounded is 1 and 2.8 rounded is 3. This means that you would now be viewing a spreadsheet that displays:

Sheet1 : Window1	
A	B
1	1
2	1
3	3
4	

and so proclaims for all the world to see that spreadsheet arithmetic makes 1+1 equal 3! It should be clear from this example that the cause certainly isn't any inaccuracy in the calculation but the difference between what is stored in a cell and what it displays. Although the format forces the cells to display their contents as whole numbers the calculations are still performed using the values actually stored in the cells.

If you think this example is a little extreme, I would agree, but it does show the problem very clearly. In real life values are often shown to rather more decimal places but the fact that they are stored to even more decimal places can still cause the result of a calculation shown on the screen to be different from the result you would obtain using a calculator.

For example, it is common to show money calculations to two decimal places. This is fine as long as the values are entered to two decimal places but if they are arrived at by some calculation they can be stored to more than two decimal places. For example, if you work out 15% of £1.99 then the result is £0.2985 which shown to 2 decimal places is £0.30. The trouble is that when this is added to another quantity it looks like adding 30p but it is in fact adding 29.85p - a small difference, but one that can accumulate. For example, imagine summing a column containing 100 such values. The result that you would expect from adding 100 30 pence values is obviously £30 but the result that the spreadsheet showed would be obtained by adding 100 29.85 pence values, i.e. £29.85. In practice it is unlikely that you would add together 100 identical values but the principle still applies when adding 100 different values.

What can be done about this problem? If all you are interested in is the accuracy of the arithmetic then you can ignore it - the final result is always accurate! The problem is really what psychologists call "face validity". Although the answer is correct it appears to be incorrect when you add up the values that the spreadsheet shows. The solution to the problem is not to allow the spreadsheet to display values that are different from what is stored in each cell. This can be achieved by following two simple rules:

» When you format a cell to show *n* decimal places never enter a value into it that has more than *n* decimal places specified.

» When you format a cell to show *n* decimal places then never allow a formula to work out a result to more than *n* decimal places.

It is easy to enforce the first rule when typing in data but what about the second one? Well this is easily enforced by use of the ROUND(*value*,*n*) function - which will round *value* to *n* decimal places. This can be used to round any value to any number of decimal places. So, for example, the problem with working out 15% of £1.99 was caused by keeping four decimal places in the answer, i.e. 0.2985, but displaying only two, i.e. .30. Instead of working out the percentage using =PRICE*.15, the formula =ROUND(PRICE*.15,2) should have been used. In this case the cell will show .30 and it will contain the value .30 - so adding up a column of 100 such entries will give the £30 and face validity has been restored! Using the ROUND function the second rule becomes:

» If you want to display the results of a calculation to *n* decimal places it is safer to use the ROUND function to actually round it to *n* decimal places than to simply format the cell.

The only problem with this solution is that you will always find someone who will argue that 15% of £1.99 isn't 30p or more seriously that 15% of 100 £1.99 values isn't £30 but £29.85! Clearly you have to know which result will be considered fair in any given situation.

» Rounding, rounding up and truncating

The use of the ROUND function to ensure that a displayed value coincides with the value used in a calculation has already been described but there are in fact three functions that can be used to modify the form of a value - ROUND, ROUNDUP and TRUNC. Using these three functions it should be possible for you to modify a value to suit the needs of the calculation.

The function ROUND(*value*, *n*) will round the value to *n* decimal places in the standard manner. The best way to think of the rounding function is that it returns a number with *n* decimal places that is as close as possible to *value*. In the same way ROUNDUP(*value*, *n*) returns the closest number with *n* decimal places that is bigger than *value*. Notice that INT(*value*) is the same as ROUND(*value*,0). TRUNC(*value*) on the other hand is much more brutal in that it simply removes the digits after the decimal point.

What is missing here is a function that allows you to round down to a given number of digits. This is easy enough to create using the TRUNC function. If you want to round down or truncate to *n* digits you simply use the formula:

=TRUNC(*value**10^*n*)/10^*n*

The following examples illustrate the use of these functions:

=ROUND(10.4321,2) = 10.43 because this is the closest number with two decimal places to 10.4321.

=ROUNDUP(10.4321,2) = 10.44 because this is the closest number with two decimal places that is larger than 10.4321.

=TRUNC(10.4321*100)/100 = 10.43 because this just ignores the digits after the second decimal place and 10^2 is 100.

These functions can also be used to round and truncate values to the left of the decimal point by preceding the n by a - sign as in ROUND(*value*,-*n*). Most users are less familiar with this idea of dealing with digits to the right of the decimal point but it follows the same principles. That is ROUND(*value*,-*n*) is the closest number to *value* with n places to the left of the decimal point set to zero. For example:

=ROUND(8194.23,-2) = 8200 because this is the closest number with two zeros to the left of the decimal point to 8194.23.

In the same way the function ROUNDUP(*value*,-*n*) returns the closest number that is larger than *value* with n places to the left of the decimal point set to zero. For example:

ROUNDUP(8194.23,-2) = 8200 because this is the closest number larger than 8194.23 with 2 places to the left of the decimal point set to zero.

Finally, =TRUNC(*value**10^-*n*)/10^-*n* simply ignores the n digits to the left of the decimal point by setting them to zero. For example:

=TRUNC(8194.23/100)*100 = 8100 because that's the result of setting all the digits up to two digits to the left of the decimal point to zero!

Converting to values

A standard problem that occurs often in spreadsheeting is to convert a set of formulae into values. You may want to do this to ensure that the results do not change if the data changes or just to "freeze" a formula like =TODAY(). No matter what the reason converting to values is easy. All you have to do is copy the data to the clipboard using Edit,Copy and then paste it back using Edit,Paste Special with the Values option selected in the Paste section of the dialog box.

» Rounding existing values

It is easy to use the ROUND, ROUNDUP or TRUNC functions to convert the results of a calculation into the correct format but values already entered in the spreadsheet are a less easy proposition. For example, if you have a column of values entered to four decimal places how do you change it to a column of values rounded to two decimal places? One possibility is to place the cursor over each value, press F2 and then edit the values to ROUND*(v,*2) before pressing return. This has the advantage of leaving the original values, entered to four decimal places, still visible but it is hard work. As this is a repetitive task it is an obvious one to convert into a simple macro.

An alternative method is to insert a column next to the column of values and enter the formula ROUND (*cell_ref*, 2) into every cell in the new column next to a value, where *cell_ref* is the cell containing the value. This converts the values to two decimal places but duplicates the data. If you don't want the duplication of data then the next step is to copy the data to the clipboard, use Edit,Copy and then use Edit,Paste Special to paste the results back as values - see the box Converting to values. After this operation you can safely delete the column containing the original data.

» A user defined RoundDn function

Although SCW lacks a TRUNC(v,n) or RoundDn(v,n) function it isn't difficult to define a user defined function that does the same job. The following instructions should be entered into the macro sheet GLOBAL.MDM

```
function RoundDn(v,n)
res=INT(v*(10^n))/(10^n)
return res
end function
```

Calculating VAT

Many businesses use a spreadsheet to help with some stage of preparing their VAT accounts, even if it is only in the production of the occasional one-off VAT invoice. For this reason it is important to know the rules for calculating VAT as prescribed by the HM Customs & Excise. At the time of writing the rules are:

1) The total VAT on a tax invoice can be rounded down, i.e. truncated, to a whole penny.

2) If the VAT is shown for each item making up a tax invoice then you can either round each value down, i.e. truncate, to the nearest .1 of a penny or you can round to the nearest penny. Whichever method you choose - truncating to .1p or rounding to 1p you have to be consistent - you can't change to alter the VAT amount in your favour!

Using these rules means that the formula that you should use to calculate VAT on each line in a tax invoice is

=TRUNC(COST*RATE*1000)/1000

assuming that COST is in pounds. The total VAT can be worked out as

=TRUNC(TOTAL*RATE*100)/100

Using this method for an item costing £1.99 at a rate of 17.5% would result in an invoice line with VAT shown as TRUNC(1.99*.175*1000)/1000 which evaluates to £0.348. An invoice with 100 such item lines giving a TOTAL of £199 would result in a total VAT of TRUNC(199*.175*100)/100 which evaluates to £34.82. Adding up the 100 separate VAT values of £0.348 gives £34.80 for the VAT which is clearly different from the more accurate calculation based on the TOTAL of goods delivered. If you calculate VAT for each item on an invoice then obviously you should work out the total VAT by summing the separate VAT amounts.

Another rule to bear in mind is that zero rated VAT items should be totalled separately from standard rated items. That is, you shouldn't total a column of mixed VAT rated items.

You can use this function to round down the value v to n places. Notice that the INT function is in fact a CA-ble arithmetic function and not the SCW INT function - see Chapter 12.

» Practical - Calculating VAT

After the discussion of percentages and dealing with the problems of accuracy, a VAT calculator is a good example. Creating a spreadsheet to produce a VAT invoice isn't difficult but there are some fine details to take care of. If you sell a mix of zero and standard rated items the two need to be totalled separately. This is just a matter of recording the VAT rate in column D and using the IF function

=IF(D4<>0,C4,0)

to pick out standard rated items in column E and

=IF(D4=0,C4,0)

to pick out the zero rated items in column G.

	A	B	C	D	E	F	G
1	VAT Calculator						
2							
3	Date	Item	List	Vat Rate	Std Rated	VAT	Zero Rated
4	03/02/1994	Camera	£450.00	17.50%	£450.00	£78.750	£0.00
5	07/02/1994	70mm lens	£99.99	17.50%	£99.99	£17.498	£0.00
6	08/02/1994	Film	£29.95	17.50%	£29.95	£5.241	£0.00
7	20/02/1994	Developer	£36.00	17.50%	£36.00	£6.300	£0.00
8	22/02/1994	Paper	£50.00	17.50%	£50.00	£8.750	£0.00
9	23/02/1994	Book	£15.00	0%	£0.00	£0.000	£15.00
10							
11				Zero rated total =	£15.00		
12				Standard rated total =	£680.94		
13				VAT=	£116.54		
14							

Calculating the VAT on each invoice line needs the use of the TRUNC function to round the answer down to three decimal places. You could also choose to round the values - the only constraint is that you can't mix the two methods. The truncation formula is

=IF(D4<>0,TRUNC(C4*D4*1000)/1000,0)

Notice that the VAT rate is entered in column D as a percentage. Finally SUMs are formed of the standard rated items, the VAT on the standard rated items and the zero rated items. If you want to turn this example into a full invoice all that is needed is some formatting to create a letterhead and some rulings for the table - and don't forget that the invoice has to quote your VAT number.

The same techniques used to deal with zero rated items can easily be adapted to work with multiple rates of tax other than zero percent.

Key points

» Dates are stored as date serial numbers corresponding to the number of days since 1/1/1900.

» Times are stored as time fractions, i.e. fractions of a day.

» Dates and times are recognised automatically, provided they are entered in the standard formats, and converted into date and time formulae which evaluate to date serial numbers.

» Any number in the correct range can be treated as a date/time serial number.

» Working with dates and times is often complicated by the need to work in so many different units - calendar months, hours, minutes, etc.

» Percentages are also recognised automatically and divided by 100 to convert them to decimal fractions. A percentage format is also applied automatically.

» If you format numbers to show a smaller number of digits than is actually stored in the cell then arithmetic performed within a spreadsheet can appear to be incorrect.

» In many cases it is important to reduce the precision of calculated values to be the same as that displayed.

Chapter 10

Database

So far we have only considered using SCW for pure spreadsheet applications. That is, we have only considered tables of numbers and the calculations they involve. You can, however, also use SuperCalc as a simple database to keep records of information that you wish to retrieve at a later date. In this context it is not the calculation of values that takes priority, but operations such as searching for particular information within a table and sorting it into order.

Although the fundamental principles of database operation remain the same in SCW as in SC5 there have been a number of enhancements that make this area easier to use. It is also worth noting that the data commands only relate to the sheet environment.

» What is a database?

The best way to think of a database is by imagining a traditional box of record cards. A card file consists a number of cards, or records, each laid out in an identical manner. For example, a name and address card file would consist of cards each laid out something like:

NAME..
ADDRESS..
....
....
TEL............................

Each area where information can be written on the card is called a "field" and its label is a "fieldname". For example, in the case of the name and address record ADDRESS is a fieldname and the space for the address is the field. Every record in a database has the same set of fields and it is this regularity that makes it possible to perform operations such as finding every card with NAME equal to "Smith".

» A database as a table

The basic idea of using a spreadsheet as a database is easy enough to understand once you have noticed that a record can be stored in a single row with each column storing a different field. You can also label the head of each column with the appropriate fieldnames. For example, the name and address database could be entered as:

	A	B	C
1	NAME	ADDRESS	TEL
2	Smith	Acacia Ave	123-4567
3	Jones	High Street	891-2345
4	Swift	Wood Lane	345-6789

Differences from SC5

The main change to the database facilities is the introduction of the Data,Form command. For most simple database tasks the form is much simpler to use and doesn't require the setting up of a Criteria range or an Extract range. All you need to define before using the data form is the Database range itself. The data form can be successfully used to browse through the database, for ad hoc editing and for data entry. Its main limitation is that you cannot specify multiple sets of criteria. You also cannot use conditions between fields in the record - but this is also true when you make use of the criteria range.

If you want to use the more powerful database commands, i.e. Data,Find, Data,Delete and Data,Extract, you do need the traditional three areas Input, Criteria and Output - which have now been renamed as Database, Criteria and Extract. Apart from the renaming these all work more or less as before. The biggest change is to the conditions that you can use. You no longer have to refer to cells in the top row of the database to perform a comparison. For example, <1000 is sufficient to select all values less than 1000. However, this also means that you cannot make use of references to the top row to specify conditions between fields.

The only other difference is that now these areas are defined by standard range names - Database, Criteria and Extract - which you are free to redefine in any way that you want.

The operation of the Data,Find and Data,Delete commands have changed in minor ways. In particular, Data,Delete will now delete ALL the records that match in one operation.

Obviously, to make the database easy to read the columns of the spreadsheet have to be set to widths that can accommodate each field, and the display formats should be set appropriately but that is really all that is needed. In other words, using a spreadsheet in this way requires no new commands it is just a matter of organisation. However, if you are going to use the spreadsheet database for typical database functions such as looking up a particular record then some new commands and new facilities are required.

» Form view

Although it is clear that a database can be considered to be a table most users are more familiar with the idea of a record card style of layout. You can view your database table one record at a time using a form view. Before you can do this, however, you have to tell SCW where the database table is within your spreadsheet. If you try to use the Data,Form command before doing this you will see an alert box appear telling you to do so!

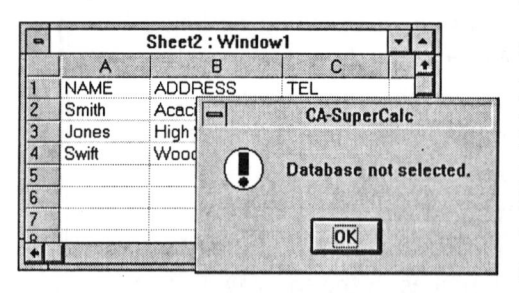

To define the database area select the entire database, including the fieldnames in the first row, and use the command Data,Set Database. This actually creates a new name Database which is defined to be the range occupied by the database. After you have done this you can use the Data,Form command successfully.

The Form that appears uses the fieldnames in the top row of your database as labels for individual entries. The fields are listed one above the other in a column layout and there is no way to alter this. The form can show only a maximum of 11 fields. If there are any formulae within the database these are shown but you can't edit them. Also if you have applied any formats in the spreadsheet these are ignored. In most cases this doesn't matter but dates, times and percentages are a particular problem.

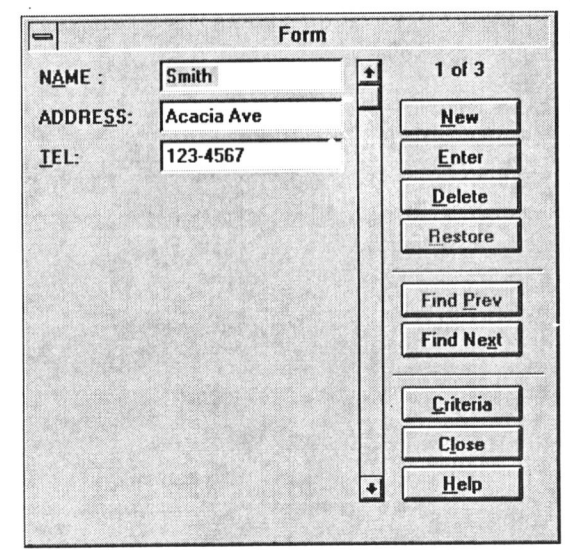

If you click on the Find Next button the form shows the next record, i.e. the next row down the table. If you click on the Find Previous button it moves back one record. You can also move through the records by dragging the scroll bar slider at the right-hand side of the field list.

» Entering data

To add a new record you can either move one place beyond the end of the last record or simply click on the New button. This results in a blank form into which you can type new values. Although the form doesn't show dates and times formatted you can still type in a date or time and it will be recognised and converted to a date and time serial number. To move from field to field you can either click the mouse on the next field or you can use the Tab key to move to it. Shift and Tab moves you to the previous field.

When you have finished entering values you can click on the Enter button or press the Enter key. At this point the values that you have entered into each field are transferred to the first blank row. If this is outside the range that you have defined as the database you will also be asked the question "Overwrite existing name 'Database'". In most cases the answer to this question will be yes because you do want the database range to be redefined to include the new record. If you don't allow the update of the range name Database then the new data that you have entered is still stored in the row but it will not be treated as part of the database for some operations. While you make use of the Form to examine and enter new data the form will continue to recognise that the new record is there and it will persist in asking you if it is OK to update the definition of the database range. However, once you close the form and re-open it the new records will not be treated as part of the database. In general, it is a good idea to allow the form to update the range name.

If the first row after the database range isn't empty you cannot add a new record. When you try to do so the form will simply display a message that it cannot extend the database. In other words, you cannot overwrite existing data that happens to be just outside the database range using the form.

» Finding and editing data

Once the record you are interested in is displayed within the form you can edit the contents of any of its fields. The more difficult problem is in finding the data that you are interested in!

Obviously to find particular records you have to know what makes them different from the other records. You need a selection criterion.

If you click on the Criteria button on the form it changes to show you a blank form. This is a Query By Example form. The idea is that you type details in each field to define the type of record you are looking for. For example if you type in Jones in the Name field this is taken to mean that you are interested only in records that have Jones in the Name field. If you then click on the Find Next button the Form reappears, positioned to show you the first record with Jones in the Name field. Clicking on the Find Next or Find Previous button moves the form to the next or previous record with Jones in the Name field.

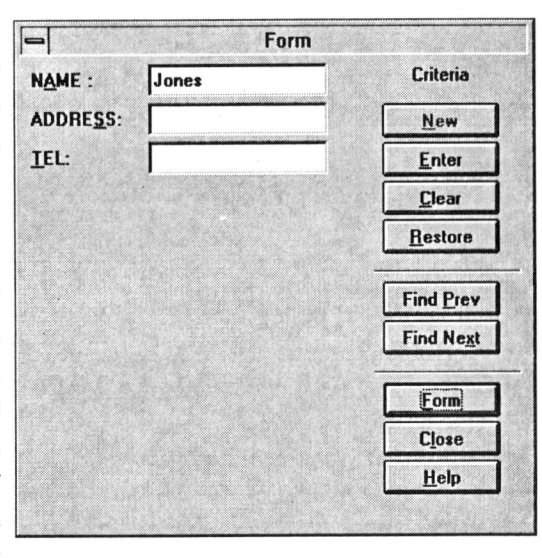

Once you have set a criterion for selection, the movement buttons only take you to records that meet the criterion.

» Criteria

Being able to find the record that you want is just a matter of being able to write the correct criteria in the fields. If you enter a constant value into one of the fields - either numeric or text - then only records which match exactly are selected. You can also enter comparison operators =, <, >,<=,>= and <> to select records. For example, to select records with SALARY greater than 3000 you would enter >3000 in the SALARY field of the Criteria form. You can also compare text values in this way as long as you remember to include the text within double quotes. For example, to select all names that come after Jones in an alphabetic list you would use the condition >"Jones".

So far you can create criteria which select exact matches or greater than less than type relationships. But what if you only want to specify that a name that begins with the letter S, say? The answer is that you would use "wildcard characters". The ? stands in place of any single character and the * stands in place of any number of other characters. So for example, Sm?th specifies a label that begins Sm, then any letter followed by th. Both Smith and Smyth fit this description. If you want to specify any word that begins with S you would use S* which means any label that begins with S followed by any number of any other letters (or digits). Once you get the hang of wildcard characters they are particularly easy to use to specify groups of words. The best way to think about them is to imagine that you are constructing a template that specifies the pattern of the words that you are interested in.

You can also use the ~ (tilde) to select records that do NOT match the criterion. So, ~S* matches everything that doesn't begin with S.

So to summarise:

» A value entered into a criterion field specifies an exact match.

» You can select on a greater than/less than basis using <,>,=<,>= and <> for both text and numeric values

» You can use wildcards to specify partial matches for text values.

» Database commands

In addition to the Data Form, SCW supports three database commands - Find, Extract and Delete. These work with a database in the same format as the Data Form, that is a table with fieldnames in the first row, but they also need two additional areas of the spreadsheet - the Criteria range and the Extract range.

The Criteria range is the area of the spreadsheet that you use to specify the selection criteria for the records that you are looking for. It plays the role of the criteria form. It has to be organised in a similar way to the main database table with fieldnames in the first row. The criteria for each field is entered in the rows below.

The Criteria range is set by selecting the area of the spreadsheet that you want and using the command Data,Set Criteria. This creates a new name, Criteria, for the range you have indicated.

The Extract range is also like the main database table but its purpose is to hold records extracted from the main table by the Data,Extract command. The extract range and the Data,Extract command work together with the criteria range to allow you to create subsets of your main data table. You set the extract range using the Data,Set Extract command.

» The database names

SCW's database facilities make use of three standard names that are automatically created when you use the Data,Set commands. However these names are perfectly standard range names and you can set and modify them using the Formula, Define Name command. If you use this command after setting the three database areas you will see their names listed in the Define Name dialog box.

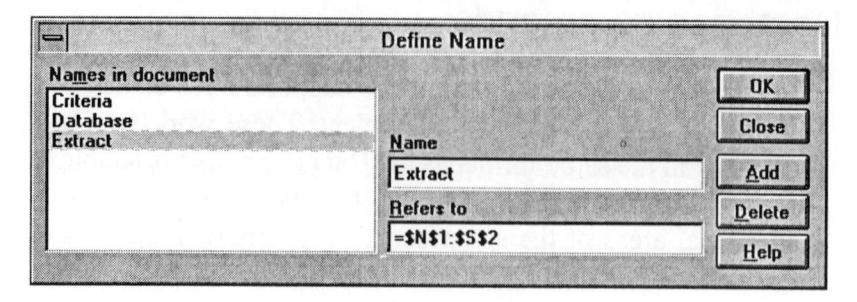

Any database commands that modify the definitions of these standard ranges always ask if it is OK to redefine the corresponding name before doing so.

» The criteria range

The criteria range can be quite tricky to set up. It must be an empty area of the spreadsheet, the first row of which names the fields that are going to be used in the selection process. These fieldnames have to match fieldnames within the database range exactly. The best way of ensuring this is simply to drag a copy of the top row across to the criteria range. You can then enter conditions to apply to the fields in the rows below the fieldnames. You don't have to include all of the fieldnames in the criteria range. For example, if you are using the name and address database described above and want to search for records that match a particular name you would set up a simple criteria range consisting of just two cells - the top cell giving the fieldname and the bottom cell ready to accept the match criteria. In most cases however it is simpler to include all of the fieldnames in the criteria range.

Once set up, you can use the criteria range much like the criteria fields in the Data Form. Any values that you enter define exact match criteria. You can use greater than and less than signs to compare field values to a constant and you can use wildcards in text criteria. In other words, you can use all of the criteria that you can in the Data Form in exactly the same way. What you cannot do is to create conditions that compare the values in two different fields. You can use formulae within the criteria range but these are evaluated once, before any database operations start, and then treated as if they were constant values.

The only extra power that a criteria range gives you is that you can include more than one line of conditions. In this case the criteria range specifies any record that satisfies any of the condition lines. For example, if you are interested in records with NAME equal to Smith at ADDRESS equal to Acacia Ave or with NAME equal to Jones at ADDRESS equal to High Street you would need a criteria range like:

G	H
NAME	ADDRESS
Smith	Acacia Ave
Jones	High Street

In general a criteria range can have any number of columns each specifying a fieldname, and any number of rows, each specifying a set of values that the records you are interested in must have. That is, if your criteria range is:

field1	field2	field3	field4
c1		c2	
c3	c4		c5

then you would select records that satisfied (c1 and c2) or (c3 and c4 and c5).

For example:

G	H
NAME	ADDRESS
Smith	
	High Street

specifies a record that has NAME equal to Smith OR an ADDRESS equal to High Street. Whereas:

	G	H
	NAME	ADDRESS
	Jones	Acacia Ave

specifies a record that has NAME equal to Jones AND an ADDRESS equal to Acacia Ave.

» Notice that if you leave a blank line in the criteria range then all the records will be selected as a blank line matches everything.

» Find and Delete

There are two Data commands that don't use an output range. The Data,Find command simply moves the cursor to the first record in the database that matches the conditions in the criteria range and the Data,Delete command will erase from the database all the records that match the condition in the criteria range.

When using the Data,Find command the up and down arrow keys move you on to the next record in the input range that matches the conditions in the criteria range. Pressing any other key ends the Data,Find command, as does selecting the command Data,Exit Data Find.

The Data,Delete command can be used to remove records that match the criteria from the database. You are given one opportunity to make up your mind that you really do want to delete the records. If you click on the OK button the records are deleted. While you might be able to reverse the delete using the Undo command, this is dependent on the amount of memory available so take great care and save the sheet before deleting records.

» Extracting data

Data,Extract is the only database command that makes use of the Extract range. The Extract range is similar to the criteria range in that its first row contains fieldnames. Only those fields named in the Extract range are copied from the database. The number of rows in the Extract range governs the maximum number of records that will be transferred.

For example, if you want to list only the names of people with salaries over 5000 you would set up a suitable criteria range and an extract range that only had the field NAME specified in its first row and then as many empty cells below it as you expected to need. If you wanted to know the person's address as well then you would include a second column headed ADDRESS in the Extract range.

The only option that you have in using the Data,Extract command is whether or not to include duplicated records in the extract range. If you check the Unique box then duplicates are eliminated.

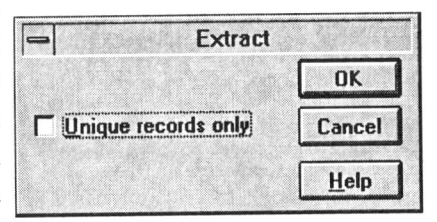

» Practical - Salary database

A simple name and salary database provides a useful example of database construction and use.

	A	B	C	D	E	F
1	NAME	ADDRESS	TEL	SALARY	DEPT	TOP SALARY
2	Smith	Acacia Ave	123-4567	5000	Sales	6000
3	Jones	High Street	891-2345	8000	Publicity	10000
4	Swift	Wood Lane	345-6789	4000	Sales	4000
5	Bloggs	Garden Ave	456-7890	3000	Sales	4000
6	Smith	Acacia Ave	123-4567	5000	Publicity	5000
7						

Having entered data, you also have to set up the database area using the command Data,Database Set or by defining the name Database as A1:F6. After this you can browse the database using the Data,Form command and set criteria to find records which you are interested in. Suppose you want to make a list of all of the personnel who earn more than 4000. For this you need a criteria range and an extract range.

The criteria range could be as simple as a pair of cells, one with the fieldname SALARY and the other containing the condition. However, it is easier to drag a copy of the entire set of fieldnames to H1:M1 and set the criteria range to be H1:M2. A single line will do for the criteria range in this instance.

	H	I	J	K	L	M	N
1	NAME	ADDRESS	TEL	SALARY	DEPT	TOP SALARY	
2				>4000			
3							
4							

Next we need an extract range. This too is most easily constructed by dragging a copy of the fieldnames to a new location but in this case we only need to list NAME, ADDRESS and SALARY and so typing the fieldnames into P1:R1 is almost as easy. Finally the extract range needs to be set to P1:R11, giving a total capacity of 10 records in the output range. The command Data,Extract will now transfer all the records that match the criteria into the extract area.

	P	Q	R
1	NAME	ADDRESS	SALARY
2	Smith	Acacia Ave	5000
3	Jones	High Street	8000
4	Smith	Acacia Ave	5000
5			
6			

If you check the Unique records only box in the Extract dialog box then duplicates will be removed from the extract range.

» Database functions

There are also a range of special database functions, similar to the list functions such as SUM, COUNT etc., which calculate their results on a given field of a database taking into account the conditions specified in a criteria range. It is not difficult to see that these database functions can be very useful in calculating quantities based only on records that satisfy some condition. For example, you could work out the total salary paid to all the employees in a particular department.

The functions are:

DAVERAGE	average
DCOUNT	count numeric cells
DCOUNTA	count non blank cells
DMAX	maximum
DMIN	minimum
DSTDEV	sample standard deviation
DSTDEVP	population standard deviation
DSUM	sum
DVAR	sample variance
DVARP	population variance

There is also one new function DGET which returns a single value from the database field specified. If more than one record satisfies the criteria then the error condition #NUM is returned.

Each database function needs three things specified:

» the input range

» the column number or name of the field in the input range to be used in the calculation

» a criteria range to select the records to be used

For example, DSUM(A1:E6,2,H1:J2) will sum all entries in the field in column B (i.e. column 2) of the records in the database block A1:E6 that meet the conditions in the criteria range H1:J2.

Notice that the database functions can use any range in the spreadsheet as the database and criteria tables and not just the ones you have defined.

» Practical - Summing salary

Using the previous salary database it isn't difficult to find the total salary bill for the sales department. To do this enter the formula

=DSUM(Database,"SALARY",Criteria)

into any free and convenient cell and enter Sales into the criteria range under the fieldname DEPT. The DSUM function will add up all of the values in the SALARY column that meet the criteria of having DEPT equal to Sales.

In this example, the predefined names Database and Criteria were used to define the database and criteria ranges in the function. If you want to, you can use any range names that you have defined or any range references. The only restriction is that the database and criteria ranges should be laid out correctly, complete with fieldnames.

If you try modifying the contents of the criteria range you will begin to see the power of the database functions. Each time you change the criteria the function is re-evaluated using only those records that match.

» Sorting

Although you can find records in a database that has any order there is a lot to be said for having records sorted into order. For example, if you are searching for a record with a NAME field equal to Smith and the records are sorted into name order then you know that the first Smith that you find is the first of a block that contains all the Smiths in the database. Although sorting is never necessary it often makes database use easier.

To sort your database all you have to do is select the block of data that you want to sort and use the command Data,Sort which displays the Sort dialog box.

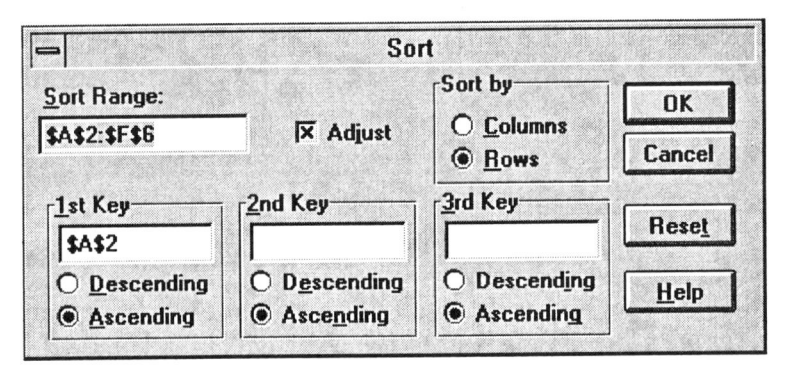

It is important that you specify the entire block that contains your data - sorting only half of each record would be a disaster. In fact, as sorting can modify your spreadsheet in a way that cannot be reversed, it is a good idea to always save your spreadsheet before any sort operation.

You can specify up to three fields to sort on. These are generally referred to as "key fields". You can also specify if the sort is to be ascending or descending and you can sort the columns or the rows in the range.

Once the keys and sort order have been specified you can click on the OK button to begin the sort. Then the database is sorted into order on the first key, then it is sorted on the second key and so on.

For example, suppose you have a database that contains the fields INITIAL and SURNAME in columns A and B you could specify 1st Key as B and 2nd Key as A. This would result in a database sorted on surname and each group of surnames sorted into order on initial. That is A.Smith would be listed before B.Smith and so on. Whenever you specify a key you are given the opportunity to alter the order of the sort. Ascending order puts A and 0 at the top of the spreadsheet and Descending order puts A and 0 at the bottom of the spreadsheet.

When columns or rows are moved during a sort there is the question of adjusting formulae, see Chapter 3. If you check the Adjust box then any formulae are adjusted. Unless you have been exact with your use of $ signs to indicate absolute and relative references you will find that the adjustment doesn't work properly.

If you want to sort on more than three keys then simply use the Data,Sort command more than once. Sort the minor keys first and work up towards the primary key. For example, if you want to sort the database on five keys - key1, key2, key3, key4 and key5, then the correct way to do it is first sort on key3 as 1stkey, key4 as 2ndkey and key5 as 3rdkey. Then sort again on key1 as 1stkey and key2 as 2ndkey.

An important fact that is sometimes overlooked is that:

》 sorting can be done on any spreadsheet range, not just database tables.

A handy tip that is worth knowing is to include a column or row of sequential numbers along with the sorted data. These can be generated using the Data,Series command, see later. If you want to return the data to its original order before the sort then all you have to do is to sort on the column or row to return the numbers to their original sequence.

» Practical - Sorting the database

Using the Salary database we can perform a sort on department as 1stkey and salary as 2ndkey. To do this select the database area but not including the fieldnames in the top row and fill in the Data,Sort dialog box as follows:

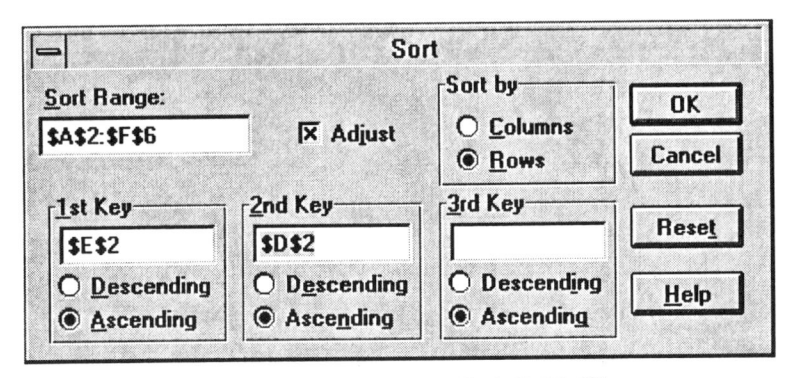

```
┌─────────────────────────── Sort ───────────────────────────┐
│  Sort Range:              ┌─Sort by──────┐    ┌────────┐   │
│  ┌──────────┐             │  ○ Columns   │    │   OK   │   │
│  │ $A$2:$F$6│  [X] Adjust │  ● Rows      │    └────────┘   │
│  └──────────┘             └──────────────┘    ┌────────┐   │
│                                                │ Cancel │   │
│  ┌─1st Key────┐ ┌─2nd Key────┐ ┌─3rd Key────┐  └────────┘   │
│  │ $E$2       │ │ $D$2       │ │            │  ┌────────┐   │
│  └────────────┘ └────────────┘ └────────────┘  │ Reset  │   │
│  ○ Descending   ○ Descending   ○ Descending    └────────┘   │
│  ● Ascending    ● Ascending    ● Ascending     ┌────────┐   │
│                                                │  Help  │   │
│                                                └────────┘   │
└─────────────────────────────────────────────────────────────┘
```

» Importing and exporting dBASE files

Although SCW provides a very easy to use database facility there are times when you want to use it in conjunction with other database programs. The best known of these is dBASE III. SCW allows you to load and save files in dBASE format. All you have to do is select DBF as the file type in the Save or Open dialog box. You can import DBF files to either sheets or models. The loading of a DBF file to a model is more complicated and often more useful than loading it to a sheet. This is discussed in *Multidimensional Modelling with CA-SuperCalc for Windows*.

» Practical - A holiday flight database

Databases are usually thought of as large and fairly permanent programs but they can actually be very useful when day to day decisions involve collecting information. This template was created to discover which of a number of possible flights to Southern Spain most closely matched the travelling requirements of a group wanting to spend Christmas in the sun. It illustrates how easy it is to search through data and sort it in meaningful ways once you have entered it into a data range. As well as providing a model for similar circumstances, it should suggest other uses for SCW's database facilities.

The data was gathered from phone calls and brochures. From the traveller's point of view the ideal flight would depart in the afternoon of 18th December from a Northern airport bound for Almeria and allow for a stay of three weeks. By the time the search was initiated no seats were available on flights that met these requirements so the database was designed to answer queries about the airport of departure, the airport of arrival, the duration of the stay up to the limit of 21 days, the date and time of departure and the price.

	A	B	C	D	E	F	G
1	NAME	DEPARTURE	DESTINATION	DATE	TIME	DAYS	PRICE
2	Horizon	Manchester	Alicante	17-Dec	07:15:00 AM	21	£199.00
3	Horizon	Gatwick	Almeria	15-Dec	03:15:00 PM	21	£97.00
4	Horizon	Glasgow	Alicante	17-Dec	08:00:00 AM	21	£145.00
5	Horizon	Birmingham	Alicante	20-Dec	07:45:00 PM	21	£180.00
6	Horizon	Gatwick	Alicante	17-Dec	07:30:00 PM	21	£187.00
7	Horizon	Newcastle	Almeria	18-Dec	02:30:00 PM	14	£195.00
8	Flight Sales	Newcastle	Alicante	20-Dec	08:00:00 AM	14	£179.00
9	Flight Sales	Gatwick	Alicante	20-Dec	04:30:00 PM	14	£174.00
10	Flight Sales	Gatwick	Murcia	20-Dec	03:10:00 PM	21	£128.00
11	Owners Abroad	Gatwick	Murcia	20-Dec	03:10:00 PM	14	£128.00
12	Owners Abroad	Gatwick	Murcia	24-Dec	03:00:00 PM	14	£132.00
13	Owners Abroad	Gatwick	Alicante	17-Dec	08:10:00 AM	14	£129.00
14	Monarch	Gatwick	Alicante	24-Dec	04:40:00 PM	21	£129.00
15	Monarch	Manchester	Alicante	17-Dec	08:40:00 AM	21	£149.00
16	Beach Villas	Gatwick	Alicante	17-Dec	06:10:00 PM	21	£144.00
17	Falcon	Gatwick	Murcia	17-Dec	03:00:00 PM	21	£157.00
18	Tarleton	Gatwick	Almeria	21-Dec	10:30:00 AM	14	£130.00
19							

Although it was quite possible to browse and search the database using the Data Form it was thought more convenient to make a list of all flights meeting the search criteria so that they could be printed out. This implies using the Data,Extract command and both a criteria and an extract range. The criteria range was set up at I1:O2 and contains an exact copy of the fieldnames. The Extract range was set up to be Q1:V16 and again all of the fieldnames were copied and suitable formats applied.

If you now enter Manchester in the DEPARTURE field of the criteria range and use the command Data,Extract you will see all the Manchester flights listed in the extract range. One problem that most users have is that of getting to the criteria or extract range quickly. The solution to the problem is to use the Goto command. Pressing F5 produces a list of range names from which you can select Criteria or Extract.

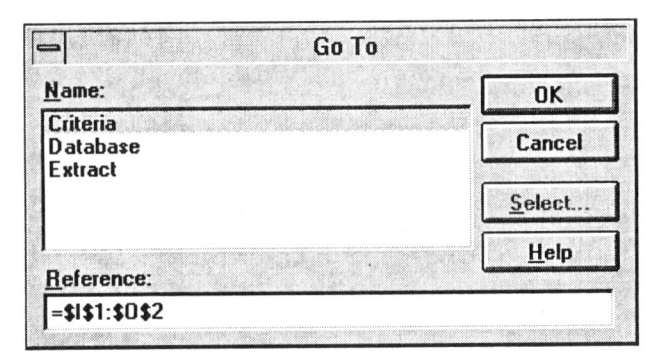

```
┌─────────────────────── Go To ───────────────────────┐
│  Name:                                  ┌────────┐  │
│  ┌──────────────────────────────┐       │   OK   │  │
│  │ Criteria                     │       └────────┘  │
│  │ Database                     │       ┌────────┐  │
│  │ Extract                      │       │ Cancel │  │
│  │                              │       └────────┘  │
│  │                              │       ┌────────┐  │
│  │                              │       │ Select.│  │
│  │                              │       └────────┘  │
│  │                              │       ┌────────┐  │
│  └──────────────────────────────┘       │  Help  │  │
│  Reference:                             └────────┘  │
│  ┌──────────────────────────────┐                   │
│  │ =$I$1:$O$2                   │                   │
│  └──────────────────────────────┘                   │
└─────────────────────────────────────────────────────┘
```

As explained earlier in the chapter, as well as searching for strings by typing in an exact match you can search for partial matches using the ? and * symbols to stand in place of one or more characters. So to look for all the flights from Birmingham you could simply type B* in the criteria table. Notice that if you want to find all the flights to Almeria you need to enter Alm* otherwise the Alicante flights will also match. You can also select records that do not match a criterion by using the ~ (tilde). For example G* would find all flights from Gatwick and Glasgow while ~G* would find flights from airports other than Gatwick or Glasgow. Notice that to exclude only Gatwick flights you would write the condition as ~Ga*.

You can select records on combinations of conditions. For example, to rule out flights costing more than £150 you would specify the condition that the price should be less than or equal to £150 by typing <=150 in the PRICE column of the criteria range. You can also use the dates and times in conditions. Suppose our intended travellers would find it difficult to catch a flight departing before 3.00p.m. - to specify this condition you would need to use the condition <15:00. Typing in <3:00 PM would fail because this is not automatically recognised as a time by SCW.

However not all conditions are so easy to specify. For example, you cannot use the function WEEKDAY to discover which flights depart on a given weekday by entering a condition. The only way of doing this is by adding a new column and working out the day of the week that each fight departs.

» Data series

A common requirement whenever you are creating a table or a database is to enter a range of values. The SCW Data,Series command can be used to automatically insert a series of values. It can do this either by extending the series that you have typed in or by being told the start, finish and increment. For example, if you have typed 1 into A1 and 2 into A2 you can automatically extend the series by selecting the range that you want the finished series to occupy, A1:A10 say, and using the Data,Series command. The Series dialog box that appears gives you the option of controlling the sequence of values.

If the Fill by Example option is checked the first two values in the range are used to predict the rest. The first value is used as the start value and the difference between it and the second value is used as the step value. This means that for numeric values the Fill by example method only works for simple arithmetic progressions such as 1,2,3 or 2,4,6,8 and so on. This makes the Data,Series command look a bit weak - but not so!

If you try the Data,Series command on text you will be pleasantly surprised to find that it knows about the days of the week and the months of the year. You can enter Mon and it will extend the series to Tue, Wed and so on. Not only this but it will extend a series of names such as Q1, Q2 to Q3, Q4 and so on. In fact any series of names ending in a numeric value will be extended in this way. So for example, if you type in Item 1, Item 2 the Data,Series command will extend this to Item 3, Item 4 and so on.

You can also automatically extend a series of dates and/or times. This almost goes without saying because a date/time series is just a sequence of numeric date/time serial numbers and in this sense no different from any other. However, the Data,Series command also applies the formatting of the first cell to all of the other cells in the range - so the sequence of dates and times does look correct.

Of course there will be times when Fill by Example isn't clever enough to work out what the pattern should be. In this case you need to use the Fill as Specified option to determine the series manually. In this case enter the start, stop and step values in the boxes provided. Notice that the series range always takes precedence over the stop value. That is, a Data,Series command will never store data outside the indicated range. If you want to change the range simply place the cursor in the text box and either type in a new value or point at the new range. If you don't enter a final value then the entire range is filled with values.

As well as a Linear fill, where the step is added to each preceding value, you can also opt for a Growth fill. In this case the step value is a multiplier. Each new value is generated from the preceding value by multiplying by the step+1. For example, if you set a start value of 1 and a step of 1 the values are multiplied by 2 each time giving the series 1,2,4,8 and so on. The only difficult part of this is remembering that the multiplier is the step value plus one!

You can also enter date series by entering a start, step and stop value but in this case you need to specify the units that step size is in. You can select day, week, month or year and the Data,Series command will generate a series of dates starting on the date entered as the start date and increasing by the specified step.

The main difficulty with generating a series of dates or times is that you cannot enter a date or time directly into the Start Value or Stop Value text box. The solution to the problem is to enter the starting date or time into the first cell in the series.

You can do this using any of the standard date or time formats and when you open the Series dialog box the corresponding date or time serial number will be entered as the default start value.

In most cases you want to fill a row or a column with data values but you can fill a rectangular range. In this case you also have to specify whether you want the range filled in row or column order. If you select column order then the data series is stored in each column of the range starting a new column only when the current one is full. Row order fills the rows first.

Key points

» A database can be thought of as either a collection of record cards or a table of values.

» SCW allows you to enter and work with a database as a table of values with fieldnames in the first row.

» The area used for the database has to be assigned the range name Database.

» You can browse, edit and enter new data into a database using the Data,Form command. This displays one line of the table at a time in record format.

» To select records using the Data,Form command you have to specify criteria.

» If you want to extract a list of records using Data,Extract or browse through the table using Data,Select you have first to assign the range name Criteria to the range used for specifying conditions. This has to contain fieldnames in the first row.

» To use the Data,Extract command you also have to assign the range name Extract to a range.

» The database functions perform operations corresponding to standard functions such as SUM but only on records that meet the conditions specified in a criteria range.

» You can sort a database or any spreadsheet range using the Data,Sort command.

» The Data,Series command will automatically generate a sequence of values from the first few example entries or you can use specified start, step and stop values.

Chapter 11

Models and 3D

So far this book has concentrated on making use of sheets. Sheets are simple, easy to use and ideal for many of the everyday tasks that spreadsheets have to handle. However, the model, the other type of spreadsheet that SCW has to offer, is a much more powerful tool. Its main strength is in working with data that has more than two dimensions but the very feature that makes it powerful also has the capacity to confuse new users.

In this chapter we examine the model in a more limited role than it is capable of - that of the multidimensional spreadsheet. We look at it mainly as a replacement for SC5's 3D spreadsheet with particular reference to importing existing multi-page .CAL files. If you want to know all about its use as a multidimensional modelling tool, and about data modelling and analysis in general, then see *Multidimensional Modelling with CA-SuperCalc for Windows.*

» Meet the model

Opening a new model is just as easy as opening a new sheet - click on the open tool or use the File,New command and select Model in the dialog box that appears. Your first, and even second, sight of a model will strike you as an odd mixture of the familiar and the unfamiliar.

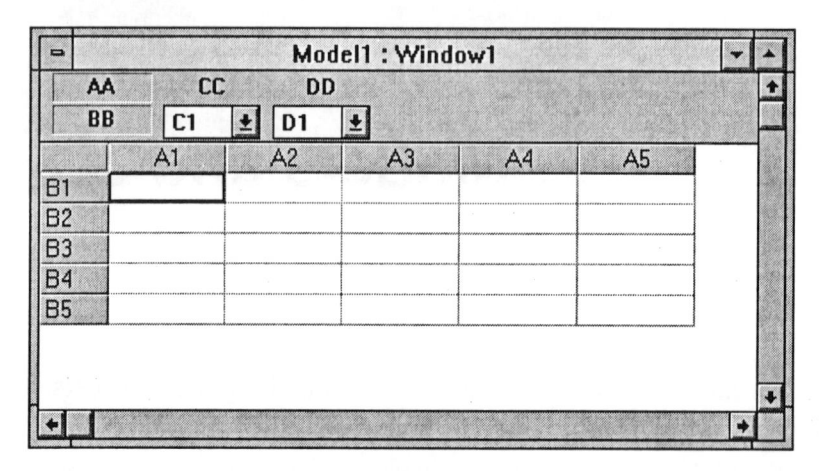

```
                    Model1 : Window1
       AA       CC       DD
       BB     C1       D1
              A1      A2      A3      A4      A5
       B1
       B2
       B3
       B4
       B5
```

There are cells visible in what looks like a 2D spreadsheet but instead of huge working area there seem to be only a few cells. There are rows and columns but instead of being named column A, B, C and row 1,2 3 they appear to have names that would be cell references in a sheet! There are also two mysterious looking boxes at the top of the model labelled CC and DD.

In fact very little of what you see needs very much by way of explanation. In a 2D sheet the rows and columns correspond to the two dimensions. In the case of a model you can work with any number of dimensions and so it isn't reasonable to call two of them row and column and then find other odd names for the rest. A more reasonable scheme is to call them dimension AA, BB, CC and so on. As the default model that is created for you has four dimensions this explains the AA, BB, CC and DD at the top of the model. Each dimension

Meet the model **277**

will have a number of items which correspond to the number of rows or columns in a 2D sheet. By default every new model is created with five items on each dimension, named by the first letter of the dimension name and a digit. So for example, dimension AA has items A1, A2, A3 and so on. You can think of these item names as playing the same role as the row and column numbers and letters.

Now you should be able to see that what we have in a model is very much the extension of a sheet beyond two dimensions. The final question is why is the number of cells limited? The answer is that once you have a multidimensional spreadsheet the number of cells grows very rapidly. For example, in the default model with four dimensions each with five items the total number of cells is 5x5x5x5 or 625. There are other and deeper reasons why the number of cells is limited but for now all you really need to know is that you can add or delete items from dimensions to increase or decrease the number of cells available and on display. You can also change the dimension and item names.

So to summarise:

» the default model has four dimensions called AA, BB, CC and DD.

» Each dimension has five items called A1 to A5, B1 to B5 and so on.

» You can add and delete dimensions and items to customise the model.

» Dimension and item names can be changed.

» A 3D model

The ideas involved in a model look a lot simpler if we reduce the number of dimensions to three. A 3D model is not only easier to understand it is very similar to the 3D spreadsheet that was introduced in SC5.

To reduce the default four-dimensional model to 3D all you have to do is delete the DD dimension. Do this using the command Edit,Delete Dimension and then select dimension DD in the dialog box that appears.

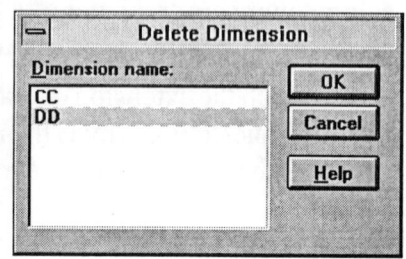

With only three dimensions you can imagine the model as being the equivalent of a "book" of sheets. You can think of the AA and BB dimensions as the rows and columns in a standard sheet and the CC dimension as governing which "page" you are looking at and working with - the current "page" number being shown in the text box at the top left of the model display.

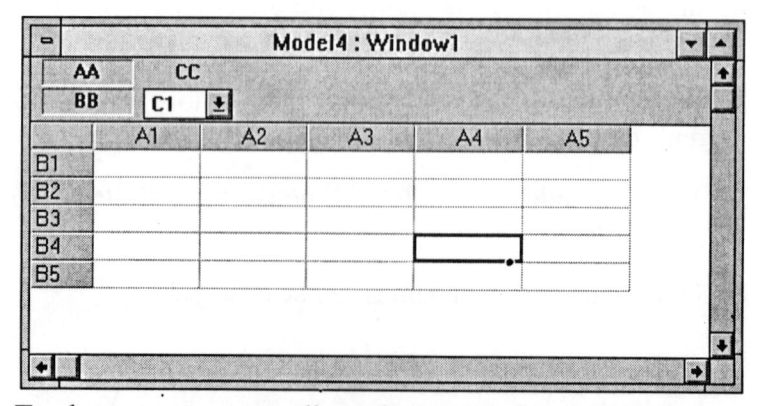

To choose a new page all you have to do is select a new item on the CC dimension - C2, C3 and so on. Each page is a complete 2D sheet just like the first.

If you already know how to use an SC5 3D spreadsheet this view of the model will be very comforting but there are still some important differences. In particular, the way that cell references are written is different. In a model you specify a cell by giving its value on each of the dimensions using a dot as a separator. So for example the cell in the top left hand corner of the first page is

    A1.B1.C1

This is easy enough and you can use cell references like this if you want to but in practice there is a shorter way to write it. SCW uses the rule that any dimension that you don't specify within a cell reference is the same as the cell that it is stored in. This is referred to as "underspecification" in SCW's jargon. As all of the cells in the C1 page have the same value on the CC dimension you don't have to quote it when writing formulae. That is, you can write A1.B1.C1 as A1.B1.

» Ranges

With this change in how cell references are written you can carry on using all of the techniques that you have learned in using sheets in writing formulae. For example,

    =SUM(A1.B1:A1.B4)

will add up the first four cells in column A1. However if you enter this formula into a model you will discover that the way that the range is written is automatically modified to read

    A1.(B1:B4)

This reflects the very different way a model handles ranges compared to a 2D sheet. If you want to ignore this difference for the time being then you can. The only penalty is that your range references will be changed to the standard model format. You can also enter range references by pointing, and again SCW uses its standard model format.

The reason for the new way of writing range references is that it works in the same way no matter how many dimensions are involved. The key idea is that of a dimension range. A dimension range is simply a range of items on the specified dimension. For example, A2:A4 is a dimension range that specifies the items A2, A3 and A4.

A1	A2	A3	A4	A5

When you write a multi-dimensional range reference you can include a dimension range for each dimension. The cells selected are the intersection of all of the dimension ranges. For example, the range

(A2:A4).(B2:B3)

is the block of cells that has cell references A2 to A4 on the AA dimension and B2 to B3 on the BB dimension. You can imagine this as being the intersection of the dimension ranges on each of the dimensions.

	A1	A2	A3	A4	A5
B1					
B2					
B3					
B4					
B5					

The same idea applies even when the dimension range is only a single item. For example, the formula given earlier

SUM(A1.B1:A1:B4)

makes use of the range (A1.A1).(B1:B4) which is more simply written A1.(B1:B4), i.e. what in a sheet would have been referred to as part of a column.

	A1	A2
B1		
B2		
B3		
B4		
B5		

A good way of thinking about this alternative approach to defining ranges is to contrast it with the method used in a sheet. In a sheet a range is defined by specifying the two opposite corners of the rectangle. In a model you specify the two sides.

» Absolute and relative

All model cell references are absolute. If you enter a cell reference to A1.B1.C1 and copy it to another cell then it will not be changed in any way and will still read A1.B1.C1. However, the idea of not quoting dimensions that are the same as the cell that the reference is stored in gives a sort of automatic relative property to cell references. For example, if you want to sum the column A1.(B1:B4) you can use the formula

=SUM((B1:B4))

as long as the formula is stored in a cell in the same column. The reason is of course that as long as the formula is stored in a cell that has a value of A1 on the AA dimension this is the default value. (SCW adds the extra brackets automatically if you don't type them.)

Now consider what happens if you copy this formula to a cell in "column" A2. The formula will read exactly the same - no adjustment will be performed - but now, because it is stored in A2, it will add up the values in its column. In other words, because the value of the AA dimension is supplied by default and is the same as the column that the formula is stored in it actually means "sum the values from B1:B4 in the current column". This makes it more or less a relative range reference.

In the same way all of the formulae written on a particular page of a 3D model refer by default to the page they are stored on. If they are copied to another page then they work on the same rows and columns on that page.

» Relative offsets

In most cases a formula will be self-adjusting as long as you leave out any dimension values that are the same as the cell the formula is stored in. However, there are still times when you need to write a truly relative reference. For example, how can you write a formula that adds 3 to the cell to the immediate left. There is no way of entering this as relative simply by omitting a dimension. For example, if the cell is A2.B1 then the formula to add 3 to the cell to its immediate left is:

=A1+3

You can omit the B1 because they are in the same row. This formula is relative in the sense that if you copy it down the same column it will add 3 to the cell to the immediate left. However if you copy it to a new column it will still read A1+3 and add 3 to the cell in the same row but still in column A1.

To enable you to write truly relative cell references, SCW allows you to write a dimension name followed by an offset in square brackets. For example, AA[-1] means one less than the value of the AA dimension in the current cell - which is of course another way of saying the cell to the immediate left. If you enter the formula

=AA[-1]+3

into A2.B1 then the reference is to A1.B1. If this is copied to cell A3.B4 then the reference is to A2.B4 and so on. Of course the form of the formula doesn't change - it reads the same no matter where it is copied - but its meaning does.

You can even make use of model style relative offsets in a sheet. In this case the dimensions are R for rows and C for columns. For example, R[1].C[1] is the cell one row down and one column to the right. If you enter a cell reference in this style into a sheet it is immediately converted into the usual "A1" form.

» Importing SC5 3D sheets

Now we know just enough to be able to understand the workings of a model in as far as they parallel those of a typical 3D spreadsheet. In particular, we know enough to be able to understand the treatment of an imported SC5 3D spreadsheet. Looking at such an imported spreadsheet is not only useful to users who want to actually do this but it provides an excellent example of how 3D models compare to 3D spreadsheets.

To import an SC5 spreadsheet all you have to do is use the File, Open command and change the List Files of Type to SuperCalc5.x .CAL and select the SC5 file you want to import. If the spreadsheet is 2D you are given the choice of importing it as a sheet or a model. In most cases a sheet will be more appropriate because it will result in a conversion that is much closer to the original. However if the SC5 sheet made use of the 3D facilities then you can only open it as a model.

In this case the model will have only three dimensions called COL, ROW and PAGE. These correspond to the rows, columns and pages in the original SC5 spreadsheet. The items on the COL dimension have column letter names A, B, and so on, the ROW dimension has row numbers 1,2, and so on and the PAGE dimension has names like PAGE1, PAGE2 and so on. This is very nearly the same as the SC5 original and therefore easy to understand.

For example, a spreadsheet summarising the sale of wine at different outlets for each of three months, one page per month and a final page of totals was constructed as a 3D SC5 spreadsheet - WINE.CAL. (This spreadsheet was described in the book *SuperCalc Professional* and is also included on the companion disk to this book.)

	A	B	C	D	E	F	G
1	Sales of Red Wine						
2	April 1991						
3		Bordeaux	Bordeaux	Burgundy	Rioja	Rioja	Total
4		78	83	86	86	87	
5	High Street	406	789	343	376	256	2170
6	Market Place	236	348	204	340	503	1631
7	Long Lane	68	134	172	38	143	555
8	Back Avenue	55	76	160	52	26	369
9							
10	Total	765	1347	879	806	928	4725

The result of importing this 3D spreadsheet looks reassuringly familiar - the row and column layouts are the same and even the individual pages correspond to the original pages. However if you look at the one of the formulae that calculate the column sums things begin to look different. For example, in the original 3D spreadsheet the formula that summed the values in column B was

> SUM(B5:B8)

in the 3D model it is

> =SUM(COL[0].(ROW[-5]:ROW[-2]))

In fact this is the formula that can be found working out each of the column sums! You should now be able to see how it works. The range reference within the sum is composed of all relative references. The COL[0] simply mean "this column" and ROW[-5]:ROW[-2] simply means five rows above to two rows above the current cell. Put the two parts together and the range reference clearly says " the cells from five rows above to two rows above this cell in the same column".

You should also be able to see that this one formula will successfully add up each of the columns when copied to the appropriate location.

All relative spreadsheet references are converted into offsets in this way and all ranges are converted into dimension ranges. Absolute references are converted to model references that look closer to the original. For example, if a 3D sheet contained the reference $A$1 then this would be converted into A.'1' in the model. The only complication is the need to surround the 1 with single quotes. This is because any dimension item that could be confused with something else, i.e. the number 1 in this case, has to be enclosed in quotes.

Once you have grasped the different form of cell and range references that's really all there is to understanding the way that imported 3D SC5 spreadsheets work. Apart from this all of the functions are more or less the same. You should be able to make sense of the row, column and page structure quite easily. The biggest problem is that you will not find any trace of any graphs or charts that were defined in the original and models cannot support database operations. The charts are easy enough to recreate and this is more a nuisance than a serious problem. The best way to handle the database problem is to import the 3D sheet as a model and then use Cut and Paste to transfer the data to a newly opened sheet which does support database operations.

» 3D spreadsheet to model

The ability to rename both dimensions and items is important when it comes to custom built multidimensional models. In a traditional spreadsheet you often make use of a set of column headings and sometimes a set of row headings. These headings identify the data stored in the adjacent cells and often play a part in the formulae that manipulate the data as range names. When you are constructing a model from scratch there is no need to include such headings within the spreadsheet because they can be used as item names on a suitably named dimension. This sounds complicated but an example will demonstrate how simple it really is.

In the case of the Wine spreadsheet each of the columns was headed by the name of a particular wine. In a sense the column dimension is in fact Wine Type - so why not give it this name rather than COLS. You can rename any dimension using the Edit, Rename command. You can select any of the dimension names in the Rename dialog box and type in its new name. Clicking on the Rename button completes the operation and gives the opportunity to rename the other dimensions. In this case it seems reasonable to change the row dimension to Outlet and the Page dimension to Month.

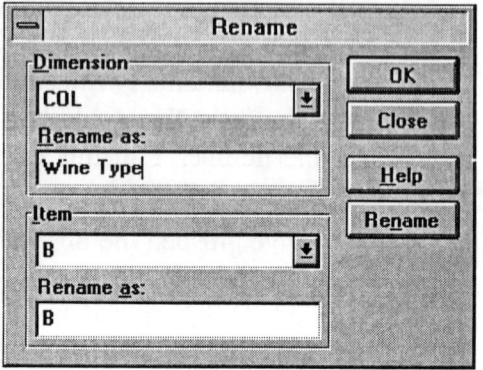

	A	B	C	D	E	F	G
1	Sales of Red Wine						
2	April 1991						
3		Bordeaux	Bordeaux	Burgundy	Rioja	Rioja	Total
4		78	83	86	86	87	
5	High Street	406	789	343	376	256	2170
6	Market Place	236	348	204	340	503	1631
7	Long Lane	68	134	172	38	143	555
8	Back Avenue	55	76	160	52	26	369
9							
10	Total	765	1347	879	806	928	4725

3D spreadsheet to model 287

With these changes the Wine 3D model now looks like a halfway house. It no longer calls its rows and columns ROW and COL but it still uses column letters and row numbers. Clearly the next step is to change the items on each dimension to be the same as the headings. You can change any dimension item name to something else simply by double clicking on it. This changes the item's box in the model border into an edit box where you can type the new name.

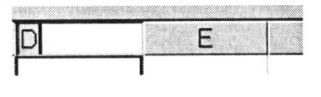

Alternatively you can use the command Edit, Rename which as well as allowing you to change dimension names also allows you to change item names. Obviously if you are transferring headings that were in the body of a spreadsheet to item names copy and paste is the way to do it - remember that Ctrl-C is copy and Ctrl-V is paste.

After changing the column letters to the wine names the next job is to convert the row numbers to the names of the shops. After this is completed, and after adjusting the column widths so that everything is visible, the result is beginning to look more like a custom built model but it still has additional rows that are used for the old headings and the pages are still called Page1, Page2 and so on.

Wine Type	Month						
Outlet	PAGE1						
	A	Bordeaux 78	Bordeaux 83	Burgundy 86	Rioja 86	Rioja 87	Totals by store
1	Sales of Red Wine						
2	April 1991						
3		Bordeaux	Bordeaux	Burgundy	Rioja	Rioja	Total
4		78	83	86	86	87	
High Street	High Street	406	789	343	376	256	2170
Market Place	Market Place	236	348	204	340	503	1631
Long Lane	Long Lane	68	134	172	143	555	1072
Back Avenue	Back Avenue	55	76	160	52	26	369
9							
Total	Total	765	1347	879	911	1340	5242

The next and final step in the transformation of the 3D spreadsheet into a model is to rename the old Page dimension items to April, May, June and Totals using the Edit,Rename command and to get rid of the rows and columns that store the now redundant headings. Getting rid of items is just a matter of selecting the items and then using the Edit,Delete Item command. If you want to add extra items you can use the Edit,Insert Item command.

		Bordeaux 78	Bordeaux 83	Burgundy 86	Rioja 86	Rioja 87	Totals by store
High Street		406	789	343	376	256	2170
Market Place		236	348	204	340	503	1631
Long Lane		68	134	172	143	555	1072
Back Avenue		55	76	160	52	26	369
Totals by wine		765	1347	879	911	1340	5242

(Wine Type: Outlet; Month: April) — WINE3.MDL : Window1

The final version of the 3D spreadsheet looks much more like a model but there is still an important difference. The formulae that it contains are still written in the old spreadsheet relative style. For example, the column sums are

=SUM(Wine Type[0].(Outlet[-4]:Outlet[-1]))

which you should recognise as the original formula with the dimension names changed. If the model had been built from scratch then a more sensible formula would have been:

=SUM((High Street:Back Avenue))

and this would have worked for all of the column sums. The row sums would have been

=SUM((Bordeaux 78 :Rioja 87))

and the totals on the final page would have been

=SUM((April:June))

The easiest way of entering these formula is to delete the originals and use the autosum tool!

» Global formulae

Surprisingly, even with these changes the model is still not as it should be if constructed from scratch. The reason is that the formula have all been copied into the cells that use them. This is a workable method but not really in the spirit of using the multidimensional model. Because any dimension that isn't specified is taken to be the same as the cell that the formula is stored in, it is very often the case that exactly the same formula will work at more than one location.

For example, in the Wine model the formula which works out the column sums is

=SUM((High Street:Back Avenue))

and this works exactly as written in each of the cells in which the column total is needed. Instead of storing a copy of this formula in each of the cells you can opt to store a single copy - a global formula and then say which cells it applies to.

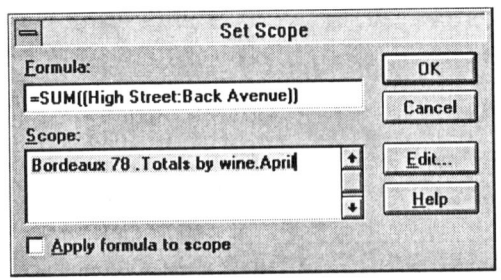

You can convert any formula into a global formula by selecting it and then clicking on the Global button. This displays the Set Scope dialog box where you can see and change the scope of the formula.

"Scope" is model jargon for the range that the formula is evaluated for. You can think of it as being the same as the range that you would copy the formula to. By default a formula's scope is just the cell into which it has been entered by clicking on the Edit button but you can change this.

The Edit Scope dialog box allows you to build up a range specification by selecting the dimension and the items to be included in the range. For example, in this case the SUM formula should be applied to all of the wine types and the

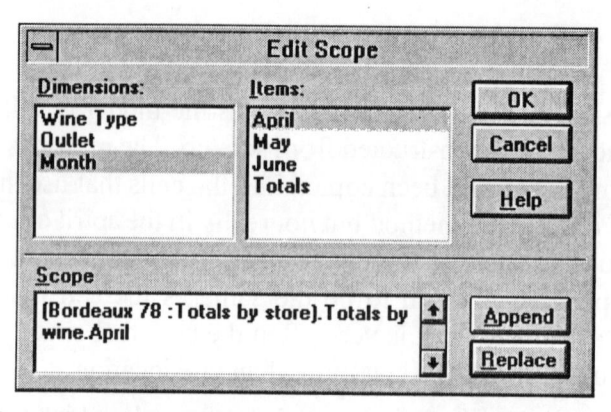

![Edit Scope dialog box showing Dimensions: Wine Type, Outlet, Month; Items: April, May, June, Totals; Scope: (Bordeaux 78 :Totals by store).Totals by wine.April; with OK, Cancel, Help, Append, Replace buttons]

totals and so the dimension range is changed to (Bordeaux 78 :Totals by store). This is achieved by selecting the range in the list of items and then clicking on the Replace button. You can add items to a dimension range by clicking on the Append button or replace the existing dimension range by clicking on the append button. As well as applying to the full range of wine types, the formula also should apply to each of the months and so the final scope is:

Month.Totals by wine.Wine Type

Finally to make the formula effective in this range you have to select the Apply Formula to Scope box in the Set Scope dialog box. If you do this you will find that the sum is formed for each wine column in each of the months. This appears to be the same as copying the formula into each of the cells indicated by its scope but the difference is that only a single copy of the global formula is used. If you edit the global formula then every cell that uses it is updated to the new version.

There are many other advantages of using a global formula but they only become apparent when you start to investigate the structure of a model and how it can be edited. For now just think of the scope of a formula as the range into which you would otherwise copy it.

» How far?

If you create a 3D model by importing an SC5 3D spreadsheet the question is how far should you go in converting it into a true model? The answer depends on your reasons for wanting to convert it. If you are only interested in using the model as if it was a 3D spreadsheet then the imported form is probably good enough and the only changes you need to make are those that occur naturally. It isn't unreasonable to continue working with the default dimension and item names and it has the advantage of keeping you closer to the original.

If, however, you want to gain the advantages of using a model then perhaps a more complete conversion is warranted. In this case you need to understand the idea of creating a model from scratch first - and this is discussed in detail in *Multidimensional Modelling with CA-SuperCalc for Windows*.

» Pivoting

To give you some idea of just how powerful models are it is worth saying that although the original dimension names are ROW, COLS and PAGES you are not forced to display them in this way. To swap any dimension with the fixed dimension simply drag it to its new location using the right mouse button.

For example, if you drag the Month dimension down to the position of the Wine type dimension they swap places. The result is a display of the model which shows you the totals for each month for a given wine type

```
┌─────────────────────────────────────────────────────────┐
│  ▬            WINE4.MDL : Window1            ▼ ▲        │
│  ┌────────┐ ┌─────────┐                                 │
│  │ Month  │ │Wine Type│                                 │
│  ├────────┤ ├─────────┤                                 │
│  │ Outlet │ │Bordeau ±│                                 │
│  └────────┘ └─────────┘                                 │
│              April    May     June    Totals            │
│  High Street  406     321     123     850               │
│  Market Place 236     208     108     552               │
│  Long Lane    68      78      57      203               │
│  Back Avenue  55      45      33      133               │
│  Totals by wine 765   652     321     1738              │
└─────────────────────────────────────────────────────────┘
```

This swapping of the dimensions is called "pivoting" and it is something that you can do no matter how many dimensions the model has. However, if you don't give the dimensions and the items proper names it can be very easy to lose your way and not be able to understand exactly what it is you are looking at.

» Models or sheets?

Most of the ideas that have been introduced with reference to a 3D spreadsheet apply to models no matter how many dimensions they have. An SCW model can have up to 12 dimensions and you will find all of the ideas - underspecification, dimension ranges, global formulae and scope - all generalise easily. This is part of the power of the model way of doing things. The rest of the power is in the way a model builds the structure of the data into itself. For example, the headings which describe the data are actually incorporated into the structure in place of the extremely general column letter and row number.

It is obvious that nearly everything that you can do with a sheet you can do with a model, the only major exception being that you cannot use the database commands. Given that this is the case why bother with sheets? The answer is that sheets are more suited to handling data with a low level of organisation. For example, where do you fit the data for a lookup table in a model? Sometimes it fits into the model naturally as part of the dimensional structure - but if it doesn't it isn't so easy to just "tuck it away somewhere". A sheet, on the other hand, makes it easy to store ad-hoc items of data in a convenient corner. Of course given that models and sheets can be linked together, the ideal arrangement is to use a model for the orderly structured data and the sheet for the ad-hoc tables of values and results.

» Importing 2D CAL files

When you import an SC5 2D spreadsheet you have the choice of importing it as a model or as a sheet. In most cases your best choice is to import it as a sheet. The reason is that there is little advantage in converting a 2D spreadsheet into a 2D model. The only exception is if you plan to extend the model to more dimensions and even in this case it is usually better to import it as a sheet, create the model from scratch and then use Copy and Paste to transfer the data from the sheet to the model. You will still have to create the model formulae to make it all work but you would have had an equal amount of effort to extend the 2D model to 3D.

Most of the features of a 2D spreadsheet import with only cosmetic changes, the notable exception being any charts that have been defined. You can even ask SCW to attempt to convert any macros that may be included - and this a topic dealt with in the next chapter.

Key points

» Models are multidimensional spreadsheets with up to 12 dimensions.

» You can use all the commands and facilities that have been introduced with reference to sheets with the exception of the database commands.

» Model dimensions and items on each dimension can be renamed. You can also add and delete dimensions and items.

» Models use a different method of cell and range reference, designed to work no matter how many dimensions are involved.

» To reference a cell you simply quote one item for each dimension separated by dots. Any dimensions that are left out of the specification are assumed to be the same as the cell in which the reference is stored. This makes the reference act like a relative reference.

» A range reference is formed by specifying a range of items on each dimension. You can think of this as specifying the sides of a rectangular area, whereas a sheet range reference specifies opposite corners.

» You can import 3D SC5 spreadsheets as 3D models and these also provide a good way of learning about models.

» As model formulae tend to be exactly the same, no matter which cell they are stored in, it makes sense to use a single global copy of the formula to be applied to its scope - i.e. the range of cells to which it is to apply.

Chapter 12

Macros with CA-ble

SCW's macro language is particularly powerful and, compared to traditional macro languages, it is very easy to use. It is a form of the Realizer language which in turn is an adaptation of Basic for Windows. If you know a little Basic you will find CA-ble familiar and there are only a few additional ideas that you need to know. If you don't know traditional Basic but do know SC5 macro language or the macro language of another MS-DOS spreadsheet then, after you have understood one or two important differences in its principle of operation, you should find no difficulty with CA-ble. Indeed compared to these applications based macro languages, CA-ble is simple, elegant and generalisable. Once you have learned CA-ble for SCW you will be quite capable of writing programs for other CA products, and even in other dialects of Basic.

In this chapter we look first the fundamentals of writing macros in CA-ble then consider what happens when you import existing SC5 macros. Particular attention is paid to using CA-ble's own online help.

» Writing macros

A macro is a list of instructions that you can ask your machine to obey. In other words, it is a program. The only difference between an SCW macro and any other program is the language that the commands are written in. In the case of the SCW macro this language is called CA-ble (Computer Associates Basic Language Extended) a dialect of the well known computer language Basic.

To write a program in CA-ble you first need to open a macro. CA-ble instructions are not stored within the cells of a sheet or a model but in a completely different kind of document that behaves more like a text processor. In fact you can use a macro to store any sort of text which you can edit at any time, not just CA-ble instructions. The range of editing commands at your disposal are limited to cut, copy, paste, find and replace - but they are adequate for writing a program.

You open a new macro by using File,New and selecting Macro from the dialog box. The macro window that appears is blank and ready for you to type in some text. As already mentioned, this text can be anything you want and you can save and load it as required.

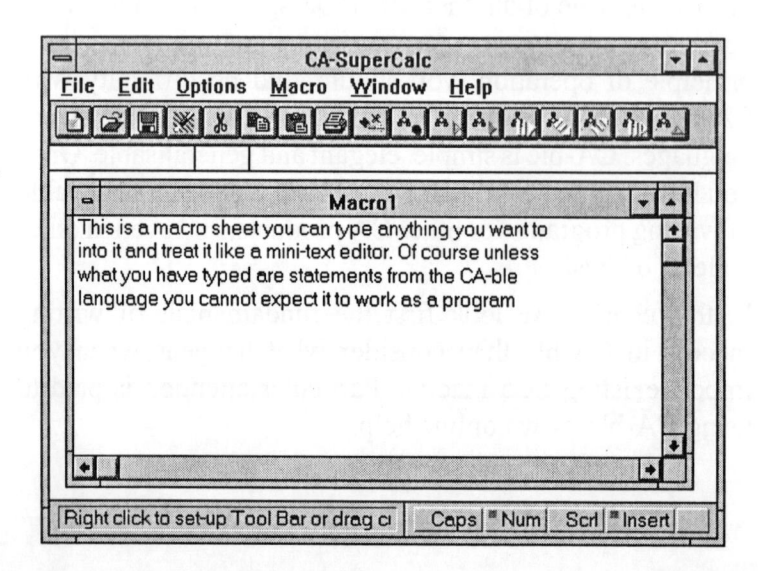

» CA-ble fundamentals

All programming languages share the same fundamental ideas. The most fundamental is that of a "variable". A variable is very much like a cell in a sheet to which you have given a name. You can store data in it and when you use the variable's name its value is retrieved for use. In CA-ble you create variables simply by using them. For example, if you write

    side=110

then this instruction does two things - it creates a new variable called 'side' and stores the value 110 in it. Notice that variables in CA-ble have in practice nothing at all to do with cells in sheets or models - it's just a helpful way of thinking about what they do.

Once you have created a variable you can continue to use it as long as the program is running. For example, the three-line program

    side=110
    otherside=232
    area=side*otherside

first creates the variable side and stores 110 in it, then creates a variable called otherside and stores 232 in it. The final instruction creates a variable called area and stores the result of multiplying side by otherside.

If you think about variables as named cells you should have no problem in understanding this three line program. Notice however that there are some important differences between this CA-ble program and the way a spreadsheet works. The most important is that each of the instructions are obeyed in turn and only when you run the program. That is, if you run this macro, by giving the command Macro,Run or by clicking on the equivalent toolbar icon then each instruction is obeyed in turn until you reach the end of the list. This only happens when the program is running and at all other times it is just static text that does nothing.

» Print and Input

Our three-line program is all very well but at the moment there is no way that we can see the result. Again variables are not like the cells in a spreadsheet, they are not "on-display" for the user to look at and modify. If you want to show the contents of a variable you have to use the PRINT command to show it. For example, adding the command

PRINT area

to the end of the previous program makes CA-ble display the value stored in area - but where? The answer is that all CA-ble output is sent to the Log Window which you can view using the command Window,Log Window.

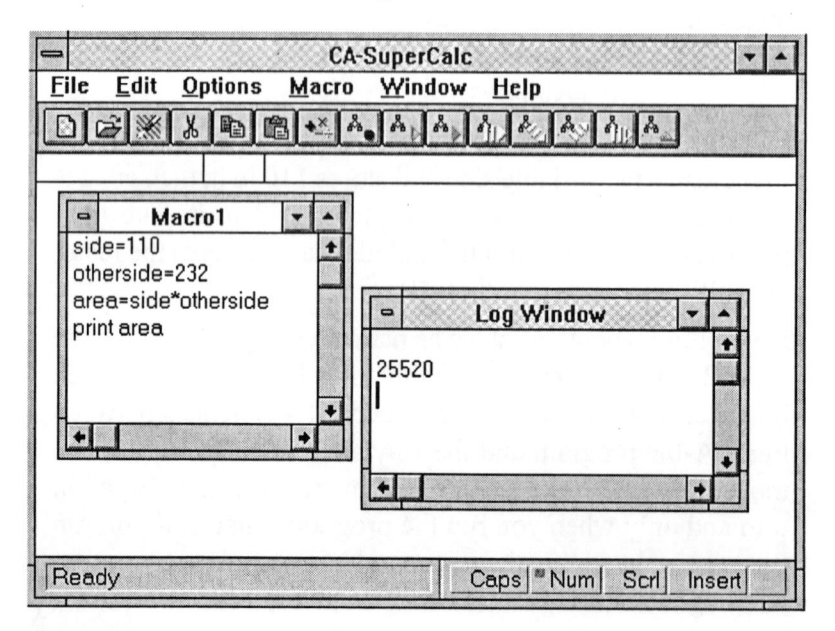

Using the PRINT command you can tell CA-ble to display the value of any variable in the Log Window. However there is still the matter of getting a value into a variable. At the moment you can store a value in a variable as the result of working out a formula but this is the same each time the program is run. What you need is some way of making the program pause while the user has the opportunity to type in a value to be stored in the variable. This is exactly what the INPUT statement does. For example, the program

    INPUT side
    INPUT otherside
    area=side*otherside
    PRINT area

pauses twice and allows the user to enter two values - one stored in the variable side and the other stored in the variable otherside. When CA-ble pauses for INPUT it displays a small dialog box that the user enters the value into. The default message and window title are reasonable for a first attempt at a program but they don't really tell the user what the value that they are typing in is for. To set your own message and window title use

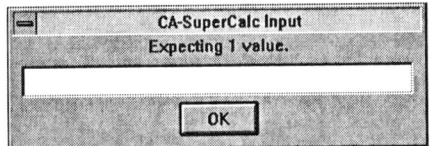

    INPUT "message","title";variable

notice that a comma is used between the message and title but a semi-colon is used between the title and the variable. For example,

    INPUT "What is the first side","Get sides";side

creates the INPUT dialog box -

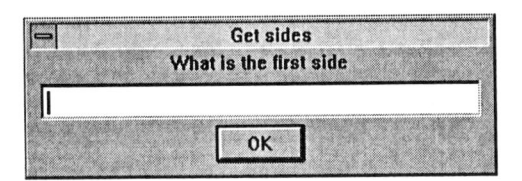

» Making choices with IF

Just as within a spreadsheet you sometimes need to select one of two formulae, within a CA-ble program you sometimes need to select between one of two sets of actions. To do this you make use of the IF command:

>IF *condition* THEN
>>*list of instructions*
>
>END IF

The list of instructions will only be carried out if *condition* is true. Notice the use of the END IF to mark the end of the list of instructions. If you want to choose between two sets of instructions you can use the slightly more complicated

>IF *condition* THEN
>>*list of instructions1*
>
>ELSE
>>*list of instructions2*
>
>END IF

In this case the first list is carried out only if *condition* is true and the second only if it is false.

For example, if the variable total contains the balance in an account you could test for it being overdrawn and print a suitable message using

>IF total<0 THEN
>>PRINT "Overdrawn"
>
>END IF

This IF statement either performs or skips the PRINT statement depending of the value of total. You could write any number of statements between the IF and the END IF and they would only be carried out if total was less than 0.

If you want to print a message if the account is healthy then you would use

>IF total<0 THEN
>>PRINT "Overdrawn"
>ELSE
>>PRINT "Credit"
>END IF

In this case the second print statement is only carried out if total<0 is false. Notice that this is not the same as

>IF total<0 THEN
>>PRINT "Overdrawn"
>END IF
>PRINT "Credit"

because in this case the PRINT "Credit" instruction is obeyed no matter what the condition evaluates to.

» Loops

Repeating a set of instructions is another fundamental idea of programming. There are a variety of facilities provided within CA-ble to allow you to repeat a set of instructions but the most general is the loop. If you have a set of instructions that you want to repeat all you have to do is enclose them between the words LOOP and END LOOP. For example,

>LOOP
>>PRINT "Hello"
>END LOOP

will repeat the instruction PRINT "Hello" forever - or rather until you press Ctrl-Break which is the signal to stop a program running. You can think of the LOOP and END LOOP as bracketing the list of instructions that you want to repeat.

The next question is how to you make the loop come to an end? There is little point in a loop that repeats forever. The answer is that you use a combination of an IF statement and a statement that stops the loop -

```
IF condition THEN
    EXIT LOOP
END IF
```

If you include these instructions within the loop they will be carried out each time through the loop and so the condition will be tested each time through the loop. If the condition is true then the EXIT LOOP command is obeyed which brings the loop to an end.

For example,

```
LOOP
    PRINT "Hello"
    INPUT "again Y/N";ans
    IF ans="N" THEN
        EXIT LOOP
    END IF
END LOOP
```

prints Hello and then asks the user if they want to go around the loop again. The IF statement tests to see what the reply is and exits the loop if it is an N. Notice that only an N will bring the loop to an end.

» Counting loops

The sort of loop that you can build using the LOOP-END LOOP instructions is completely general - you don't need any other sort of loop to be able to write any program. You may not need any other type of loop but one type is so common that it is worth adding an extra command to make life easier. A common requirement is for a loop that repeats the set of instructions a given number of times. For example, you might want to print Hello exactly five times. This sort of loop is called a "counting" or "enumeration" loop and the easiest way of writing such a loop is to use the FOR statement

>FOR *variable=start* TO *finish*
>*instructions*
>NEXT *variable*

This looks complicated but an example will quickly show you how simple it actually is

>FOR i=1 to 10
>PRINT "Hello"
>NEXT i

You can almost grasp the meaning of this section of program from the way it sounds. The loop really is repeated for values of i from 1 to 10. Each time the instructions between the FOR and the NEXT are obeyed and i is incremented by 1. The variable used in the loop to count each time it is repeated is called the "index variable". Obviously you shouldn't change the value of the index variable as this would confuse the issue but you can make use of it within the loop. For example, if you change the PRINT "Hello" statement to PRINT i you will see the values 1, 2, 3 ... up to 10 printed.

There are more complicated versions of the FOR loop but this simple counting loop is what you actually need in most situations.

» The link with SCW

CA-ble is a completely general programming language and you could use it to write almost any program you wanted to. However, it is SCW's macro language and so the next question to be answered is how does it work with SCW? In a traditional macro language this question would not arise because the commands of the language are the commands of the application. That is, for each of the menu commands there are commands within the macro language which do the same thing. In addition the macro language would make use of spreadsheet for its data storage and so the connection between the two is intimate. However, this isn't the case with CA-ble. Its commands have nothing to do with a spreadsheet or any other application for that matter - because they are Basic!

The solution to the problem of providing commands which are similar to the command that you get with SCW is provided by the Cmd functions. There are a long list of functions (fully described in the online help) that add to CA-ble the SCW specific features that it needs. If you use CA-ble with other CA applications all you will have to learn is another set of Cmd functions - and this is the great advantage of this method of providing a macro language.

Roughly speaking there is a Cmd function for each of the SCW menu commands. For example, the menu command Edit,Copy corresponds to the Cmd function CmdEditCopy. If you use this function within a CA-ble program the contents of the currently selected area in the currently selected sheet or model are copied to the keyboard.

Each of the menu commands have a similarly named Cmd function and this will enable you to find the function in the online help and discover its detailed workings. All of the menu commands are there but at present the Chart menu commands are not. This makes it impossible to construct macros that work with charts.

Being able to use menu commands within a macro is only half of the problem. There are many ways in which the user can change a sheet or a model without using a menu command. For example, they can select cells, move the current location, enter data and formulae and so on. To provide these features within CA-ble there are a range of Cmd functions which do not correspond to menu commands. Although these are listed and described in the online help it is worth presenting them here as logical groups organised according to what they do and are used for.

One of the most important actions is selecting cells and ranges and the following two commands are provided:

CmdSetSelection(*range*)

selects the range *range*.

CmdSetActiveCell(*ref*)

sets the active cell in a selected range. These commands are often used together and usually before any command that modifies or makes use of the contents of a cell. If you want to select a relative range then use the R[1]C[1] style of notation introduced for models. For example,

CmdSetSelection("R[0]C[-1]")

sets the selection to the cell to the left of the current cell.

To know which range or cell to select you often need to know the current selection or the reference of the first used cell in a given direction and there are two relevant commands:

ref=CmdCell

will return the cell reference of current cell and the command

range=CmdGetSelection

returns the range reference of current range.

You can use CmdCell to returns the reference of the first non-empty cell in given direction using

ref=CmdCell*direction*

where *direction* is up, down, left or right.

Once you have specified the cell or range reference in which you are interested you need to gain access to that data. There are two commands which allow you to store something in the current selection:

CmdSetFormula(*formula*)

which stores *formula* in the current cell and

CmdSetFormulaFill(*formula*)

which stores copies of *formula* in the currently selected range. The command:

CmdSetFormulaRef(*ref, formula*)

stores *formula* in the cell specified by *ref* without changing the current selection. Notice that, despite their names, these commands can be used to store values as well as formulae in cells or ranges. For example,

>CmdSetFormulaRef("A1","123.45")

will store 123.45 in cell A1 and

>CmdSetFormulaRef("A1","=A2+4")

will store the formula =A2+4 in cell A1.

There are four commands that will return the contents of a cell - two return the value and two return the formula that generates the value. The commands:

>val=CmdCellValue
>val=CmdCellValueRef(*ref*)

return the value stored in the current cell or the cell *ref* and

>form=CmdGetFormula
>form=CmdGetFormulaRef(*ref*)

return the formula at the current location or at the cell *ref*.

There are also two commands that will let you discover the type of data stored in a cell:

>type=CmdCellStatus
>type=CmdCellStatusRef(*ref*)

return a code (0 = empty, 1 = error, 2 = logical, 3 = number and 4=text) that indicate what sort of thing is stored in the current cell or at cell *ref*.

Finally, there are a set of commands concerned with scrolling the screen right, left, up or down. These are:

CmdHLine(*n*)	scroll *n* columns left or right
CmdVLine(*n*)	scroll *n* lines up or down
CmdHPage(*n*)	scroll screen *n* pages left or right
CmdVpage(*n*)	scroll *n* pages up or down
CmdHScroll(*n*)	scroll screen to column *n*
CmdVScroll(*n*)	scroll screen to row *n*

This is by no means an exhaustive list of CA-ble Cmd functions which do not correspond directly to a menu option but it gives some of the most useful ones and will serve as a good guideline to your exploration of the online help.

» CA-ble functions and SCW functions

When you are writing a CA-ble macro you cannot make use of the familiar SCW functions. For example, there is no SUM function and no WEEKDAY function. In most cases there will be an equivalent CA-ble function or facility. For example, there is no IF function but this is more than replaced by the IF..THEN..END IF statement. For many of the ordinary arithmetic functions such as ABS, COS and SIN, the CA-ble functions not only have the same name they also do the same job. But don't let this fool you into thinking that you are working in SCW. There are also lots of CA-ble specific functions that take you well beyond what SCW has to offer.

However if you really need to evaluate an SCW function within a CA-ble program you can use either

result=CmdEvaluate(*formula*)

which evaluates a numeric formula or

result=CmdEvaluateText(*formula*)

which evaluates a text formula.

» Dialog boxes

This is an advanced topic and can be skipped on first reading.

Although using the Cmd equivalents of the SCW menu commands is relatively easy, specifying all the values that would be set in a dialog box can be tedious. It is also sometimes that case that you only want to change one or two values and leave the rest set as they are. You may even want to present the user with one of the standard dialog boxes and allow them to make the selections. CA-ble allows you to achieve both of these objectives via the dialog box record. This is a special variable, one for each dialog box, which stores all of the settings that the dialog box controls.

To find out about these dialog box record variables you have to look in the online help under the entry for the Cmd command that is the equivalent of the menu command that displays the dialog box.

For example, if you use the Format,Alignment command you see the Alignment dialog box. The Cmd equivalent of Format,Alignment is CmdFormatAlignment. If you look this up in the online help you will discover that the command has two parameters:

>FormatAlignment(faAlignment,faWrap)

where faAlignment controls alignment with the default setting 0 being General and the other options of 1 left, 2 centre, 3 right, and 4 repeating text and faWrap has two settings - 1 to wrap text and 0 not to wrap.

The online help gives the following snippet as an example of how to use the command:

>DIM LOCAL fa AS CmdFormatAlignmentRecord
>CmdUpdateParams(fa)
>fa.faAlignment=1
>fa.faWrap=1
>CmdFormatAlignment(fa)

Some explanation will help you to understand not only this example but also other similar ones for other commands. The first instruction is a CA-ble instruction which creates the special dialog box record. The variable is called fa and you can define any variable to be a dialog box record using a command like

>DIM LOCAL *name* AS *type*

where *name* is the name of the new variable and *type* is the dialog box record type as looked up in the online help example.

The second instruction in the example, CmdUpdateParams, will transfer the current settings of the dialog box into the dialog box record variable that has just been created. After this instruction the variable fa contains all of the settings in the current Alignment dialog box.

Now that you have all the dialog box settings it is possible to change just those parts that you want to. The only question is how, because the dialog box record variable stores all of the settings as one monolithic chunk? The answer is that you can use the parameter names given in the definition of the command to gain access to the individual parts. In this case the two parameters are faAlignment and faWrap and so fa.faAlignment is the alignment part of the dialog box and fa.faWrap is the wrap part. Now you should be able to see that the next two statements in the example set the alignment to left and the wrap to on. Finally you can use the dialog record variable in place of the parameters of the Cmd function. Hence CmdFormatAlignment(fa) sets both the alignment and the wrap with one variable.

In the example both the alignment and the wrap settings were changed but this was simply to illustrate that it is possible to change both. In practice you are more likely to get the current settings and then change a subset of them.

Finally you can also use the dialog box record to display the dialog box to the user and return the values that they set. The command:

CmdDialog(*record*)

displays the dialog box corresponding to the dialog box record. When the user has finished with the dialog box the values that have been specified are stored in the record for further use. For example

CmdDialog(fa)

displays the Alignment dialog box and when the user has finished entering settings they are returned in fa and can be used in CmdFormatAlignment(fa).

» Recording a macro

One of the easiest ways of creating a macro is to record one as you work. If you select the Macro,Record command or click on the Record icon then a new macro sheet is opened and macro commands corresponding to all of the menu commands and actions that you perform are stored in it. The recording continues until you use the Macro,Stop command.

Macro recording is a good way to learn about macros and a good way to capture portions of a macro that you then edit into something larger. However, recording a macro has a number of problems. In particular, it is very "absolute" about every action. For example, suppose you want to create a macro that will enter three values A,B,C into three cells in a column. If you record this macro and start in cell A1 the macro will read:

    CmdSetFormula ("A")
    CmdSetSelection ("$A$2")
    CmdSetFormula ("B")
    CmdSetSelection ("$A$3")
    CmdSetFormula ("C")

If you run this macro starting off from another cell you will find that the A is entered into the current cell but the B and C are entered into A2 and A3 as before. This is a fairly literal replay of your actions but presumably your intention was to create a macro which would enter A,B,C into three cells in the current column. To do this you require:

    CmdSetFormula ("A")
    CmdSetSelection ("R[1].C[0]")
    CmdSetFormula ("B")
    CmdSetSelection ("R[1].C[0]")
    CmdSetFormula ("C")

The R[*n*].C[*m*] notation is the relative cell reference style introduced earlier. It means *n* cells to the right and *m* cells down from the current cell - with negative values of *n* and *m* corresponding to left and up. You should be able to see that

CmdSetSelection ("R[1].C[0]")

moves the current selection one cell down no matter where it is in the spreadsheet and so allows the macro to work at any location.

» Importing SC5 macros

If you import an SC5 spreadsheet that contains a macro then SCW will give you the opportunity to have this automatically converted to CA-ble. As you might expect, the resulting translation is not likely to be as good as a CA-ble program that you have written from scratch but it can save a great deal of time in getting something working. It is also important to realise that the task of translating macros is a very difficult one that benefits greatly from a little human intelligence. What might be slavishly translated into hundreds of very similar lines can often be converted into a single instruction once you realise that there is a better way of achieving the same end.

When you import an SC5 2D spreadsheet any macros that it contains will be automatically detected and you will be asked if you want to convert them. If you do then a sheet will be created which contains everything that the original SC5 spreadsheet did - including the text of the macro - and a macro sheet will be created containing the translation of the macro.

Although it looks as if the sheet contains the original macro don't try to run it because it is actually just a list of text items! The working part of the macro is actually in the macro sheet. However, the listing of the original macro is useful in trying to understand what it was doing and how it did it.

The macro translation process mostly occurs line by line. To every line of instructions in the original macro there will be a little block of CA-ble instructions in the macro sheet. The block of CA-ble instructions attempts to be a complete implementation of what the original SC5 macro instruction did. In other words, you can for the most part judge the correctness of the translation on a line by line reading of the program. However, SCW also attempts to detect the division of the original macro into subroutines and will create a CA-ble procedure for each subroutine it detects.

A CA-ble procedure is very like an SC5 subroutine but it starts with PROC *name* and ends with END PROC. After it has been defined the procedure can be called simply by using its name. For example,

    PROC hello
        PRINT "Hello"
    END PROC

is a procedure that will print Hello in the Log Window. If you want to use this procedure you simply use its name, i.e. hello. The only confusing part of CA-ble procedures is that they are listed at the start of the program and they are not obeyed by SCW when the program is run until the "main program" calls them.

In a converted program one of the procedures will be the place where the original macro started, i.e. its first instruction. Working out where a program starts may sound easy but in fact it is very difficult and so SCW shows you a list of all of the procedures that it has created and asks you to select the one that starts the program off. Often the list will contain a lot of "nonsense" procedures which correspond to bits of text that never actually belonged to the macro.

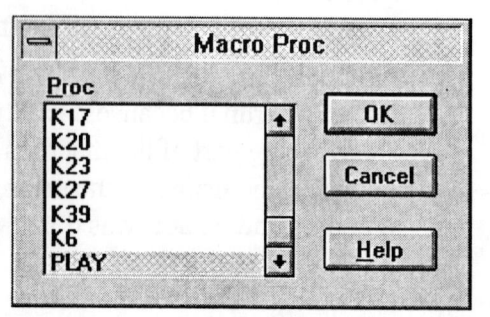

The procedures are named according to the cell that their first instruction was stored in. So if the first instruction was stored in K21 the procedure will be called PROC K21. If the cell was assigned a range name then this is used to name the procedure and so some of the newly created procedures will have meaningful names.

» Notice that if the macro was assigned to a keystroke then its name was originally *letter* and will be translated to A*letter*.

Once you have identified the procedure that initiates the program, a main program is constructed right at the end of all of the procedure definitions. This main program consists of a single line which calls the subroutine that starts the macro.

This means that the general structure of a translated CA-ble program is

> PROC *name1*
> > *instructions*
>
> END PROC
> PROC *name2*
> > *instructions*
>
> END PROC
> > etc
>
> *name2*

assuming that you have specified *name2* to be the start of the macro. If you make a mistake about where the macro starts simply go to the end of the CA-ble program and change the name of the procedure that is called first.

SCW often fails to translate a macro subroutine into a CA-ble procedure. In this case when it reaches the {return} command marking the end of the subroutine it translates it into EXIT PROC rather than END PROC.

» Translation - an example

To give you some idea how macro translation works consider the following simple SC5 keystroke macro.

>   John{right}
>   Mike{right}
>   Janet{right}
>   Mark~
>   /FE{left}:{left}{left}{left}~TC~

This enters the names in a row, moving to the right after each entry and then formats the text so that the names are centered.

If you import this macro the first question you will be asked is which procedure starts it - AC or Z214 - both of which seem unlikely! The reason you are being offered Z214 is that this cell contained some explanatory text which has been mistakenly converted into a procedure. Procedure AC is the correct choice because the macro was originally assigned to the Alt-C key press by naming it \C which is translated to AC.

The result of the translation can be seen opposite. Each line of the original macro has been translated into a group of CA-ble instructions. The original commands are also present in the program as comments. Any line that starts with a single quote is treated as a comment and ignored when the program is run. Notice that the last line of the translation is simply AC - which looks very strange until you realise that this is just a call to procedure AC which is defined above.

Three procedures are defined. The first is PROC Z214 which is harmless mistaken translation of some comments in the original macro - it can be deleted or left in without danger. PROC AC is where the translation of the macro really starts.

Translation - an example

```
Proc Z214    'From Z214
Line1:
' NOTE: PRESS ALT C TO RUN THE MACRO
Line2:
' ALSO GLOBAL NEXT HAS TO BE ON FOR THIS MACRO
Line3:
' TO WORK CORRECTLY I.E. /GLOBAL,+,NEXT
End Proc    'Z214

Proc AC    'From AA200
Line4:
' John{right}
CmdSetFormula("John")
CmdFormulaGoTo("R[0].C[1]")
Line5:
' Mike{right}
CmdSetFormula("Mike")
CmdFormulaGoTo("R[0].C[1]")
Line6:
' Janet{right}
CmdSetFormula("Janet")
CmdFormulaGoTo("R[0].C[1]")
Line7:
' Mark~
CmdSetFormula("Mark")
CmdSetSelection("R[0].C[1]")

Line8:
' /FE{left}:{left}{left}{left}~TC~
VSave = CmdGetSelection()
CmdSetSelection("Z209:R[0].C[0]")
CmdFormatAlignment(2, 0)
CmdSetSelection(VSave)
End Proc    'AC

Proc InitOpen    'Initialization
Line9:
' InitOpen
   CmdFormulaDefineName(2, \C, "$R[200].$C[27]:$R[200].$C[27]")
End Proc    'InitOpen

AC
```

You can see that the original macro instruction John{right} has been translated into

>Line4:
>' John{right}
>CmdSetFormula("John")
>CmdFormulaGoTo("R[0].C[1]")

which is a correct translation. The other data entry commands are also correctly translated. However, the format command isn't. The reason is that SCW has become confused about the way the range is specified. The format command uses the left keypress to mark out the range that holds the data just entered by reversing the cursor's movements. But the CA-ble instructions try to mix an absolute cell reference with a relative one in a way that not only doesn't work but actually generates an error message.

>Line8:
>' /FE{left}:{left}{left}{left}~TC~
>CmdSetSelection("Z209:R[0].C[0]")
>CmdFormatAlignment(2, 0)
>CmdSetSelection(VSave)
>End Proc   'AC

Unfortunately the number of ways that it is possible to use SC5 macros makes it very difficult to ensure that a translation will always work, let alone be faithful to the original intention. In this case the correct translation is

>CmdSetSelection("R[0].C[-1]:R[0].C[-4]")

but if you think that this is easy ask yourself the question of why three left moves in the original translate to four in the CA-ble instruction. If you can work this out you will begin to see why the translation is difficult to automate!

Also notice that at the start of the procedure the current selection is saved in a variable called VSave and at the end of the procedure it is restored using the command CmdSetSelection(VSave). You will discover that a great many of the commands introduced in translation are concerned with saving the current state and restoring it. By deciding if these are necessary or not you can often reduce the length and complexity of a translated macro.

You may also be puzzled by the inclusion of the third procedure InitOpen. This is created for every macro translation but it isn't automatically used. Its purpose is to create range names and perform other initialisation procedures within the sheet. In most cases it isn't necessary to use it but if you do need to define a range name include a call to it before the call to the procedure that starts the macro.

» Debugging

The CA-ble debugging facilities are useful during the development of a brand new macro and especially useful in getting translated macros working. If you select Debug when you are first running the macro you can step through it one instruction at a time. By setting up the windows so that the macro can be seen at the same time as the sheet, you can follow the course of the macro execution.

When a macro is running in debug mode you can use the Trace In command to single step through each instruction. Each time you use the command, or click on its toolbar icon, a single instruction is carried out. The trouble with this approach is that you have to single step through the internals of procedures that you already know are working. In this case use the Step command which single steps until it encounters a procedure call when it allows the procedure to run normally and only pauses again after it is completed. If you are stepping through a procedure and want to run it normally to completion then use the Step Out command. This runs the remainder of the procedure at normal speed and only pauses again when it is finished. Finally you can use the Reset command to restore the whole macro and start if off again and you can use Go, or "Play" as its toolbar icon is labelled to run the rest of the macro without pausing.

Normally stepping though a macro, and seeing what each instruction actually does, is sufficient to find out what is going wrong. However, it is worth knowing that you can type any CA-ble command into the Log Window and it will be executed immediately. This can be used to test instructions but if you make use of it while a macro is running in debug mode you can print, and even alter, the current contents of variables.

» Assigning to keys and menus

If you want to give the user a simple and direct access to a macro then you can use the Macro, Assign to Key command. However, you can only assign a macro to a keypress that uses the Ctrl key. That is Ctrl-A and Ctrl-F1 can be assigned to a macro but you cannot assign one just to F10. You can also assign a macro to a menu using the Macro,Assign to Menu command. In this case the macro's name is listed in a special section at the end of the selected menu. In both cases the macro assigned to the menu or key has to be loaded into memory before it will run. The simplest way of ensuring this is to save the sheet or model along with the macro as a workspace and load them as a workspace.

» User defined functions

If you look back to Chapter 8 where user defined functions were introduced you will now recognise these are being nothing more than CA-ble programs. To be more precise, a user defined function is a CA-ble function and you can use all of the CA-ble commands and variables that you can use in a CA-ble procedure. This explains some of the initial difficulty in writing a simple user defined function because once in the function you are restricted to CA-ble language and you cannot use any of the SCW built-in functions unless they have a CA-ble equivalent. However, now that you know about the Cmd functions, and CmdEvaluate in particular, you should find it easier to create new functions that work without restriction. For example, the function

```
Function test(a)
    ans=CmdEvaluate("=SUM(A1:A10)")
    return ans
end func
```

will sum A1:A10, even though CA-ble doesn't have a SUM function.

» Example 1- Auto 3D

The following example will convert the default model that appears when you use File,New into a 3D model of the type that results when you import a 3D spreadsheet.

```
CmdFileNew ("Model")
CmdEditDeleteDimension ("DD")
CmdEditRename ("AA", "COL", "A1", "A")
CmdEditRename ("COL", "COL", "A2", "B")
CmdEditRename ("COL", "COL", "A3", "C")
CmdEditRename ("COL", "COL", "A4", "D")
CmdEditRename ("COL", "COL", "A5", "E")
CmdEditRename ("BB", "ROW", "B1", "1")
CmdEditRename ("ROW", "ROW", "B2", "2")
CmdEditRename ("ROW", "ROW", "B3", "3")
CmdEditRename ("ROW", "ROW", "B4", "4")
CmdEditRename ("ROW", "ROW", "B5", "5")
CmdEditRename ("CC", "PAGE", "C1", "PAGE1")
CmdEditRename ("PAGE", "PAGE", "C2", "PAGE2")
CmdEditRename ("PAGE", "PAGE", "C3", "PAGE3")
CmdEditRename ("PAGE", "PAGE", "C4", "PAGE4")
CmdEditRename ("PAGE", "PAGE", "C5", "PAGE5")
CmdOptionsModelBar (1, 1, "7")
```

This is a fairly straightforward macro and one of the few examples of a macro that can be created using the Macro,Record command without having to edit the result!

» Example 2 - Age in years

The following user defined function demonstrates how date calculations can be performed in CA-ble. As the parameter passed to a user defined function is always evaluated to a numeric or string value the function has to be called as

=Age("12/3/1983")

that is, with the date as a string. The function is:

```
Function Age(d)
birthdate=DateInfo(StrToDate(d))
today=DateInfo(QDate)
thisyear=today[_DI_Year]
birthyear=birthdate[_DI_Year]
birthmonth=birthdate[_DI_Month]
birthday=StrToDate(sprint(birthmonth)+
        "/"+sprint(birthdate[_DI_DayOfMonth])+
        "/"+sprint(thisyear))
calyears=thisyear-birthyear
IF QDate<birthday THEN
        calyears=calyears-1
END IF
return calyears
end func
```

The first instruction converts the date string to a date array containing all of the information about the date you need. (See DateInfo in the online help.) The next section of the function gets the current year number and builds up the date of this year's birthday as a string which is immediately converted to a date. The IF statement subtracts one from the age in calendar years if the birthday hasn't happened yet.

» Example 3 - Codebreaker

This is an example of a sophisticated CA-ble macro that plays a guessing game. It generates three different random numbers in the variables dig1, dig2 and dig3. The user guesses the digits and the result is reported back as M meaning miss, H meaning a hit or correct digit but wrong place, and P meaning correct digit and position. The results are reported in a sheet called CODE.MDS which must be open when the macro is run. You can add formatting and other embellishments to this sheet to make the game look better.

```
PROC TARGET
dig1=INT(RND*10)
LOOP
       dig2=INT(RND*10)
IF dig1<>dig2 THEN
       EXIT LOOP
END IF
END LOOP
LOOP
       dig3=INT(RND*10)
IF dig3<>dig1 AND dig3<>dig2 THEN
       EXIT LOOP
END IF
END LOOP
PRINT dig1,dig2,dig3
End PROC

PROC GUESS
INPUT "first digit","GUESS";guess1
INPUT "second digit","GUESS";guess2
INPUT "third digit","GUESS";guess3
END PROC

PROC REPORT
win=0
state1="M"
IF guess1=dig2 OR guess1=dig3 THEN
       state1="H"
END IF
IF guess1=dig1 THEN
       state1="P"
END IF

state2="M"
IF guess2=dig1 OR guess2=dig3 THEN
       state2="H"
END IF
IF guess2=dig2 THEN
       state2="P"
END IF
```

```
state3="M"
IF guess3=dig1 OR guess3=dig2 THEN
        state3="H"
END IF
IF  guess3=dig3 THEN
        state3="P"
END IF
CmdSetFormulaRef("B4",state1)
CmdSetFormulaRef("C4",state2)
CmdSetFormulaRef("D4",state3)

IF dig1=guess1 AND dig2=guess2 AND dig3=guess3 THEN
        win=1
END IF
END PROC


'START OF PROGRAM PLAY
LOOP
goes=0
CmdActivate("Code.MDS : Window1")
CmdFormulaGoTo("$R[1].$C[1]")
TARGET
LOOP
goes=goes+1
GUESS
REPORT
IF win<>0 THEN
 EXIT LOOP
END IF
END LOOP
ans=MESSAGEBOX("You did that in only "+SPRINT(GOES)+" tries
Another go?","You WIN!!",_MB_YESNO)
IF ans=7 THEN
 EXIT LOOP
END IF
END LOOP
```

This macro is a conversion of the SC5 Code breaker macro listed in my book *SuperCalc Professional* and also included on the disk that accompanies this book. You should compare the difference between this rewritten macro and the translated macro. The biggest difference in style between the two is that the CA-ble macro makes use of variables in preference to cells in the sheet. This is a general difference of approach between the two macro languages. In SC5 macro language the spreadsheet was easily accessible, in CA-ble it is less accessible but there are more powerful ways of doing the same thing.

Key points

》 SCW macros are written in CA-ble which is a dialect of Basic.

》 When you are working in CA-ble you cannot make use of the SCW functions.

》 Every SCW menu command has a related CA-ble CMD function.

》 There are a range of CMD functions which allow a CA-ble program to access the contents of cells and set selections within a sheet.

》 You can record a CA-ble macro but in most cases the result is best treated as a starting point for a more general macro.

》 SC5 macros can be imported but the translation process generally produces something that can serve as the basis for editing rather than a finished macro.

》 User defined functions are simply CA-ble functions stored in GLOBAL.MDM.

Index

A
absolute references	40, 281
accuracy	239
Adobe fonts	78, 163
alignment	66, 76, 172
Alignment dialog	76
am/pm indicator	219
ampersand	170, 193
AND	183
appearance	66
Application	145
applying names	54
area chart	104
argument	44
arithmetic functions	178
arithmetic operators	38
ASCII code	198
Assign Data	106, 116
Assign to Menu	318
assigning macros to keys	318
asterisks	11, 71
ATAN	180
auditing	154
Auto Save option	16
Automatic colour	84
autoscaling on axes	109
autosum	10, 61, 288
AVERAGE	180
axis control	109

B
background colour	81
background printing	161
backup	15
bar chart	102
Best Fit	86
biorhythms	234
blanking cells	83
bold	78
borders	66, 78
borders in charts	108
brackets	38

C
CA-ble	208, 296
CAL Files	283
Calculation dialog	60
Calendar	231
capitalisation	197
case sensitivity	182
categorical axis	110
categorical data	101
Category Selection	98
cell notes	151
Cell Protection dialog	147
cell reference	21, 279
centred headings	172
CHAR	198
Character Map	70
Chart icon	96
chart overlays	116
Chart Selection dialog	106
chart templates	114
Chart Toolbar	97
Chart Type	107, 116
Chart, Assign Data	98
Chart, X Error Bars	120
checking validity	187
checksums	157, 188, 190
CHOOSE	202, 219
circular references	59
CLEAN	194
clearing cells	83
clipboard	21, 141
Cmd functions	304
CODE	198
codes for headers/footers	169
colon	21
Color Overrides dialog	84
colour	77
colour in charts	112
colour in formats	72
colour schemes	112
column headings	167
column relative	43
column width	85
columns	58
combination charts	116
comma	69
comparing text values	182
compound conditions	184
COMPREF	127, 142
computed cell references	142
concatenation	193
conditional format	72
conditions	182, 270
consolidation	139
Control Panel	6, 69, 78, 160, 162, 213
copying	21, 23, 287
COUNT	180
Create Backup Copy	15
Create Names dialog	53
Criteria range	257
Ctrl key	14, 28, 49
Ctrl-C	27, 34, 287
Ctrl-D	27, 34
Ctrl-F6	130
Ctrl-L	27
Ctrl-N	151
Ctrl-R	27
Ctrl-Shift-F3	53
Ctrl-U	27
Ctrl-V	27, 34, 70, 287
Ctrl-X	27
Ctrl-Z	17
currency symbol	70, 194
current date	221
cursor	5, 9
CurveFit	123
customising charts	107
customising models	277
cut	21
Cycle	59

D

data series	98, 270
Data,Form	251
Data,Set Database	252
database	249
database - example	268
database commands	261
database functions	263
date arithmetic	221
date base	212
date fill	272
Date Format dialog	213
date serial number	212, 236
dates and times	216, 253
DAY	219
Day of the month	229
DAYS360	227
dBASE files	267
DDE	144
debug mode	317
default font	85
Define Name dialog	50
defining a style	88
delete key	23, 83
deleting	133
deleting dimensions	278
deleting items	288
deleting names	55
dependents	154
destination range	24
DGET	263
dialog boxes	307
DIM LOCAL	308
dimension range	280
dimensions	276
directories	17
DISPLAY	194, 197, 236, 240
displaying cell contents	66
displaying zeroes	83
DOLLAR	194
dollar signs	40
dot	33
double clicking	6
double rulings	80
double X chart	118
double Y chart	103
drag and drop	27
dragging	20, 85
drawing tools	107
drivers	160
DSUM	264
Duplicated Category names dialog	115
Dynamic data exchange	144

E

Edit mode	8
Edit Scope dialog	289
Edit, Insert Item	288
Edit,Add Depth	114
Edit,Add Value Labels	114
Edit,Attributes	107
Edit,Bring to Front	113
Edit,Clear	23, 83, 134
Edit,Copy	34, 141
Edit,Cut	22, 23
Edit,Delete	133
Edit,Delete Dimension	278
Edit,Delete Item	288
Edit,Fill	26
Edit,Insert	133
Edit,Paste	22, 34
Edit,Paste Link	145
Edit,Paste Special	127, 141, 145, 244
Edit,Remove Depth	114
Edit,Remove Plot Frame	114
Edit,Rename	286
Edit,Series	117
Edit,Switch Axis	114
ELSE	300
End func	207
END IF	300
End key	14
END LOOP	301
END PROC	312
equals sign	12
error bars	120
errors	150, 157
EXACT	197
exchanging data	144
exclamation mark	140
exclusive OR	183
EXIT LOOP	302
explanatory text	172
exploded pie segment	126
exponent	75
exponential format	74
extended range	31
Extract range	257

F

F2	8
F4	41
F5	32
F9	60, 221
face validity	240
factorial	180
false	190
faster printing	161
field	250
fieldname	250
File Manager	16
File,Links	140, 146
File,Merge	139
File,Open	16
File,Save	15
File,Save Workspace	132
File,Search	17
Fill by Example	271
Fill by Specified	272
Fill Down	34
fill pattern	81
fill patterns in charts	108
financial functions	209
finding files	17
Fit largest font	86

FIX	194	Info window	153
Fixed Decimal option	238	INPUT	299
font	66, 70, 77, 163	Insert key	5
Font dialog	77	inserting	133
footers	168	installing printer	160
FOR	303	international settings	213
foreground colour	81	interpolation	123
form view	252	ISCONSISTENT	191
format	194, 197, 236	ISERR	192
Format,Alignment	76	ISLOGICAL	192
Format,Borders	78	ISNUMBER	191
Format,Cell Protection	147	ISTEXT	192
Format,Column Width	85	italics	78
Format,Number	67	items	277
Format,Patterns	81, 150	**L**	
Format,Row Height	86	labels	53
Format,Style	87	LEFT	195, 231
formatting	66, 197, 221, 240	legends	111, 112
formatting negative numbers	72	LEN	196
formula adjustment	40	line chart	103
formula names	57	linear axis	110
Formula,Apply Names	54	linear fill	272
Formula,Create Names	53	lines	66
Formula,Define Name	50	lines in charts	108
Formula,Goto	32	links	146
Formula,Note	151	locked cells	148
Formula,Paste Name	52	Lock Indicator box	148
Formula,Replace	55	log axis	110
Formula,Select Special	155	Log Window	298, 299, 312, 318
Formulas mode	152	logical functions	191
frame	79	LOOKUP	231
functions	44	Lookup functions	199
G		loops	301
General alignment	76	**M**	
global formulae	289	Macro	296
GLOBAL.MDM	207	macro functions	208
goodness of fit	124	macro help	308
Goto dialog	32	macro translation	314
grid lines in charts	109	Macro,Record	310
gridlines	82, 167	Macro,Stop	310
growth fill	272	major ticks	109
H		manual calculation	60
hash symbol	71	Map mode	153
headers	168	MATCH	203, 206
help with macros	308	MEDIAN	180
Hi-Lo charts	122	merging sheets	139
hiding legends	112	MID	195
HLOOKUP	201, 203	MINUTE	219
Home key	14	mixed charts	116
HOUR	219	mixed references	43
I		MOD	222
icons	29	Model	276
IF	181, 185, 300	model functions	209
IF..THEN..END IF	307	MONTH	219, 222
importing DBF files	267	mouse	3, 6, 20, 28, 141
importing from SC5	283	movement keys	32
importing SC5 macros	311	moving formulae	41
inaccuracy	240	MS Sans Serif	70, 85
Include Charts	167	multi-dimensional range reference	280
inclusive OR	183	multiple copies	23
indenting	173	multiple print areas	166
INDEX	203, 204, 206	multiple selections	49

N
name	50
naming formulae	57
NEXT	303
non-categorical data	101, 104
NOT	183
notes	151
NOW	221
Number dialog	67
number format	66
numeric place holders	68

O
offsets	282
online help	308
opening a sheet	16
operators	38
Options	9, 15
Options,Calculation	60
Options,Display	82, 84, 137
Options,Preferences	27, 239
OR	183
Outline	78
overlaying charts	116

P
page break	170
page setup	166
PageDown	14
PageUp	14
paragraphs	172
password	149
paste	22, 287
Paste Function dialog	45
Paste Name dialog	52
Paste Special dialog	127
Paste,Link	141
patterns	66
Patterns dialog	81
percentage	237
PI	178, 235
Pie chart	99, 104, 125
pivoting	292
place holders	67
Play	318
Plot Axis Attributes dialog	110
Plot Symbol Attributes dialog	111
point	78
pointing	20, 46, 141
polar chart	104
polynomial	123
pop-up menu	29, 82, 83, 147
positioning cell entries	76
Precedents	153
precision	66
Preferences	9, 15, 84
Preview	165
Print	298
Print Manager	161
print preview	165
printer drivers	160
printer setup	162
printing charts	167
PROC	312
procedure	312
Program Manager	2
PROPER	197
protecting cells	147
protecting structure	149

Q
Query by Example	255

R
R^2	124
radians	178, 235
raising to a power	39
RAND	180
range	166
range expressions	48, 179
range names	50
range reference	21
ranges in models	279
Realizer	295
recalculate	60, 221
records	250
recording macros	310
regression	124
relative cell references	40
relative names	52
relative references	281
renaming dimensions	286
REPLACE	195
Replace dialog	56
Reset macro	318
RIGHT	195
right mouse button	29, 82
rounding	241
Rounding values	244
ROUNDUP	242
Row & Column Headings	82
row height	85
Row Labels	99
Row Numbers	99
row relative	43
rows	58
rulings	79, 92

S
Saving	15
SC5	9, 20, 107, 142, 251, 283, 311
scale on axes	109
scatter chart	103
scatter diagram	107
scientific format	74
Scope	289
scroll bars	14
scroll lock	14
SEARCH	194, 196
search and replace	194
searching for a file	17
SECOND	219
Select Special dialog	155
selecting a range	20
selecting cells	5
Series Attributes dialog	117
Series dialog	270
Set Scope dialog	289

setting colours	84	**U**	
setup	162	underline	78
sharing structure	136	underspecification	279
Sheet	4	Undo	17
sheet links	140	user defined functions	207, 318
sheet merging	139	**V**	
sheet windows	130	validity checks	187
shift-click	32	VAR	180
Shift key	31, 49	variance	180
Shift-Ctrl-F6	130	VAT	245
Shift-F3	45	vectors	179
SIN	235	verification	156
single quotes	140	VLOOKUP	201, 203
size of type	77	**W**	
slash	11	WDAY	219, 229
slider	14	wildcard characters	256, 269
slope	105	Window,Cascade	131
sort key	266	Window,Hide	132
sorting	265	Window;Info Window	153
source range	24	Window,New Window	130
standard deviation	180	Window,Tile	131
statistical functions	180, 209	Window,Unhide	132
STDEV	180	Windows printing	160
Step Out	317	Windows Tutorial	2
Step through macro	317	workspace	141
String functions	192	Wrap	172
style	67, 174	Wrap Text	76
Style dialog	87	WYSIWYG	65
subroutine	312	**X**	
SUBSTITUTE	194, 196	XY chart	103
SUM	11, 61	**Y**	
symbols in formats	69	YEAR	219, 222
system clock	214, 221	**Z**	
T		Zero Values	83
templates	147	Zoom	165
Text	192, 194	**!**	
text in charts	108	!	140
text in formats	69	3D effect in charts	114
THEN	300	3D model	278
thousands separator	69	# (hash symbol)	71, 183
tick marks	109	$	40, 256
tilde	269	&	193
time	215, 226	*	11, 256, 269
time arithmetic	224	.	33
time serial number	215	/	11
title lock	137	:	21
Titles	168	=	12
TO	303	?	269
TODAY	221	@	71
toolbar	29, 31	\ (slash)	69
Topic	145	^	39
transcribing formulae	38	~	256, 269
translating keystroke macros	314		
transposing data	127		
trigonometric functions	178		
TRIM	197		
true	190		
TrueType fonts	78, 163		
TRUNC	222, 226		
Truncate	241		
typeface	77		

Other books of interest

Multidimensional Modelling with CA-SuperCalc for Windows
by Janet Swift
CA-SuperCalc for Windows is more than a spreadsheet; it is also a powerful multidimensional modeller. While most users recognise a spreadsheet, the idea of a multidimensional model is less obvious, and the first question that this book answers is what is a multidimensional model. It also demonstrates that the opportunities to make use of MDMs are much wider than you might think. In fact data that would be easier to work with as an MDM is everywhere - it's just a matter of recognising it. In this book Janet Swift demonstrates how simple MDMs are to build and how existing data in a conventional database can be converted into an MDM. Dimension and category, global formula and scope are discussed and examples are included for you to be able to see the relevance of MDMs to your own data. The final part of the book shows how novel and powerful applications can be created using MDMs and 2D spreadsheets together.
ISBN 1-871962-26-9

The SuperProject Expert
by Andrew C Johnson
Project management is a sphere in which computers have revolutionised the way businesses operate - but the impact has not been as far reaching as might have been expected due to the complexity of the software itself. In initial chapters Andrew Johnson explores the basics of creating and viewing a model using CA-SuperProject. He then goes on to show methods and techniques in dealing with the complexity inherent in large projects. Later chapters deal with tracking and costing projects and allocating material resources, and include a discussion of rescheduling in the light of actual data, earned value analysis and inventory costing.
ISBN 1-871962-23-4

The 386/486 PC: A Power User's Guide (Updated Second Edition)
by Harry Fairhead
Windows applications such as CA-SuperCalc for Windows require a computer based on a 368/486 processor. Harry Fairhead provides the technical information you need to make the most of this hardware, explaining aspects such as extended and expanded memory, LIM, hard disk seek rates, caching, memory interleave and shadow RAM. He also shows you how to configure and optimise your system for the applications you are interested in. The final chapter covers latest developments - the Pentium chip, the local bus, superscalar architecture and Windows NT.
ISBN 1-871962-22-6

In Preparation

Financial Functions Using a Spreadsheet
by Mike James and Janet Swift
Calculations concerning percentages and interest rates are at the heart of every financial decision. Most spreadsheet users are unaware that there is a complete financial calculator built in to their software. You can work out repayments on almost any type of loan and determine the interest earned on almost any type of investment. Starting from simple ideas this book shows how you can quickly master financial calculations and get to grips with seemingly impenetrable financial functions. Each technique is explained and illustrated with working templates dealing with practical problems. **ISBN 1-871962-01-3**

Programming in CA-Realizer and CA-ble
by Mike James and Janet Swift
Realizer 2.0 is a complete development language for Windows and OS/2. It is easy to use, powerful and the language that is, the basis for CA's application macro language CA-ble. If you are interested in writing macros for CA-SuperCalc for Windows or for CA-SuperProject then you will find all the help you need in this title. **ISBN 1-871962-37-4**

Companion Disk

All the examples discussed in this book - plus a few extras - are included on a 3.5" (720K) disk. This disk costs £5 (including VAT, if applicable, and postage) and can be ordered directly from I/O Press. Please enclose cheque, postal order or your VISA or Access details when ordering.

Update Service

To keep you up-to-date with changes and revisions in SCW we plan to produce an update booklet as a service to readers. If you would like a free copy then send us a self addressed envelope large enough to hold an A5 booklet stamped with postage for 100gms and marked (SCW Update service). There is no need to include any proof of purchase. Your envelope will be kept on file until the update becomes available

For more information or a catalogue contact:

I/O Press, Oak Tree House, Leyburn, North Yorkshire DL8 5SE
Tel: (0969) 24402 Fax: (0969) 24375